T0271309

SUSTAINABLE MATERIALS PROCESSING AND MANUFACTURING

Material, Processing, and Manufacturing

SUSTAINABLE MATERIALS PROCESSING AND MANUFACTURING
Material, Processing, and Manufacturing

Edited by
Lin Zhu
Tien-Chien Jen

CRC Press
Taylor & Francis Group
Boca Raton London New York

CRC Press is an imprint of the
Taylor & Francis Group, an **informa** business

First edition published 2024
by CRC Press
4 Park Square, Milton Park, Abingdon, Oxon, OX14 4RN

and by CRC Press
2385 NW Executive Center Drive, Suite 320, Boca Raton FL 33431

© 2024 selection and editorial matter, Lin Zhu and Tien-Chien Jen; individual chapters, the contributors

CRC Press is an imprint of Informa UK Limited

The right Lin Zhu and Tien-Chien Jen to be identified as the authors of the editorial material, and of the authors for their individual chapters, has been asserted in accordance with sections 77 and 78 of the Copyright, Designs and Patents Act 1988.

All rights reserved. No part of this book may be reprinted or reproduced or utilised in any form or by any electronic, mechanical, or other means, now known or hereafter invented, including photocopying and recording, or in any information storage or retrieval system, without permission in writing from the publishers.

For permission to photocopy or use material electronically from this work, access www.copyright.com or contact the Copyright Clearance Center, Inc. (CCC), 222 Rosewood Drive, Danvers, MA 01923, 978-750-8400. For works that are not available on CCC please contact mpkbookspermissions@tandf.co.uk

Trademark notice: Product or corporate names may be trademarks or registered trademarks, and are used only for identification and explanation without intent to infringe.

British Library Cataloguing-in-Publication Data
A catalogue record for this book is available from the British Library

ISBN: 978-1-032-88599-5 (pbk)
ISBN: 978-1-003-53864-6 (ebk)

DOI: 10.1201/9781003538646

Typeset in Times LT Std
by Aditiinfosystems

This conference was jointly organised by University of Johannesburg (UJ, South Africa) and Anhui Agricultural University (AHAU, P.R. China). We hope that this conference will contribute to advanced researches in sustainable materials processing and manufacturing.

Lin Zhu

Sustainable Materials Processing and Manufacturing – Lin Zhu et al. (eds)
© 2024 Taylor & Francis Group, London, ISBN 978-1-032-88599-5

Contents

Sustainable Materials Processing and Manufacturing – Lin Zhu et al. (eds)
© 2024 Taylor & Francis Group, London, ISBN 978-1-032-88599-5

List of Figures

Sustainable Materials Processing and Manufacturing – Lin Zhu et al. (eds)
© 2024 Taylor & Francis Group, London, ISBN 978-1-032-88599-5

List of Tables

Sustainable Materials Processing and Manufacturing – Lin Zhu et al. (eds)
© 2024 Taylor & Francis Group, London, ISBN 978-1-032-88599-5

Preface

The conference on 'Substantial Materials Processing and Manufacturing (SMPM)' aims to bring together scientists, researchers, and companies to attend and share their vision, ideas, recent developments as well as advanced scientific and technical knowledge in the field of materials processing and manufacturing. The conference is concerned with sustainable engineering, life cycle engineering, sustainable manufacturing systems and technologies, sustainable materials and processing, sustainable product design and development, sustainable supply chain and business models, renewable energy and sustainable development, Industry 4.0 and Internet of Things, modelling and simulation of sustainable manufacturing, intelligent agricultural equipment, etc. The conference has invited some academicians and research leaders in related fields to give the keynote report. Based on the theme of this book, eighteen outstanding and high-quality manuscripts have been selected for the publication in this book. The detailed information is presented below.

Biomechanical Analysis on the In-situ Three-point Jump Shooting Technique in Basketball; Production Strategy for Electric Vehicle and Power Battery in a Closed-loop Supply Chain with Loss Aversion and Green Preference; The Effects of Proactive Strategic Orientation on Manufacturing SMEs' Performance; An Investigation into Industrial Manufacturing and Sustainable Production Implementation in sub-Saharan Africa; Parameter optimisation and cost analysis of lavender oil production using steam distillation; Water Purification Using Freshwater Algae; Drying of Biomass in a Multistage Auger Pyrolysis Reactor; Design, Prototyping and Testing of Biodegradable Sanitary Pads; Assessment of Recycling Plastic Bottle Waste Considering Public Behavior and Attitude: Case Study Ibadan, Nigeria; Production and Biodegradation Testing of Bioplastics; Design of an Automatic Soya Beans Cake-cutting Machine; Investigating Settleability Properties of Different Sludges to Enhance Optimum Performance of an Upflow Anaerobic Sludge Bed Reactor; Wireless Charging System for Unmanned Aerial Vehicle Using Lightweight and Compact Receiver Module; Research and Design of Adaptive Control System for Driver's Seat; Comparison of Three Sludge Cuts for Biomethane Potential From Selected Municipal Wastewater Treatment Plant; Methane Solubility in Effluent Wastewater from Anaerobic UASB Reactor Treatment - A Theoretical Perspective; Agriculture Monitoring System Improvement Utilizing Wireless Sensors Networks; Failure Analysis and Improvement of the Sliding Door Opening and Closing of the Multiple Unit.

The book is very helpful to researchers, students, and scientists who are interested in the study of sustainable material processing and manufacturing, for various excellent viewpoints proposed by famous scholars. It is worth reading for researchers and scientists to gain insights into advanced research in this field.

Lin Zhu,
Anhui Agricultural University,
P.R. Chian

Tien-Chien Jen,
University of Johannesburg,
South Africa

Sustainable Materials Processing and Manufacturing – Lin Zhu et al. (eds)
© 2024 Taylor & Francis Group, London, ISBN 978-1-032-88599-5

Acknowledgements

On behalf of conference committee, Professor Lin Zhu and Professor Tien-Chien Jen would like to thank scholars, colleagues, and volunteers of both universities for their participation and support. Professor Lin Zhu and Professor Tien-Chien Jen also thank Ms. Xiao-Rui Zou and Mr. Wen-Xuan Zhou from Laboratory of Mechanical Structure and Biomechanics of Anhui Agricultural University for hard work on the conference, especially for Zou's work on the overall coordination of the conference and Zhou's work on the editing and proofreading for this book. Professor Lin Zhu acknowledges financial support from School of Engineering, Anhui Agricultural University, especially by Professor Li-qin Chen and Secretary Qi Ren for the conference.

Sustainable Materials Processing and Manufacturing – Lin Zhu et al. (eds)
© 2024 Taylor & Francis Group, London, ISBN 978-1-032-88599-5

About the Authors

Professor Lin Zhu is a professor at the Department of Mechanical Engineering of Anhui Agricultural University, P, R. China, He received his PhD in Precision Machinery and Precision Instrumentation from the University of Science and Technology of China (USTC), specialising in flowing characteristics and structural analysis of a silicon-based micro-combustor, And he was ever a postdoctoral research associated in mechanical engineering at the University of Wisconsin-Milwaukee and a visiting scholar of the State University of New York at Stony Brook, respectively.

The main research interests of Professor Lin Zhu are focussed on the following three aspects: (1) performances and structures of plants and animals using mechanical Engineering Methods. (2) optimisation structures and performances of mechanical components, and (3) micro-fluids and micro-structure. He also has an interest in additive manufacturing technologies including laser-based manufacturing and fused deposition modelling. He has received several competitive grants for his research, including those from the National Science Foundation of China (NSFC). Currently, he has over 80 publications and has written three books.

Professor Lin Zhu mentors several postgraduate students in the field of fluid mechanics. He is currently supervising five masters and one PhD students on liquid-solid interaction. spray mechanism, and additive manufacturing, He is a member of the Vibration Society of China.

Professor T. C. Jen was a faculty member at the University of Wisconsin, Milwaukee, and then joined the University of Johannesburg in August 2015. Prof Jen received his PhD in Mechanical and Aerospace Engineering from UCLA, specialising in thermal aspects of grinding. He has received several competitive grants for his research, including those from the US National Science Foundation, the US Department of Energy and the EPA. Dr Jen has brought in $3.0 million of funding for his research, and has received various awards for his research including the NSF GOALI Award. Prof Jen has recently established a Joint Research Centre with Nanjing Tech University of China on the "Sustainable Materials and Manufacturing." Prof Jen is also the director of Manufacturing Research Centre of the University of Johannesburg. Meanwhile, SA National Research Foundation has awarded Prof Jen a NNEP (National Nano Equipment Program) grant worth of USD l million to acquire two state-of-the-art Atomic Layer Deposition (ALD) Tools for ultra-thin film coating. These two ALD tools will be the first in South Africa and possibly the first in Africa continent.

In 2011.Prof Jen was elected as a fellow to the American Society of Mechanical Engineers (ASME), which recognised his contributions to the field of thermal science and manufacturing. As stated in the announcement of Prof Jen fellow status in the 2011 International Mechanical Engineering and Congress Exposition, "Tien-Chien Jen has made extensive contribution to the field of mechanical engineering, specifically in the area of machining process. Examples include, but not limited to, environmentally benign machining, atomic layer deposition, cold gas dynamics spraying, fuel cells and hydrogen technology, batteries, and material processing." Prof Jen has written a total of 198 peer-reviewed articles, including 84 peer-reviewed journal papers, published in many prestigious journals such as *International Journal of Heat and Mass Transfer*, *ASME Journal of Heat Transfer*, *ASME Journal of Mechanical Design*, and *ASME Journal of Manufacturing Science and Engineering*, He also has written many chapters in special topics book, for example, a chapter in *Numerical Simulation Proton Exchange Membrane Fuel Cell*, published by WIT Press, and another chapter in *Application of Lattice Boltzmann Method in Fluid Flow and Heat Transfer in Computational Fluid Dynamics-Technology and Application*.

Sustainable Materials Processing and Manufacturing – Lin Zhu et al. (eds)
© 2024 Taylor & Francis Group, London, ISBN 978-1-032-88599-5

Biomechanical Analysis on the In-situ Three-point Jump Shooting Technique in Basketball

Xuefeng Wang*

Associate Professor, Anhui Finance and Trade Vocational College,
Hefei, 230601, Anhui, China

ABSTRACT: This study aims to probe into biomechanical characteristics presented in different steps of the in-situ three-point jump shooting technique in Basketball. To monitor the whole process of the in-situ three-point jump shooting, six basketball athletes, two of whom are the second-grade basketball players, are tested with high-speed camera and 3-D force measuring platform, during which the APAS 3-D video system will be used to analyze the captured video images. And, the results of the study are as follows: (1) before the stage of take-off, the better coordination between the upper limbs of the athletes and their lower ones, the faster the take-off speed will be, which will effectively enhance their take-off height; (2) at the stage of take-off, the strength in the athletes' muscles and the speed of their shootings are closely related to the angle of the shooting; (3) at the stage of landing buffer, fewer changes in the angle of the hip joint will contribute to a better performance of the body's steadiness, mainly because the impact on landing phase will be substantially reduced with the help of the hip joint.

KEYWORDS: Basketball, In-situ three-point jump shooting technique, biomechanics in Sports

1. Introduction

Basketball is loved by the public for its unique form of activity. Jump shot is a common method of precise shooting with basketball. The main purpose of jump shot is to defeat the opponent's defense, increase scoring efficiency and ultimately win the game. With the continuous development of basketball technique, the intensity of basketball games is increasing with each passing day. The in-place three-point jump shot technique can break through other interference situations, and at the same time, it also produces an impact effect, which has a certain impact on the shooting accuracy. This technique also focuses on the physical quality of athletes. This paper takes basketball Techniques of in-situ three-point jump shot as the research object from the perspective of sports biomechanics, and analyzes the joints in its technical action, providing a certain reference for guiding athletes to practice technical action correctly.

2. Research Object and Method

2.1 Object of the Study

Basketball players performing basketball in-situ three-point jump shot technique.

2.2 Research Methodology

Experimental method

(1) Experimental subjects

Two basketball players at the national second-level and four ordinary basketball players (all male) shot with their right hands. Athletes who did not participate in strenuous exercise within 24 hours before the test were selected as subjects and all were in good athletic condition.

(2) Experimental tools

Two high-speed cameras, three-dimensional force measurement platform.

*396914004@qq.com

DOI: 10.1201/9781003538646-1

(3) Experimental procedures

(a) Number athletes;

(b) Explain the action specifications and experimental content;

(c) The two cameras were arranged 12 meters apart and the height is set to 1.3 meters. The main optical axis is perpendicular to the measurement point, and the shooting frequency is set to 100 frames/second

(d) Mark and paste positions: acromion, lateral elbow joint, lateral wrist joint, hip joint, lateral knee joint, lateral ankle and toe.

(e) Complete the whole shooting action according to the numbered sequence, five times in each group, and take the most standardized data as experimental data.

(4) Video processing

The video images were digitally processed by using a three-dimensional analysis system and smoothed by 8 Hz digital filtering to obtain the data of Fx, Fy, Fz in three directions in three-dimensional force measurement platform.

Mathematical and statistical method

Excel and SPSS softwares were used to make data analysis of the video images according to the action stages and thereupon charts were created.

3. Research Results and Analysis

3.1 Technique of Basketball in-situ Three-point Jump Shot and Description of Sports Biomechanics

Technique of basketball in-situ three-point jump shot

The basketball in-situ three-point jump shot technique can be divided into three phases.

The athlete holds the ball and moves his weight upward until his feet are completely off the ground, which is the take-off stage.

The soaring phase begins when the athlete's feet are off the ground and ends when the athlete's center of gravity reaches its highest point of the soaring technique.

The landing buffer phase begins when the athlete's center of gravity is at its highest point in the air during the landing buffer phase and lasts until the foot strikes the ground..

Sports Biomechanics

The joint angle is the angle formed when the joint of each part is the center point and the joint of the same limb is connected to the center point at the same time.

The shooting angle created by the tangent of the ball's center track and the horizontal plane at the shooting point after the player throws the ball while lifting it into the air is referred to as the shooting angle.

The speed of the shot is the speed at which the ball leaves the hand when the player is taking off in the air.

3.2 Sports Biomechanical Characteristics of Takeoff Technique

Characteristics of joint angles

It can be seen from Table 1.1 that the angles of each joint of elbow, shoulder, hip, knee and ankle are different in the takeoff stage of the in-situ three-point jump shot.

The players were holding the ball in their hands during this process, and the angle between the shoulder and waist joints is 18.763.10° 46.313.28°. The range of the shoulder joint's angle is somewhat limited. It is feasible to quicken the jumping process by extending the distance of the upper arm swing. The physical strength and speed of the jump from the ground enhanced the athlete's movement coordination. The elbow joint angle ranged from 69. 19 ± 1.84° to 98.96 ± 2.10°. The elbow joint angle of contestant No. 4 was 98.96 ± 2.10°, while that of other contestants was less than 90°. It was an acute angle. In the take-off stage, the swing speed of the upper limbs has a certain impact on the strength and speed of the jump, and the more stable the basketball player's upper limbs are, the more stable the shot will be.

Table 1.1 Angles of each joint when jumping from the ground (unit:)

	NO.1	No.2	NO.3	NO.4	NO.5	NO.6
Right elbow join	77.32±1.20	76.13±2.53	78.94±1.69	98.96±2.10	46.31±3.28	84.47±2.61
Right shoulder joint	33.21±3.14	18.76±3.10	23.68±1.34	34.27±2.64	113.36±5.46	19.02±4.38
Left hip joint	109.12±4.21	118.56±1.20	122.54±1.95	121.28±1.03	127.56±3.10	115.52±1.35
Right hip joint	117.89±2.23	126.63±3.42	138.85±2.10	126.79±4.37	104.21±1.97	125.13±4.13
Left knee joint	122.96±4.18	124.79±0.98	127.00±1.30	130.00±4.37	154.20±4.61	130.04±5.48
Right knee joint	136.51±1.03	145.56±1.59	148.30±3.25	115.09±5.62	98.24±1.69	142.94±4.12
Left ankle joint	97.35±0.35	80.36±1.30	95.41±5.31	87.95±2.18	91.25±4.81	90.41±1.58
Left ankle joint	95.73±1.57	79.99±3.42	91.29±1.82	69.33±1.94	46.31±3.28	94.03±4.17

The players' left hip angles were 109. 12 ± 4.21° - 122.54 ± 1.95° and 117.89 ± 2.23° - 109.138.85 ± 2.10°. The player no. 1 had the smallest angle, while the player No.3 has the highest angle. Among the six basketball players, the left hip angle was about the same as the right hip angle, which was better synchronized. If the hip angle is over 90 degrees, it indicates that the upper body does not tilt forward excessively.

The analysis of the left knee angle revealed that the left knee angle and the right knee angle of player #5 ranged from 104.211.97° to 154.20~4.6°, with a significant angle difference that was greater on both sides. The reason for the different angles of the left knee and right knee segments of player No.5 is that the player leaned his center of gravity to the right side. The angle values of the other basketball players' knee joints were not significantly different, and the left and right knees were more synchronized.

Through the comparative analysis of left ankle angle and right ankle angle of 6 basketball players, the data of 6 basketball players are 80.36 ± 1.30 ~ 98.24 ± 1.69° , 69.33 ± 1.94 ~ 95.73 ± 1.57°. It indicates that the function of the left ankle is more consistent with that of the right ankle.

Characteristics of angular velocity of lower limb joints

Table 1.2 shows the angular velocity characteristics of the lower limb joints at the takeoff stage. It can be seen that four ordinary basketball players were less than two basketball players at the second level. Compared with other players, the angular velocity of hip joint, knee joint and ankle joint of No.3 player was relatively low and the other five athletes had no significant differences in lower limb angular velocity. During the takeoff stage, the strength of the lower limbs was the main source of energy. The average angular velocity of the joints varied to different degrees, which determined their explosive capacity, indicating the muscle function of the lower limb movement. In terms of coordination ability of muscle groups

in the current stage, the second level basketball players were much better than the ordinary basketball players.

Mechanical characteristics of takeoff stage

Within the range of taking off, the athletes first lowered the body's center of gravity, and then generated force on the ground by moving their leg bones, bending and extending joints, and contracting their muscles so as to form a force in a certain state of flight on the ground when they were jumping. When a basketball player landed, he would exert a greater force on the ground, and the counter-force on the ground against the player would increase correspondingly. It can be seen from the results of the table that the vertical force of the athletes on the ground had a positive relationship with the ground reaction force of the players when it was pushed out. The more kinetic energy the body obtains, the higher the body would jump. The smaller the lateral and longitudinal forces were, the more they helped to increase the force in the vertical direction and thus increase the height of the flight. In daily exercise, to strengthen the muscle strength training of the left and right legs and balance the muscle strength of the left and right legs can achieve a higher height of flight. The smaller the lateral and longitudinal forces are, the more they help to increase the force in the vertical direction and thus increase the height of the flight. In daily exercise, to strengthen the muscle strength training of the left and right legs and balance the muscle strength of the left and right legs can achieve a higher height of flight.

3.3 Sports Biomechanical Characteristics of Shot Techniques

The height of the shot point is determined by the height of the player and the height of the elevation, therefore there is some difference in the angle of the shot. Only the correct direction of aiming towards the basket, the correct angle of the shot and

Table 1.2 Angular velocity of the joints of the lower limbs (unit: rad/s).

	No.1	No.2	No.3	No.4	No.5	No.6
Hip joint	328.46±4.28	296.92±1.37	187.48±1.12	282.62±2.08	202.27±5.41	234.07±4.08
Knee joint	284.84±3.07	286.64±3.86	201.93±0.89	288.70±4.81	260.75±3.64	269.43±3.64
Ankle joint	285. 15±1.51	287.87±6.41	242.31±3.36	282.49±5.37	234.95±2.94	283.29±1.69

Table 1.3 Characteristics of the instantaneous force at takeoff stage (N/kg)

	No.1	No.2	No.3	No.4	No.5	No.6
Forward and backward forces (Fx)	0.62±0.11	0.24±0.03	0.17±0.05	0.12±0.01	0.34±0.05	0.12±0.02
Lateral force (Fy)	0.09±0.01	1.77±0.05	0.82±0.03	0.17±0.05	0.57±0.02	0.52±0.04
Vertical force (Fz)	34.93±0.08	27.67±0. 12	23.28±0.15	26.96±0.08	25.63±0. 11	40.86±0.06

Table 1.4 Angle of the shot and speed of the shot

	No.1	No.2	No.3	No.4	No.5	No.6
Shot angle (°)	56.45±0.51	60.72±0.63	64.02±0.47	45.44±0.85	47.77±0.45	64.09±0.75
Shot speed (m/s)	6.35±0.51	6.18±0.12	6. 14±0.25	5.79±0.21	5.94±0.23	5.87±0.15

the corresponding speed of the shot can improve the accuracy of basketball throwing.

According to the relevant mathematical model analysis, the optimal angle for a long shot from the 3-point line is 50 to 55 °, and the best shooting speed for a mid-range shot, such as from 5 meters, is about 70 °. At the same time, the angle of the athlete's shot was not fixed and it depended on the height of the athlete, the way of the shot and the speed of the shot. According to the data in Table 1.4, player No. 1's shooting angle was the closest to the best shooting angle from the 3-point line. The shooting angles of No.2, No.3 and No.6 were relatively large within the range of 60 – 65, while the shooting angles of No.4 and No.5 were less than 50. In general, the shot angle of the players is different from one another. The shot angle of No. 1 player is more reasonable, while the shot angle of other players is relatively unreasonable with a higher speed of shots. Pushing the ball out of the fingers is the speed of the shot, and it is related to the strength of the arm muscle and the elasticity of the finger, according to the data in the table. Two national level basketball players shot at the basket more swiftly than four ordinary basketball players.

3.4 Sports Biomechanical Characteristics of Shot Techniques

Characteristics of lower limb joint angle

The angle of athlete's joints and angular velocity will change as he progressively descends to the earth throughout this period. Through studying the angle changes in hip joint, knees and ankle joint, the writer will do some analysis about the joints and muscle groups.

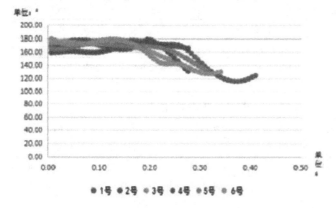

Fig. 1.1 Characteristics of hip joint angle changes

Figure 1.1 shows the characteristics of changes in hip angle during the landing buffer for six athletes. As shown in Fig. 1.3, the joint angle varied from 140° to 180° for each athlete

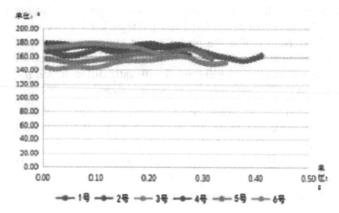

Fig. 1.2 Characteristics of knee joint angle changes

Figure 1.2 shows the change in knee angle of the six basketball players during the landing buffer phase. The athlete's joint angle changed over time due to different heights of flight.

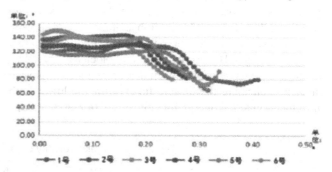

Fig. 1.3 Characteristics of ankle joint angle changes

Figure 1.3 shows that the instability of the ankle joint angle was periodical when six basketball players landed on the ground. The angle of the ankle joint changed with the process of their descending to the ground and gradually decreased, with a wide range of from 60 ° to 140 °.

The analysis on the changes of lower limb angles of the athletes during the landing buffer period shows that in this period, the athletes' joint angles varied the most on the ankle, followed by the knee and the least on the hip. At the end of the elevation stage, the athlete's body fell from the air and the feet touched the ground for the first time. The joints of the lower limbs in the ankle joint were closest to the ground and had the best reflexes. Bending the knee joint reduced the ground reaction force on the knee joint and reduced the possibility of joint changes. Meanwhile, the curvature of the knee joint decreased as did the change in the hip joint. The hip, knee and ankle joints of No. 1 and No.6 changed significantly, thus reducing the reaction force of the ground on the knee and ankle joints, mitigating knee and ankle injuries and effectively avoiding the impact of landing.

Angular velocity characteristics of lower limb joints

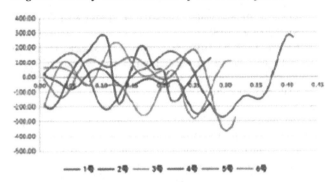

Fig. 1.4 Angular velocity variation characteristics of the hip joint (unit: rad/s)

As can be seen from the graph in Fig. 1.4, there are three peaks in the hip joint angle of the player No. 1 during this phase. Each peak occurred at slightly different times, because each player had a different joint angle.

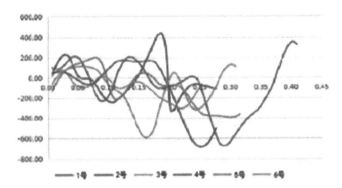

Fig. 1.5 Angular velocity variation characteristics of the knee joint (unit: rad/s)

Figure 1.5 shows the characteristics of the variation of the angular velocity of the knee joint for the six tested basketball players. It can be seen from the figure that the knee angular velocity also fluctuated three times during the landing buffer phase, and the knee angular velocity changed further with a greater magnitude than the hip joint during this phase. This indicates that the knee joint bends and extends faster during the landing buffer phase, and the sharp change in the knee joint during this period can effectively mitigate the ground reaction force on the knee joint, thus protecting the joint.

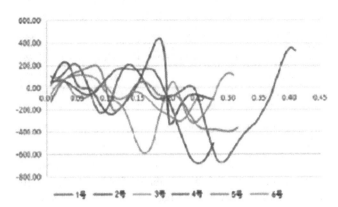

Fig. 1.6 Angular velocity variation characteristics of the ankle joint (unit: rad/s)

Figure 1.6 shows the variation characteristics of the ankle angular velocity of the athletes tested in the landing buffer phase. As can be seen from the figure, the athletes' ankle angular velocity showed a tendency to change in synchronization with the ground, with very little change in angular velocity before 0.15 seconds, and after 0.15 seconds the angular velocity of the ankle joint became larger and the foot landing on the ground leaded to the dorsiflexion of the ankle joint.

According to the data of the angular velocity of the hip, knee and ankle of the six players who landed on the ground, it was found that the change of the angular velocity of the ankle joint was the largest, followed by the knee, and the angular velocity of the hip joint, which was found to be the smallest, in addition, the rapid change of the joint angle also had a positive relationship with the speed of joint bending and expansion. At this stage, the ankle joint of the lower limb plays a very important role, so it is important to pay attention to muscle strengthening exercises around the ankle to further protect it.

Mechanical characteristics of the landing buffer phase

The landing buffer stage is the ultimate phase of the entire basketball in-situ three-point jump shooting technique. In this phase, when the athlete's body descended and touched the ground, the ankle joint changed from a toe flexion state to a foot back extension state; the muscle groups around the ankle joint completed the change from an active state to a passive state; the knee joint moved from extension to flexion, and the peripheral muscle groups changed from active contraction to passive contraction.

According to the data in Table 1.5, the reason for the differences of the vertical force (Fz) of the athletes in this phase was mainly due to the effect of height and weight on the vertical force. The lateral force (Fy) which depended on whether the force between the athlete's feet was balanced when the body was falling or whether the movements of the

Table 1.5 Characteristics of the force at the moment of landing (N/kg)

	No.1	No.2	No.3	No.4	No.5	No.6
Forward and backward forces (Fx)	0.62±0.11	0.24±0.03	0.17±0.05	0.12±0.01	0.34±0.05	0.12±0.02
Lateral force (Fy)	0.09±0.01	1.77±0.05	0.82±0.03	0.17±0.05	0.57±0.02	0.52±0.04
Vertial force (Fz)	34.93±0.08	27.67±0.12	23.28±0.15	26.96±0.08	25.63±0.11	40.86±0.06

left and right legs were synchronized when the body was falling.

There are some differences in athletes' exercise habits, as well as in the degree of slip resistance of athletic shoes, so the force (Fx) from forward and backward varied. The strength of the athlete's falling depended heavily on the weight of the athlete itself and the height of the fall.

4. Conclusion

1. In the takeoff stage, the higher the coordination between upper and lower limbs is, the better the jumping speed is. Therefore, the height of elevating in the air increases more effectively.

2. In the elevation stage, because of the individual differences, several athletes shot without considering a reasonable shot angle. The smaller the angle of shot is, the faster the speed of the basketball.

3. In the landing buffer stage, the changes of the lower limb joints are changing with the ankle, knee and hip joints in the process of the impact from the ground, showing a trend from large to small. Among all the joints, the angle and angular velocity of the ankle joint change most, then comes after the knee joint. All in all, the hip joint connects the upper and lower part of the limb, and the trend of changes would have a certain impact on the stability of the athlete's body.

Acknowledgements

This research was financially supported by Anhui Vocational College of Finance and trade (tzpysj059, tzpysj240, and tzpyxj076)

REFERENCES

1. ZHENG Song-ling, MAN Xi.(2021).Knee Isokinetic Characteristics of Men's Basketball Players.Journal of Medical Biomechanics, 36(S01): 1. DOI:CNKI:SUN:NMSB.0.2020-01-018.
2. CHEN Xiangzi.(2019).Measurement of Muscle Discharge and Kinematic Analysis of Joints in Basketball Players' Spike. Journal of Suzhou University, 34(6):5.DOI:10.3969/j.issn.1673-2006.2019.06.013.
3. Song Jin-hua, Zhang Fan. (2019).Biomechanical Analysis of the Jump Shot in Basketball. Contemporary Sports Technology, 26+28. DOI:10. 16655/j.cnki.2095-2813.2019.07.026
4. Bao Chunyu, Meng Qinghua, Yan Mingming. (2019).Analysis of Biomechancial Characteristics of Ankle during Stop-jump for Basket Player. Chinese Journal of Applied Mechanics, 36(02):492-498+518.DOI:10. 11776/cjam.36.02.D1 16.
5. Qiu Jie. (2017) Application of Sports Biomechanics in Basketball Teaching. Contemporary Sports Technology, 7(32): 57-58. DOI:10. 16655/j.cnki.2095 -2813.2017.32.057.
6. Wang Jingyi.(2017).Application of Physiological and Biochemical Indexes in Amateur Basketball Training in Colleges.Sport, (16):21-22.DOI:10.3969/j.issn.1674-151x.2017.16. 011.
7. Ye Zexi.(2017).Biomechanical Analysis of Single Handed Over Shoulder Shoot Technique in Basketball. Contemporary Sports Technology, 7(14): 14+16. DOI: 10. 16655/j.cnki.2095-2813.2017.14.014.
8. Niu Chenglong, Zhao Shipeng, Han Chengshuang, Zhu Xuran.(2017). Biomechanical Analysis of the Jump Shot in Basketball[J]. Youth Sport,(02):46-47.DOI:10.3969/j.issn.2095-4581.2017.02.025.

Note: All the figures and tables in this chapter were compiled by the author.

Sustainable Materials Processing and Manufacturing – Lin Zhu et al. (eds)
© 2024 Taylor & Francis Group, London, ISBN 978-1-032-88599-5

Production Strategy for Electric Vehicle and Power Battery in a Closed-Loop Supply Chain with Loss Aversion and Green Preference

2

Yifan Hou[1]

Assistant Professor, Guangzhou, Guangdong, China, School of Business Administration, Guangdong University of Finance & Economics

Jie Zhang[2]

Professor, Guangzhou, Guangdong, China, School of Business Administration, Guangdong University of Finance & Economics

ABSTRACT: This paper analyzes the interaction between electric vehicle (EV) manufacturers' loss aversion and consumers' green preference towards the production decision of electric vehicles (EVs). We construct a closed-loop supply chain consisting of EV manufacturers, power battery manufacturers, recycling centers and consumers. By using the newsvendor model in the research, we find that with EV manufacturers' loss aversion, EV manufacturers will increase their production quantities when the production quantity is below a certain level and the shortage cost is large. When consumers have the green preference, there is an optimal value for the green level of EVs, and EV manufacturers will also enhance the production quantities. When considering EV manufacturers' loss aversion and consumers' green preference together, consumers' green preference inhibits the impact of loss aversion of EV manufacturers on their production.

KEYWORDS: Electric vehicles, Closed-loop supply chain, Loss aversion, Green preference, Newsvendor model

1. Introduction

Under the background of carbon emissions peak and carbon neutrality goals, the development of technology and the rising cost of fuel and materials have spurred customers to become more aware of environmental consumption. EVs have become the preferred choice for car buyers. Previous scholars have conducted many empirical studies on EVs, considering aspects such as policies, subsidies and usage costs.

How can EV manufacturers make the best production decisions as the market for EVs expands? On the one hand, EV manufacturers would take losses such as orders not being delivered on time owing to auto parts shortages. On the other hand, excessive inventory can lead to increased stock costs and a large risk of inventory damage. Thus, decision bias exists in the newsvendor problem, in other words, a manager may

have preference other than risk neutrality (Schweitzer ME, 2000). In this paper, we attempt to use loss aversion behavior to describe the newsvendor decision bias. In summary, the loss aversion behavior of EV manufacturers affects their production decisions, profits, and expected utilities.

There is an increasing number of factors influencing EV purchasers' behavior, such as characteristics of green consumers' preference impact on supply chain decisions and pricing, Du et al (2018) and Cirillo et al (2017) have shown that low-carbon awareness has a regulatory effect on purchasing behavior. As a result, an environmental buyer should be more inclined to buy an EV. However, most studies on consumers' green preference have focused on single-channel, dual-channel, or closed-loop supply chains only for EV manufacturers, with sparse mention of the impact on the closed-loop supply chain with consideration of power batteries. A large power battery pack in an EV covers 38% of

[1]houyifan0609@foxmail.com, [2]Jiezh@gdufe.edu.cn

DOI: 10.1201/9781003538646-2

the overall vehicle cost, which is a crucial component of EVs, so that worth more attention.

Existing research on the supply chain of EV batteries are mainly from the perspective of closed-loop and reverse supply chain to achieve equilibrium and profit maximization. Some scholars have conduct related studies on the production path of EVs, battery swap stations, and related planning, and some have predict the need of raw materials, batteries, etc. In short, the battery supply chain has been a hot topic of research among scholars in recent years, but fewer scholars have studied the impact of members' preference of the supply chain for power batteries. In this paper, we propose that recycling centers would recycle the batteries and realize cascade utilization.

This paper considers the production decisions of EV manufacturers more important than pricing issues and ignores their price decisions. We construct a closed-loop supply chain for power batteries, considering the impact of the green preference of consumers and the loss aversion of EV manufacturers on the production decisions of EV manufacturers. We list some of the problems that may occur in the closed-loop supply chain for EV power batteries.

(1) Does EV manufacturers' loss-aversion affect production decisions and expected utility? How do overstock and shortage losses affect EV manufacturers' production decisions and expected utility?

(2) What is the relationship between the green level of EV and manufacturers' production decisions and expected utility? Will consumers' green preference inspirit EV manufacturers to build greener vehicles?

(3) How would their production decisions be changed when considering both EV manufacturers' loss aversion and consumers' green preference? Will consumers' green preference promote EV manufacturers to overcome their irrational decisions so that they can avoid losses?

To answer these research questions, we analyze three scenarios: considering the loss aversion behavior of EV manufacturers and the green preference of consumers respectively, and then the interaction of these two preferences on the production decisions of EV manufacturers. We find that: first, with loss aversion, the greater the loss aversion degree is, the less expected utility will become before the production volume exceeds a certain amount $\left(\dfrac{(Pv + h)\int_{x=0}^{q_1(Q_{\lambda x})} xf(x)dx}{(Pw + h)} \right)$. Then, with consumers' green preference, the increase of consumers' green preference incentives the EV enterprises to produce more green EVs before the green level of EVs reaches the optimal amount $\left(\dfrac{\rho P_v F(Q_{\lambda x})}{\sigma} \right)$. Finally, the green preference of consumers inhibits the loss aversion of EV manufacturers.

2. The Model

Our model assumes the following decision sequence. First, EV manufacturers place orders with power battery manufacturers to produce and sell EVs to consumers. Then, power battery manufacturers organize production according to the number of orders. They are two channels of materials for battery production, energy companies that supply raw materials for new batteries and recycling centers that provide class I batteries. Finally, recycling centers recycle waste batteries from consumers before disposing of them for echelon utilization. The above-mentioned sequence is shown in Fig. 2.1.

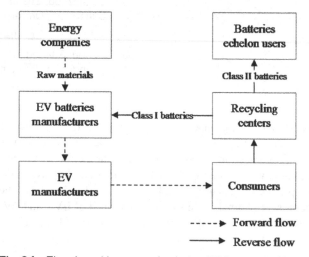

Fig. 2.1 The closed-loop supply chain of EV power batteries
Source: Author's compilation

It is assumed that enterprises in the closed-loop supply chain consist of a single enterprise. The main value of the EV lies in the power battery, and hence we assume that the wholesale price of the EV is identical to the wholesale price of the power battery P_w. The value of the EV is exactly the value of the power battery P_v, and $P_w < P_v$. For the convenience of analysis, the cost of producing a battery by using a used one is less costly than manufacturing a new one, that is, $C_r < C_m$, with the same performance and quality. We also set the market demand $D = \alpha - \beta P_v$, where α, β, P_v are positive parameters. α is basic market capacity, β represents the sensibility to the price of EVs. x is the indeterminate random customer demand in the sales cycle, which probability density function is f(x), and the cumulative distribution function is F(x). To simplify the calculations, f(x) in this section follows a uniform distribution.

This paper sets the number of batteries recycled by an EV manufacturer as $Q = m + nW$, where m, n, W are positive parameters. m represents the number of waste batteries that consumers voluntarily return to the recycling centers driven by environmental awareness and self-restraint, rather than the recycling price. n stands for sensitivity to battery recycling price W. The retired power batteries are divided into class I batteries and class II batteries after detection (Moore et al., 2020. Zheng et al., 2018). The recycling centers acquire class I batteries with a quantity of θQ for remanufactures, and the other classified category as ladder utilization, they can obtain P_u by selling a unit of class II batteries. This article omits the cost of transferring batteries from consumers to recycling centers and recycling centers to power battery manufacturers. The following notations are used through the paper (Table 2.1).

Table 2.1 Notations of the model

Variables	Notations
P_w	The wholesale price of a unit power battery (the wholesale price of the EV)
P_v	The value of a unit power battery (the value of the EV)
P_u	Price of selling a unit of class II battery
C_m	The manufacture cost of producing a unit power battery using raw materials
C_r	The remanufacture cost of a unit recycled battery
D	The market demand for EVs
W	The price of recycling a unit of battery
X	The indeterminate random customer demand in the sales cycle
f(x)	The probability density function of x
F(x)	The cumulative distribution function of x
$Q_{\lambda x}$	The production decision of EV manufacturers
Q	The amount of the power batteries recycled
θQ	The number of I batteries remanufactured by recycling centers
s	Losses due to the inability to meet consumers demand
h	Losses due to overstocking
ρ	The degree of consumers' green preference
g	The green level of EVs
λ	The degree of loss-aversion
$\pi(Q_i)$	The profit function for i. The subscript i will take values λx,b, c, which denote EV manufacturer, power battery manufacturer, and the recycling center, respectively

Source: Author's compilation

3. Considering Electric Vehicle (EV) Manufacturers' Loss Aversion

This section analyzes the impact of the loss-averse behavior of EV manufacturers on their decisions, including losses due to the inability to meet consumers demand and losses due to overstock. The profit functions of EV manufacturer, power battery manufacturer and recycling center are as follows.

$$\pi(Q_{\lambda x}) = \begin{cases} \pi_{(Q_{\lambda x})} = P_v x - P_w Q_{\lambda x} - h(Q_{\lambda x} - x), \\ \qquad x < Q_{\lambda x} \\ \pi_+(Q_{\lambda x}) = P_v Q_{\lambda x} - P_w Q_{\lambda x} - s(x - Q_{\lambda x}), \\ \qquad x \geq Q_{\lambda x} \end{cases} \quad (1)$$

$$\pi(Q_b) = (P_w - C_m)(Q_{\lambda x} - \theta Q) + (P_w - C_r)\theta \quad (2)$$

$$\pi(Q_c) = (1 - \theta)QP_u + C_r\theta Q - QW \quad (3)$$

The profit of the EV manufacturer should be greater than zero, and then the break-even point is

$$q_1(Q_{\lambda x}) = (P_w + h)Q_{\lambda x}/(P_v + h) \quad (4)$$

When the EV manufacturer does not produce enough to meet the demand of the consumer, the break-even point is

$$q_2(Q_{\lambda x}) = (P_v - P_w + s)Q_{\lambda x}/s \quad (5)$$

Assuming that EV manufacturer is loss-averse, the degree of loss-aversion is represented by parameter λ, and π_0 is the reference point of decision-makers. Generally, we set the profit reference level for decision-makers as zero ($\pi_0 = 0$). EV manufacturer utility function is

$$u(\pi) = \begin{cases} \pi - \pi_0, & \pi \geq \pi_0 \\ \lambda(\pi - \pi_0), & \pi < \pi_0 \end{cases} \quad (6)$$

The expected utility of the loss-aversion decision-maker is

$$EU(\pi_{Q_{\lambda x}}) = (P_v + h)\int_{x=0}^{Q_{\lambda x}} xf(x)dx - s$$

$$\int_{Q_{\lambda x}}^{\infty} xf(x)dx - (P_v + s + h)Q_{\lambda x}F(Q_{\lambda x}) + (\lambda - 1)$$

$$(P_v + h)\int_{x=0}^{q_1(Q_{\lambda x})} xf(x)dx - (\lambda - 1)s$$

$$\int_{q_2(Q_{\lambda x})}^{\infty} xf(x)dx + \lambda(P_v - P_w + s)$$

$$Q_{\lambda x} - (\lambda - 1)(P_w + h)Q_{\lambda x}F(q_1(Q_{\lambda x}))$$
$$- (\lambda - 1)(P_v + s - P_w)Q_{\lambda x}F(q_2(Q_{\lambda x})) \quad (7)$$

Therefore, the optimal production strategy for EV manufacturers satisfies the following equation.

$$F(Q^*_{\lambda x}) = \frac{\lambda(P_v + s - P_w)}{(P_v + s + h)}$$
$$- \frac{(\lambda - 1)\begin{bmatrix} (P_w + h)F(q_1(Q_{\lambda x})) \\ + (P_v + s - P_w)F(q_2(Q_{\lambda x})) \end{bmatrix}}{(P_v + s + h)} \quad (8)$$

Let L_{under} be the loss of expectations because of under-production, $L_{under} = (P_v - P_w + s)[1 - F(q_2(Q_{\lambda x}))]$, which is the product of loss and probability of loss due to shortage. And let L_{over} be the loss of expectations for over-production,

$L_{over} = (h + P_w)F(q_1(Q_{\lambda x}))$, which is the product of loss and probability of loss owing to overstock.

Proposition 1 The impact of EV manufacturers' loss aversion coefficient on the optimal decision and expected utility are as follows.

(i) When $L_{under} > L_{over}$, $\dfrac{\partial Q^*_{\lambda x}}{\partial \lambda} > 0$. When $L_{under} < L_{over}$, $\dfrac{\partial Q^*_{\lambda x}}{\partial \lambda} < 0$;

(ii) When $Q_{\lambda x} > \dfrac{(Pv+h)\int_{x=0}^{q_1(Q_{\lambda x})} xf(x)dx}{(Pw+h)}$, $\dfrac{\partial EU(\pi_{Q_{\lambda x}})}{\partial \lambda} < 0$.

Proposition 1 shows that if the expected loss caused by the shortage is greater than over-product loss, the number of EVs produced by EV manufacturers increases as the loss aversion increases to avoid the loss of shortage. When $Q_{\lambda x}$ exceeds a certain number, in the case of overproduction, the greater the degree of loss aversion the EV manufacturers have, the less their expected utility get.

Proposition 2 The impact of EV manufacturers' shortage cost and inventory overstock cost on the optimal decision and expected utility are as follows.

(i) $\dfrac{\partial Q^*_{\lambda x}}{\partial s} > 0$, $\dfrac{\partial EU(\pi_{Q_{\lambda x}})}{\partial s} < 0$;

(ii) $\dfrac{\partial Q^*_{\lambda x}}{\partial h} < 0$, $\dfrac{\partial EU(\pi_{Q_{\lambda x}})}{\partial h} < 0$.

Based on proposition 2, the higher the shortage cost is, the more EVs would be produced by EV manufacturers and the greater the demand for parts appears. Due to the current complex and changeable economic environment, parts suppliers and OEMs (Original equipment manufacturers) have also been actively working on production layout. At the same time, EV manufacturers expect utility falls as the cost of shortages increases.

The larger the inventory backlog cost is, the fewer EVs would be produced and the expected utility of EV manufacturers would decrease. For dealers and direct-sale auto companies, inventory cars take up too much cash flow and garage space, which leads them to be prone to financial problems and unable to raise better EVs for sale, so that suffering inventory losses. As a result, EV companies increase motor exhibition halls or urban experience stores in supermarkets to master customers' preferences and adopt customized strategies so that they can avoid inventory losses.

4. Considering Consumers' Green Preference

When considering green consumption preference, the consumers demand function D' for EVs is the indeterminate random customer demand that adds the green preference coefficient ρ multiplied by the green level of the vehicle g. The number of recycled batteries Q' is the product of Q and the consumers' green preference coefficient ρ. The unit cost of recycling batteries is W, and we assume EV manufacturers invest $\dfrac{1}{2}\rho g^2$ in green technologies. The profit function of EV manufacturer, power battery manufacturer and the recycling center of power batteries are as follows.

$$\pi(Q_{\lambda x}) = \begin{cases} P_v D' - P_w Q_{\lambda x} - \dfrac{1}{2}\sigma g^2, D' < Q_{\lambda x} \\ P_v Q_{\lambda x} - P_w Q_{\lambda x} - \dfrac{1}{2}\sigma g^2, D' \geq Q_{\lambda x} \end{cases} \quad (9)$$

$$\pi(Q_b) = (P_w - C_m)(Q_{\lambda x} - \theta Q') + (P_w - C_r)\theta Q' \quad (10)$$

$$\pi(Q_c) = (1-\theta)Q'P_u + \theta Q C_r - WQ'$$
$$= (1-\theta)P_u + \theta C_r - WQ' \quad (11)$$

We can obtain the optimal production decision and expected utility for EV manufacturers as follows.

$$F\left(Q'^*_{\lambda x}\right) = g\rho f(Q_{\lambda x}) + \dfrac{P_v - P_w}{P_v} \quad (12)$$

$$EU^*\left(\pi(Q_{\lambda x})\right) = \int_{x=0}^{Q_{\lambda x}} P_v xf(x)dx + g\rho P_v$$
$$\left[F(Q_{\lambda x}) - Q_{\lambda x}f(Q_{\lambda x})\right] - \dfrac{1}{2}\sigma g^2 \quad (13)$$

The optimal amount of battery recycling and the cost of recovery are as follows.

$$Q'^* = 1/2\left[(1-\theta)n\rho P_u + \theta C_r n\rho + \rho m\right] \quad (14)$$

$$W^* = \dfrac{(1-\theta)nP_u + \theta nC_r - \rho m}{2n\rho}$$
$$= \dfrac{(1-\theta)P_u + \theta C_r}{2\rho} - \dfrac{m}{2n} \quad (15)$$

Proposition 3 The impact of the green level of the EVs and consumers' green preference coefficient on the optimal decision and expected utility are as follows.

(i) $\dfrac{\partial EU(\pi_{Q_{\lambda x}})}{\partial \rho} > 0$, $\dfrac{\partial g}{\partial \rho} > 0$;

(ii) When $g < \dfrac{\rho P_v F(Q_{\lambda x})}{\sigma}$ and x follows evenly distributed,

$\dfrac{\partial Q^*_{\lambda x}}{\partial g} > 0$, $\dfrac{\partial EU(\pi_{Q_{\lambda x}})}{\partial g} > 0$.

According to Proposition 3, consumers' green preference promotes the expected utility of EV manufacturers and the green level of EVs designed. As a result, EV manufacturers are more environmentally friendly. The green preference of consumers presents the willingness of customers to buy EVs with the elevated green degree. When the green level of the EVs is below a certain level $\left(\dfrac{\rho P_v F(Q_{\lambda x})}{\sigma}\right)$, the number of EVs produced and the expected utility of EV manufacturers grows as the degree level increases. In this situation, the EV manufacturer's production decision $F(Q_{\lambda x})$ is $\dfrac{P_v - P_w}{P_v}\dfrac{\sigma}{\sigma - \rho^2 P_v f(Q_{\lambda x})}$.

Proposition 4 The impact of consumers' green preference and the number of recycled batteries on profits of recycling centers are as follows, when $Q' < (1 - \theta)P_u \rho n + \theta C_r \rho n + \rho m$, $\dfrac{\partial \pi(Q_c)}{\partial \rho} > 0$ and $\dfrac{\partial \pi(Q_c)}{\partial Q'} > 0$.

According to this proposition, when the number of batteries recycled is less than a certain number, as consumers' preference increases, the number of recycled batteries and the profit of the recycling center arguments. It is important to note that the revenue from cascaded utilization of recycled batteries must be greater than the cost of manufacturing the batteries. Otherwise, battery recycling centers will be reluctant to recycle the batteries.

5. Interaction between EV Manufacturers' Loss Aversion and Consumers' Green Preference

When considering EV manufacturers' loss aversion and consumers' green consumption preference, the profit functions of the EV manufacturer, the power battery manufacturer and the recycling center of power batteries are as follows.

$$\pi(Q_v) = \begin{cases} \pi_-(Q_v) = P_v(x + \rho g) - P_w Q_{\lambda x} - h \\ \qquad (Q_{\lambda x} - x - \rho g) - \dfrac{1}{2}\sigma g^2, \ x < Q_{\lambda x} \\ \pi_+(Q_v) = P_v Q_{\lambda x} - P_w Q_{\lambda x} - s \\ \qquad (x + \rho g - Q_{\lambda x}) - \dfrac{1}{2}\sigma g^2, \ x \geq Q_{\lambda x} \end{cases} \quad (16)$$

$$\pi(Q_b) = (P_w - C_m)(Q_{\lambda x} - \theta Q') + (P_w - C_r)\theta Q' \quad (17)$$

$$\pi(Q_c) = (1 - \theta)Q' P_u + \theta Q' C_r - W Q'$$
$$= [(1 - \theta)P_u + \theta C_r - W]Q' \quad (18)$$

In a similar way, the break-even point is

$$q_1(Q_{\lambda x}) = \dfrac{(P_w + h)Q_{\lambda x} + \rho g(-h - P_v) + \dfrac{1}{2}\sigma g^2}{(P_v + h)} \quad (19)$$

$$q_2(Q_{\lambda x}) = \dfrac{(P_v - P_w + s)Q_{\lambda x} + \rho g(-h - P_v) - s\rho g - \dfrac{1}{2}\sigma g^2}{s} \quad (20)$$

The production decision of the loss-averse EV manufacturer is

$$Q_{\lambda x} = \dfrac{\lambda\big[(P_v + h + s)\rho g + (P_v - P_w + s)\big] + \dfrac{(\lambda - 1)\sigma g^2}{2}\left[\dfrac{(P_v - P_w + s)}{s} - \dfrac{(P_w + h)}{(P_v + h)}\right]}{(P_v + h + s) + (\lambda - 1)\left[\dfrac{(P_v - P_w + s)^2}{s} + \dfrac{(P_w + h)^2}{(P_v + h)}\right]} \quad (21)$$

Proposition 5 The impact of the EV manufacturers' loss aversion on the optimal decision and expected utility are as follows.

(i) when $Q' > \dfrac{(P_v - P_w + s)(1 - \rho g) + (P_w - h)\rho g + \dfrac{1}{2}\sigma g^2\left[\dfrac{(-h - P_w)}{(P_v + h)} + \dfrac{(P_v - P_w + s)}{s}\right]}{\left[\dfrac{(-h - P_w)^2}{(P_v + h)} + \dfrac{(P_v - P_w + s)^2}{s}\right]}$,

$\dfrac{\partial Q^*_{\lambda x}}{\partial \lambda} < 0$;

(ii) when $(P_v + h) > s$, and $Q_{\lambda x} > \dfrac{s\rho g + \dfrac{1}{2}\sigma g^2}{(P_v - P_w + s)}$,

$\dfrac{\partial EU(\pi_{Q_{\lambda x}})}{\partial \lambda} < 0$.

This proposition's result is similar to the conclusion that without the green preference of consumers, as the number of production decisions of EV manufacturers reaches a certain number, the number of optimal decisions of production decreases as the level of loss aversion of EV manufacturers increases. If the inventory loss after selling the inventory car is greater than the out-of-stock loss and the production volume reaches a certain value, as the EV manufacturers' loss aversion increases, the expected utility decreases. However, after adding the factor of consumers' green preference, the boundary value of the number of decisions that EV manufacturers need to achieve has changed. We summarize optimal decisions in four situations in Table 2.2.

Proposition 6 Consumers' green preference inhibits the loss aversion of EV manufacturers.

Considering only the loss aversion of EV manufacturers, the expected utility of EV manufacturers will decline when the production quantity reaches a critical value

Table 2.2 The optimal production decisions in different situations.

$Q^*_{\lambda x}$	Without loss-aversion	With loss-aversion	
Without green preference	$F(Q^*_{\lambda x}) = \dfrac{P_v - P_w}{P_v}$	$F(Q^*_{\lambda x}) = \dfrac{\lambda(P_v + s - P_w) - (\lambda - 1)(P_w + h)F(q_1(Q_{\lambda x})) - (\lambda - 1)(P_v + s - P_w)F(q_2(Q_{\lambda x}))}{(P_v + s + h)}$ $Q_{\lambda x} = \dfrac{(P_v - P_w + s) + \frac{(\lambda - 1)\sigma g^2}{2}\left[\frac{(P_v - P_w + s)}{s} - \frac{(P_w + h)}{(P_v + h)}\right]}{(P_v + h + s) + (\lambda - 1)\left[\frac{(P_v - P_w + s)^2}{s} + \frac{(P_w + h)^2}{(P_v + h)}\right]}$	
With green preference	$F(Q^*_{\lambda x}) = g\rho f(Q_{\lambda x}) + \dfrac{P_v - P_w}{P_v}$	$Q_{\lambda x} = \dfrac{\lambda\left[(P_v + h + s)\rho g + (P_v - P_w + s)\right] + \frac{(\lambda - 1)\sigma g^2}{2}\left[\frac{(P_v - P_w + s)}{s} - \frac{(P_w + h)}{(P_v + h)}\right]}{(P_v + h + s) + (\lambda - 1)\left[\frac{(P_v - P_w + s)^2}{s} + \frac{P_w + h^2}{(P_v + h)}\right]}$	

Source: Author's compilation

$\dfrac{(P_v + s - P_w)}{\left[\frac{(P_v - P_w + s)^2}{s} + \frac{(P_w + h)^2}{P_v + h}\right]}$. But when considering consumers' green preference, the boundary condition is

$$\left(\frac{(P_v - P_w + s)(1 - \rho g) + (P_w - h)\rho g + \frac{1}{2}\sigma g^2\left[\frac{(-h - P_w)}{(P_v + h)} + \frac{(P_v - P_w + s)}{s}\right]}{\left[\frac{(h + P_w)^2}{(P_v + h)} + \frac{(P_v - P_w + s)^2}{s}\right]}\right).$$

The threshold is widened so that the EV manufacturers can produce more cars and gain more profits. Hence, consumers' green preference inhibits the loss aversion of EV manufacturers. Indeed, under the goal of double carbon, EV manufacturers increase investment in EVs' body performance and green production. For example, NIO launched the new car ES7 in May 2022, this vehicle 's system carried, the seat material, and the color of the parts all show the design of green and environment-friendly trends.

6. Conclusion

This research works on the impact of EV manufacturers' loss aversion and consumers' green preference on the decisions of the EV power battery supply chain. Firstly, EV manufacturers should increase inventories of batteries and other components when the expected shortage losses are greater. When the production volume exceeds a certain amount, the greater the loss aversion degree is, the fewer expected utility they gain. Next, the improvement of the consumers' green preference (willingness to buy cleaner cars) promotes the production of EVs and the desired utility of EV manufacturers before the green level of EVs reaches a certain level. At the same time, consumers' green preference drives more investment in

EV green technology research and development. Finally, we find consumers' green preference inhibits the loss aversion of EV manufacturers.

The paper also offers some recommendations for enterprises and government. First, developing the digitization of the supply chain can help EV manufacturers predict sales under multiple factors and adjust capacity and inventory to avoid losses, can support parts suppliers to capture inventory information and ensure timely supply. Then, EV manufacturers should invest more in green technologies and try to diversify their sales models. For example, the model of battery swap is a safe, green, and efficient way to manage batteries. It will reduce the pressure of using EV chargers and avoid the peak of public electricity consumption. The mode of leasing the battery pack reduces the cost of car purchase, charging, and time for drivers. Finally, encouraging consumer awareness of green environmental protection will contribute to the sales of EVs, promote corporate social responsibility, and help achieve the double carbon goal sooner.

Acknowledgements

The authors are grateful to the managing editor and the anonymous reviewers for their helpful comments and suggestions. This research was supported by the National Natural Science Foundation of China (No. 71871067) and Innovative Team Project of Guangdong Universities (Nos. 2019WCXTD008, 2020WCXTD011).

REFERENCES

1. Maccrimmon, K. R., Wehrung, D. A., & Stanbury, W. T. (1986). Taking risks: the management of uncertainty. taking risks the management of uncertainty.
2. Schweitzer, M. E., & Cachon, G. P. (2000). Decision bias in the newsvendor problem with a known demand distribution: experimental evidence. Management Science. 46(3):404-420.

3. Zhang, X., & Zhang, C. (2015). Optimal new energy vehicle production strategy considering subsidy and shortage cost. Energy Procedia. 75:2981-2986.
4. Cirillo, C., Liu, Y., & Maness, M. (2017). A time-dependent stated preference approach to measuring vehicle type preferences and market elasticity of conventional and green vehicles. Transportation Research Part A Policy & Practice. 100(6):294-310.
5. Zheng, Z., Chen, M., Wang, Q., Zhang, Y., Ma, X., & Shen, C., et al. (2018). High performance cathode recovery from different electric vehicle recycling streams. ACS Sustainable Chemistry & Engineering. 6(11).
6. Du, H., Liu, D., Sovacool, B. K., Wang, Y., Ma, S., & Li, R. (2018). Who buys new energy vehicles in china? assessing social-psychological predictors of purchasing awareness, intention, and policy. Transportation Research. 58(8):56-69.
7. Moore, E. A., Russell, J. D., Babbitt, C. W., Tomaszewski, B., & Clark, S. (2020). Spatial modeling of a second-use strategy for electric vehicle batteries to improve disaster resilience and circular economy. Resources Conservation and Recycling. 160, 104889.
8. Sun, Q., Chen, H., Long, R., Li, Q., Huang, H. (2022) Comparative evaluation for recycling waste power batteries with different collection modes based on stackelberg game. sciencedirect. Journal of Environmental Management. 312.

Sustainable Materials Processing and Manufacturing – Lin Zhu et al. (eds)
© 2024 Taylor & Francis Group, London, ISBN 978-1-032-88599-5

The Effects of Proactive Strategic Orientation on Manufacturing SMEs' Performance

Peter Onu*

College of Engineering, Landmark University
Faculty of Engineering and the Builth Environment, University of Johannesburg

Anup Pradha, Charles Mbohwa

Faculty of Engineering and the Builth Environment, University of Johannesburg

ABSTRACT: Despite sustainability advancements in manufacturing, there is still no conclusive evidence on whether and how the interaction between technological, entrepreneurial, environmental, and learning orientations influences innovation results, and particularly business performance. Using a survey of over 400 manufacturing small and medium-sized enterprises (SMEs) from sub-Saharan Africa, we evaluate the impacts of technological, learning, entrepreneurial, and environmental orientations on organizational innovation (OI) and the mediating influence of OI on these relationships. The quality of our structural model was evaluated using Pearson's correlation coefficient (r). OI plays a statistically significant role in the interaction between SME performance and technology, learning, and entrepreneurial orientation. Our research contributes to the literature on corporate responsibility strategies in developing economies by highlighting the critical role of innovation in businesses seeking to benefit from diverse proactive strategic orientations. Consequently, manufacturing SME s' must be proactive, innovative, and willing to improve their performance to contribute to society, environment, and economy.

KEYWORDS: Manufacturing, Proactive strategic innovation, SME performance, Developing economies

1. Introduction

Globalization has been more prevalent throughout time, and diverse business sectors enjoy faster growth rates, resulting in a better competition that helps the economy expand. These considerations consequently inspire the need for strategic orientations in the industrial sector in developing countries (Onu et al., 2023). These industries are more likely to welcome international investors and encourage innovation. Innovation is crucial since it helps explore areas for development (Ahmed & Shepherd, 2010). It highlights the firm's strength, allows organizations to evaluate their performance, assists in figuring out the cause for poor implementation, and helps identify new possibilities. According to studies, innovation process is characterized by the compression of input and output components (Forsman, 2011; Vasconcellos & Marx, 2011). Small and medium- sized enterprises (SMEs) are

the backbone of the global economy, accounting for the great majority of firms in practically every industry (Onu & Mbohwa, 2019, 2021a, 2021b). While conglomerates and small and medium-sized enterprises (SMEs) may vary in how they integrate various elements such as expertise, information, and innovation into a unique strategic dimension, the ability of SMEs to develop a distinctive strategy could be a crucial factor in competing with conglomerates.

According to research (Gatignon & Xuereb, 1997), strategic orientation is linked to developing appropriate behaviors to attain superior performance. Strategic orientation assists companies in developing appropriate strategies for achieving their objectives (Noble et al., 2002). It is typically separated into multiple aspects such as technological, environmental, entrepreneurial, and learning orientations (Ardito et al., 2021; Real et al., 2014). Few studies have researched the role

*Corresponding author: onup@uj.ac.za

DOI: 10.1201/9781003538646-3

of organizational innovation in mediating the associations between technological, learning, entrepreneurial, and environmental orientations and SME performance. Consequently, we add to our current understanding by filling the research gaps listed below (Shamsudin et al., 2017) . First, past research attempting to determine if strategic orientation influences company performance has shown mixed findings. One explanation might be that most prior research has focused on not more than two strategic orientation factors and their indirect and direct correlations. We use an integrated and comprehensive approach to define and analyze environmental, technological, entrepreneurial, and learning approaches. Our strategy is a novel approach to proactive strategic orientations. By using organizational innovation as a mediating variable, we investigate probable circumstances underlying (or influencing) the strategic orientation–SME performance link.

2. Literature Review

2.1 Technology Orientation and Organizational Innovativeness

According to the resource-based view (RBV), enterprises directed by technology orientation acquire rich technological knowledge by collecting up-to-date specialized information that may be utilized to create a new technological solution to fulfil a new market need (Gatignon & Xuereb, 1997; Onu & Mbohwa, 2020). According to another study, technology orientation is connected to technology-based innovation but has a negative impact on market-based innovation (Zhou et al., 2005). As a result, incorporating advanced technology into a firm's decision-making and organizing process could be considered a valuable resource. The higher an organization's level of technology orientation, the more likely it is for that corporation to innovate. Thus, we developed our hypothesis as follows:

H1: *Technology orientation has a significant positive impact on organizational innovativeness.*

2.2 Learning Orientation and Organizational Innovativeness

Learning orientation is described as a basic attitude toward learning as well as organizational and managerial characteristics that aid learning. (Real et al., 2014). Learning orientation has been demonstrated to substantially influence the performance of SMEs in previous research (Real et al., 2014; Wang, 2008). For example, Maes and Sels (2014) believe that learning is essential for any endeavors to increase competitive advantage and organizational performance (Maes & Sels, 2014). According to several types of research, learning orientation is positively connected to company innovativeness (Hult et al., 2004; Keskin, 2006). They argue

that information sharing is critical for company innovation since it allows companies to improve their whole innovation process. Thus, we developed our hypothesis as follows:

H2: *Learning orientation has a significant positive impact on organizational innovativeness*

2.3 Entrepreneurial Orientation and Organizational Innovativeness

Entrepreneurial Orientation (EO) is a process of organizational-level entrepreneurial engagement. The EO and strategic management are often synonymous. According to Miller (2011), businesses that engage in entrepreneurial activity are more likely to produce new products, take on hazardous initiatives, be first to market, take a proactive strategy, and gain a competitive edge (Miller, 2011). Miller (2011) defines entrepreneurial orientation as a term that encompasses risk-taking, innovation readiness, and proactiveness (Miller, 2011). As a result, EO is seen as a crucial organizational activity that aids a company's survival and improvement (Miller, 1983; Tajeddini et al., 2006). According to their findings, proactive entrepreneurs who take risks generate new ideas and distinctive products, improving the firm's innovativeness. Thus, we developed our hypothesis as follows:

H3: *Entrepreneurial orientation has a significant positive impact on organizational innovativeness*

2.4 Environmental Orientation and Organizational Innovativeness

Environmental orientation aids businesses in attracting, motivating, and retaining environmentally conscious employees. These individuals are more inclined to aim for continual development, particularly in environmentally sensitive processes and products, and search for new methods to incorporate environmental issues into the company (Cheng, 2020). Environmental orientation enables businesses, particularly SMEs, to "successfully respond to new green market possibilities by rapidly dedicating important resources to research new green knowledge and technology to build new business solutions" (Ardito et al., 2021; Danso et al., 2020). That is, businesses become better equipped to identify efficient resource combinations and utilization for innovation, lowering the high uncertainty and significant changes typical of enterprises that 'go green'. According to this logic, we developed our hypothesis as follows:

H4: *Environmental orientation has a significant positive impact on organizational innovativeness*

2.5 Organizational Innovativeness and SMEs' Performance

Fostering a creative attitude, encouraging research and development, developing new procedures, launching emerging products/services, and technical leadership are examples of innovation (Dibrell et al., 2015). According to research, a firm's innovativeness is linked to its competitive advantage and performance (Peter et al., 2023a). Innovation helps companies gain a competitive advantage and provide better results (Hult et al., 2004). According to previous research, innovative businesses will provide exceptional results, drive economic growth, and employ creativity in the workplace (Laforet, 2016; Peter et al., 2023b; Szopik-Depczyńska et al., 2018). These empirical data suggest that company innovativeness may predict SME performance. Thus, we developed our hypothesis as follows:

H5: *Organizational innovativeness has a significant positive impact on SME performance*

2.6 Mediation by Organizational Innovation

Environmental orientation denotes the strategic choice to include environmental goals into a business's tactical, operational, and productivity actions to meet corporate values while also responding to external market constraints (Danso et al., 2020; Klassen et al., 2016). Entrepreneurial Orientation is an essential notion to consider when discussing business strategies. Entrepreneurial orientation (EO) is a critical aspect that assists an organization in discovering new market possibilities (Caseiro & Coelho, 2019; Chang, 2018). It is argued that a business that uses EO is more likely to identify new market possibilities (Adomako et al., 2021; Gawke et al., 2019) and manage new obstacles such as an unpredictable environment and competition (Clausen, 2020). Learning orientation is a fundamental attitude toward learning, i.e., organizational and management traits that enhance the corporate learning process (Real et al., 2014).

Accordingly, learning orientation reflects a company's values that impact the company's propensity to produce and use knowledge for business development (Onu et al., 2023; Real et al., 2014), which is a significant predictor of SME performance (Peter et al., 2023b). Learning orientation, Entrepreneurial orientation, and innovation performance in the setting of SMEs have all been studied in the literature (Shaher & Mohd Ali, 2020). Following the above discussion, we developed our hypothesis as follows:

H6: *Organizational innovativeness mediates the significant positive impact of technology orientation on SME performance.*

H7: *Organizational innovativeness mediates the significant positive impact of environmental orientation on SME performance.*

H8: *Organizational innovativeness mediates the significant positive impact of entrepreneurial orientation on SME performance.*

H9: *Organizational innovativeness mediates the significant positive impact of learning orientation on SME performance.*

3. Research Methodology

This section presents the sampling technique, data collection process, and measures.

3.1 Sample, Data Collection, and Measures

The data for this study comes from SMEs in Sub-Saharan Africa that are technology-intensive and innovative. These manufacturing SMEs are included in the Africa Business Directory and are registered in their respective nations (contain contact information for the firms). A random sample of over 1,842 businesses was chosen, and the survey was mailed to the respondents. After contacting over 1,000 businesses, 465 valid surveys were returned. The companies were chosen based on their year of creation and staff count. These companies comprise basic metal manufacturing (e.g., metal and fabricated metal products), wood manufacturing (e.g., manufacturing of wood and wood products, pulp and paper and paper products), and other manufacturing enterprises (e.g., non-metallic mineral products, rubber and plastic products, and textile and textile products). A seven-point Likert scale was utilized to assess proactive strategic orientation and SMEs' performance. The four elements of proactive strategic orientations were measured using indicators taken from previous research (Ardito et al., 2021; Lee et al., 2014; Lei et al., 2019). Meanwhile, performance metrics for SMEs were adopted from research (Llivisaca et al., 2020; Stasielowicz, 2019; Wiklund & Shepherd, 2005).

4. Empirical Results

Internal consistency, convergent, and discriminant validity checks are used to filter the measures in IBM SPSS version 26. Cronbach's Alpha was used to check for scale internal consistency. The Cronbach's alpha coefficient was calculated to determine the reliability (Creswell, 2003) of technical, entrepreneurial, environmental, and learning orientation measures. These values were higher than the prescribed 0.7 by 0.789, 0.831, 0.759, and 0.981, respectively (Pallant, 2016). We believe the model construct has appropriate convergent validity since factor loading on their target constructs was strong, ranging from 0.634 to 0.937 and larger than the 0.5 recommended (Hair et al., 2010). The structural model's quality was evaluated using the Pearson correlation coefficient (r). Because the square root of the AVE between each pair of factors is greater than the expected correlation between factors, it demonstrates discriminate validity, which we further confirm by examining variance inflation factors. The means, standard deviations, and intercorrelations of the variables and square root of AVE in our model are presented in Table 3.1.

Table 3.1 Descriptive statistics and correlation matrix

Scale	Mean	SD	1	2	3	4	5	6
1. Technology Orientation	4.13	0.784	1					
2. Learning Orientation	3.73	0.810	0.721**	1				
3. Entrepreneurial Orientation	3.27	1.732	0.654**	0.654**	1			
4. Environmental Orientation	3.98	0.831	0.165*	0.745**	-0.544**	1		
5. Organizational innovation	4.01	2.427	-0.583**	0.743**	0.643**	0.531**	1	
6. SME Performance	3.04	0.794	0.498**	0.532**	-0.462**	0.384*	0.544**	1

* $p<0.05$; ** $p<0.01$.

The findings reveal a strong correlation between the proactive strategic orientations, organizational innovation, and SME performance. None of the pairwise correlations are high enough to cause a multi-collinearity concern. Therefore, it proves the hypotheses of the present study.

4.1 Assessment of Structural Model

The results of structural equation modelling were used to confirm the various hypotheses reported in this study, as indicated in Table 3.2. The results showed that technology ($\beta = 0.534$, $p < 0.01$), learning ($\beta = 0.371$, $p < 0.01$), Entrepreneurial ($\beta = 0.472$, $p < 0.01$), and environmental orientation ($\beta = 0.698$, $p < 0.01$) were positively related to organizational innovativeness in the direct effects. Thus, H1, H2, H3, and H4 significantly influence organizational innovativeness. The present research posits that organizational innovation positively impacts SME performance ($\beta = 0.401$, $p < 0.001$).

As such, corporate innovation can influence organizational success and supports research findings (Ardito et al., 2021; Hult et al., 2004; Rhee et al., 2010). As a result, H5 is recommended. The data reveal that technological, learning, and entrepreneurial orientations all positively affect business performance via organizational innovativeness ($\beta = 0.604$,

$p < 0.05$; $\beta = 0.444$, $p < 0.05$; $\beta = 0.397$, $p < 0.01$). The findings show that organizational innovativeness mediates the links between technological, entrepreneurial, and learning orientations and firm success. As a result, H6, H7, and H8 are recommended. The mediating impact of firm innovativeness is negligible ($\beta = 0.184$, $p > 0.05$), thus, H9 is not supported.

5. Conclusion

The relevance of adopting a more integrated approach to evaluating the effects of strategic orientations on SMEs performance in developing economies through innovation using a new model is highlighted in this study. We give a more detailed explanation of how proactive strategic orientation (technological, learning, entrepreneurial, and environmental) affects manufacturing SME performance, both positively and negatively. Furthermore, the study's research approach examines the mediating influence of innovation. The findings were encouraging, with all proactive strategic oriented variables having a significant impact on SME performance. This conclusion is consistent with previous study findings (Ahmed & Shepherd, 2010; Amin, 2015; Hult et al., 2004; Pesämaa et al., 2013). Because organizational innovation has a partial mediating effect on the link between proactive

Table 3.2 Mediating effect of organizational innovation

Model	Direct effect	Indirect effect	t-value	p-value	Hypothesis
Technology Orientation —> Organizational innovation (H1)	0.534***	-	6.324	0.004	Supported
Learning Orientation —> Organizational innovation (H2)	0.371***	-	4.312	0.007	Supported
Entrepreneurial Orientation —> Organizational innovation (H3)	0.472***	-	4.980	0.001	Supported
Environmental Orientation —> Organizational innovation (H4)	0.698***	-	6.781	0.003	Supported
Organizational innovation —> SME performance (H5)	0.401***	-	3.873	0.004	Supported
Technology Orientation —> SME performance (H6)	-	0.604***	8.324	0.040	Supported
Learning Orientation —> SME performance (H7)	-	0.444***	3.932	0.026	Supported
Entrepreneurial Orientation —> SME performance (H8)	-	0.397***	4.007	0.003	Supported
Environmental Orientation —> SME performance (H9)	-	0.184*	1.734	0.104	Not supported

* $p<0.05$; ** $p<0.01$; *** $p<0.001$.

strategy orientations and SMEs' performance, it is proposed that companies use it to execute strategic orientations more proactively. The present study emphasizes the need to look at innovation from a broad viewpoint that may help companies bolster their business performance. There are various limitations to this study that point to future research opportunities: to generalize the outcomes of the survey across other organizations, future studies should use the suggested research paradigm across large businesses.

REFERENCES

1. Adomako, S., Amankwah-Amoah, J., Danso, A., Danquah, J. K., Hussain, Z., & Khan, Z. (2021). R&D intensity, knowledge creation process and new product performance: The mediating role of international R&D teams. *Journal of Business Research.* https://doi.org/10.1016/j.jbusres.2019.08.036

2. Ahmed, P. K., & Shepherd, C. (2010). Innovation management: context, strategies, systems, and processes. *New York (NY): Pearson Prentice Hall.* Amin, M. (2015). The effect of entrepreneurship orientation and learning orientation on SMEs' performance: an SEM-PLS approach. *J. for International Business and Entrepreneurship Development.* https://doi.org/10.1504/jibed.2015.070797

3. Ardito, L., Raby, S., Albino, V., & Bertoldi, B. (2021). The duality of digital and environmental orientations in the context of SMEs: Implications for innovation performance. *Journal of Business Research.* https://doi.org/10.1016/j.jbusres.2020.09.022

4. Caseiro, N., & Coelho, A. (2019). The influence of Business Intelligence capacity, network learning and innovativeness on startups performance. *Journal of Innovation and Knowledge.* https://doi.org/10.1016/j.jik.2018.03.009

5. Chang, C. H. (2018). How to enhance green service and green product innovation performance? The roles of inward and outward capabilities. *Corporate Social Responsibility and Environmental Management.* https://doi.org/10. 1002/csr.1469

6. Cheng, C. C. J. (2020). Sustainability Orientation, Green Supplier Involvement, and Green Innovation Performance: Evidence from Diversifying Green Entrants. *Journal of Business Ethics.* https://doi.org/10.1007/s10551-018-3946-7

7. Clausen, T. H. (2020). Entrepreneurial thinking and action in opportunity development: A conceptual process model. *International Small Business Journal: Researching Entrepreneurship.* https://doi.org/10.1177/0266242619872883

8. Creswell, J. W. (2003). Research Design Qualitative, Quantitative and Mixed Methods Approaches 2nd ed. *Research Design Qualitative Quantitative and Mixed Methods Approaches.* https://doi.org/10.3109/08941939.2012.723954

9. Danso, A., Adomako, S., Lartey, T., Amankwah- Amoah, J., & Owusu-Yirenkyi, D. (2020). Stakeholder integration, environmental sustainability orientation and financial performance. *Journal of Business Research.* https://doi.org/10.1016/j.jbusres.2019.02.038

10. Dibrell, C., B. Craig, J., Kim, J., & J. Johnson, A. (2015). Establishing How Natural Environmental Competency, Organizational Social Consciousness, and Innovativeness Relate. *Journal of Business Ethics.* https://doi.org/10.1007/s10551-013-2043-1

11. Forsman, H. (2011). Innovation capacity and innovation development in small enterprises. A comparison between the manufacturing and service sectors. *Research Policy.* https://doi.org/10.1016/j.respol.2011.02.003

12. Gatignon, H., & Xuereb, J. M. (1997). Strategic orientation of the firm and new product performance. *Journal of Marketing Research.* https://doi.org/10.2307/3152066

13. Gawke, J. C., Gorgievski, M. J., & Bakker, A. B. (2019). Measuring intrapreneurship at the individual level: Development and validation of the Employee Intrapreneurship Scale (EIS). *European Management Journal.* https://doi.org/10.1016/j.emj.2019.03.001

14. Hair, J., Black, W., Babin, B., & Anderson, R. (2010). Multivariate Data Analysis: A Global Perspective. In *Multivariate Data Analysis: A Global Perspective.*

15. Hult, G. T. M., Hurley, R. F., & Knight, G. A. (2004). Innovativeness: Its antecedents and impact on business performance. *Industrial Marketing Management.* https://doi.org/10.1016/j.indmarman.2003.08.015

16. Keskin, H. (2006). Market orientation, learning orientation, and innovation capabilities in SMEs: An extended model. *European Journal of Innovation Management.* https://doi.org/10.1108/14601060610707849

17. Klassen, R. D., Mclaughlin, C. P., Klassen, R. D., & Mclaughlin, C. P. (2016). The Impact of Environmental Management on Firm Performance The Impact of Environmental Management on Firm Performance. *Strategic Management Journal.* Laforet, S. (2016). Effects of organisational culture on organisational innovation performance in family firms. *Journal of Small Business and Enterprise Development.* https://doi.org/10.1108/JSBED-02- 2015-0020

18. Lee, D. H., Choi, S. B., & Kwak, W. J. (2014). The Effects of Four Dimensions of Strategic Orientation on Firm Innovativeness and Performance in Emerging Market Small- and Medium-Size Enterprises. *Emerging Markets Finance & Trade.*

19. Lei, L., Wu, X., & Fu, Y. (2019). Effects of sustainability and technology orientations on firm growth: Evidence from Chinese manufacturing. *Sustainability (Switzerland).* https://doi.org/10.3390/su11164406

20. Llivisaca, J., Jadan, D., Guamán, R., & ... (2020). Key Performance Indicators for the Supply Chain in Small and Medium-Sized Enterprises based on Balance Score Card. *Test Engineering and ... .*

21. Maes, J., & Sels, L. (2014). SMEs' Radical Product Innovation: The Role of Internally and Externally Oriented Knowledge Capabilities. *Journal of Small Business Management.* https://doi.org/10.1111/jsbm.12037

22. Miller, D. (1983). The Correlates of Entrepreneurship in Three Types of Firms. *Management Science.* https://doi.org/10.1287/mnsc.29.7.770

23. Miller, D. (2011). Miller (1983) revisited: A reflection on EO research and some suggestions for the future. *Entrepreneurship: Theory and Practice.* https://doi.org/10.1111/j.1540-6520.2011.00457.x

24. Noble, C. H., Sinha, R. K., & Kumar, A. (2002). Market orientation and alternative strategic orientations: A longitudinal assessment of performance implications. *Journal of Marketing*. https://doi.org/10.1509/jmkg.66.4.25.18513

25. Onu, P., & Mbohwa, C. (2019). Sustainable Production: New Thinking for SMEs. *Journal of Physics: Conference Series, 1378*(2). https://doi.org/10.1088/1742-6596/1378/2/022072

26. Onu, P., & Mbohwa, C. (2020). *Green strategies and Techno-innovation Penetration: Sustainability Advancement and Manufacturing Sector in Perspective.*

27. Onu, P., & Mbohwa, C. (2021a). Agricultural Waste Diversity and Sustainability Issues. In *Agricultural Waste Diversity and Sustainability Issues*. https://doi.org/10. 1016/c2020-0-02631-9

28. Onu, P., & Mbohwa, C. (2021b). Industry 4.0 opportunities in manufacturing SMEs: Sustainability outlook. *Materials Today: Proceedings*. https://doi.org/10.1016/j.matpr.2020.12.095

29. Onu, P., Pradhan, A., & Mbohwa, C. (2023). Potential to use Metaverse for future teaching and learning. *Education and Information Technologies, Springer Nature*. https://doi.org/10. 1007/s10639- 023- 12167-9

30. Pallant, J. (2016). SPSS Survival Manual: A step by step guide to data analysisusing spss 6th edition. In *Book*. https://doi. org/10. 1046/j.1365- 2648.2001.2027c.x

31. Pesämaa, O., Shoham, A., Wincent, J., & Ruvio, A. A. (2013). How a learning orientation affects drivers of innovativeness and performance in service delivery. *Journal of Engineering and Technology Management - JET-M*. https://doi.org/10.1016/j.jengtecman.2013.01.004

32. Peter, O., Pradhan, A., & Mbohwa, C. (2023a). Industrial internet of things (IIoT): opportunities, challenges, and requirements in manufacturing businesses in emerging economies. *Procedia Computer Science, 217*, 856–865. https://doi.org/10.1016/j.procs.2022.12.282

33. Peter, O., Pradhan, A., & Mbohwa, C. (2023b). Industry 4.0 concepts within the sub– Saharan African SME manufacturing sector. *Procedia Computer Science, 217*, 846–855. https://doi.org/10.1016/j.procs.2022.12.281

34. Real, J. C., Roldán, J. L., & Leal, A. (2014). From entrepreneurial orientation and learning orientation to business performance: Analysing the mediating role of organizational learning and the moderating effects of organizational size. *British Journal of Management*. https://doi.org/10. 1111/j.1467- 8551.2012.00848.x

35. Rhee, J., Park, T., & Lee, D. H. (2010). Drivers of innovativeness and performance for innovative SMEs in South Korea: Mediation of learning orientation. *Technovation*. https://doi.org/10.1016/j.technovation.2009.04.008

36. Shaher, A. T. H. Q., & Mohd Ali, K. A. (2020). The effect of entrepreneurial orientation on innovation performance: The mediation role of learning orientation on Kuwait SMEs. *Management Science Letters*. https://doi.org/10.5267/j.msl.2020.7.030

37. Stasielowicz, L. (2019). Goal orientation and performance adaptation: A meta-analysis. *Journal of Research in Personality*. https://doi.org/10.1016/j.jrp.2019.103847

38. Szopik-Depczyńska, K., Kędzierska-Szczepaniak, A., Szczepaniak, K., Cheba, K., Gajda, W., & Ioppolo, G. (2018). Innovation in sustainable development: an investigation of the EU context using 2030 agenda indicators. *Land Use Policy*. https://doi.org/10.1016/j.landusepol.2018.08.004

39. Tajeddini, K., Trueman, M., & Larsen, G. (2006). Examining the Effect of Market Orientation On Innovativeness. *Journal of Marketing Management*. https://doi.org/10.1362/026725706777978640

40. Vasconcellos, L. H. R., & Marx, R. (2011). Understanding how innovation takes place in service companies - An exploratory study of companies in Brazil. *Gestao e Producao*. https://doi.org/10.1590/s0104-530x2011000300001

41. Wang, C. L. (2008). Entrepreneurial orientation, learning orientation, and firm performance. *Entrepreneurship: Theory and Practice*. https://doi.org/10.1111/j.1540-6520.2008.00246.x

42. Wiklund, J., & Shepherd, D. (2005). Entrepreneurial orientation and small business performance: A configurational approach. *Journal of Business Venturing*. https://doi.org/10.1016/j.jbusvent.2004.01.001

43. Zhou, K. Z., Gao, G. Y., Yang, Z., & Zhou, N. (2005). Developing strategic orientation in China: Antecedents and consequences of market and innovation orientations. *Journal of Business Research*. https://doi.org/10.1016/j.jbusres.2004.02.003

Note: All the tables in this chapter were compiled by the author.

Sustainable Materials Processing and Manufacturing – Lin Zhu et al. (eds)
© 2024 Taylor & Francis Group, London, ISBN 978-1-032-88599-5

An Investigation into Industrial Manufacturing and Sustainable Production Implementation in sub-Saharan Africa

Peter Onu*

College of Engineering, Landmark University

Faculty of Engineering and the Builth Environment, University of Johannesburg

Anup Pradha, Charles Mbohwa

Faculty of Engineering and the Builth Environment, University of Johannesburg

ABSTRACT: The euphoria of the Fourth Industrial Revolution and Sustainable Production, concerning the endorsement of new technological innovations, operational practices, standards, models, and policies to effectively achieve increased productivity, is mostly noticed in the industrial manufacturing sector and calls for more insight. This study conducted an empirical survey of case companies based on the growing interest in how sustainability initiatives may impact corporate effectiveness from an engineering perspective conducted among nine companies in three sub-Saharan African states. The results show crucial areas in industrial operations where the adoption of sustainability practices is required, with access to standardization guidance for manufacturing enterprises to drive quality, risk, and environmental management concerns. The findings present an outlook of what should be the focus of industrial sustainability practitioners and educational and governmental institutions with regard to proactive sustainable production measures in the manufacturing industries of developing countries.

KEYWORDS: Sustainable production, Manufacturing, Developing countries, Africa

1. Introduction

Sustainable production principles combine environmental and socio-economic considerations to meet optimal product, process, and organizational effectiveness. It also considers operational performance, from raw material development to end-of-life disposal. The contribution of SMEs to international environmental protection obligations through new methodologies and technology- innovation processes is critical to long-term development (OCDE, 2014). And doing so to facilitate zero-waste production or no harmful emissions while employing universal sustainable principles (Wu et al., 2015) during manufacturing processes that necessitate conservative techniques (Onu & Mbohwa, 2021a; Rajeev et al., 2017). Sustainable production practices in the coverage of energy savings, audits, heat recovery, or material selection/substitution, including alternative or renewable resources, are studied for effectiveness in the industrial manufacturing sector. Also, waste prevention, reduction, reuse, recycling, and harmful emission control have become critical issues among SMEs to operate sustainably. However, they lack clarity on the strategic approach and the basis for implementation. The purpose of the present paper is to survey how companies in three countries in sub- Saharan Africa adopt sustainable production practices, focusing on industrial sustainability practitioners and educational and governmental institutions concerning proactive measures in the manufacturing industries of developing countries.

The above concept and strategies have been developed in literature (Joung et al., 2013; Lindsey, 2011; Machado et al., 2017; Peter & Mbohwa, 2019) over the years and prompt the present empirical investigative study to assess SME responsiveness to sustainability and its impact on industrial

*Corresponding author: onup@uj.ac.za

DOI: 10.1201/9781003538646-4

manufacturing activities for operational excellence to lead to sustainable development in Africa in perspective. The body of the current paper follows a brief literature review, which precedes the methodology used to arrive at the juxtaposition discussed in section four, and then the concluding part, which is a capsule of the result of the investigation and the way forward on sustainability for manufacturing SMEs in developing countries.

2. Literature Review

Bocken et al. (2014) (Bocken et al., 2014) have identified challenges within sustainability practices to forester technical excellence inline with the triple bottom line approach and suggest a business model innovation where drivers that ensure sustainable operations are introduced to proffer a solution. Conservative considerations: materials, energy, waste, renewables versus natural processes, etc., which form part of the sustainability practices explored in this text. It also establishes the baseline for industrial ecology and the concern for sustainable production and consumption (Lifset & Graedel, 2015).

Innovative thinking is crucial for companies to meet the expectations of systematically enhancing value creation through sustainable operations (Bocken et al., 2015). For example, the development of refractories for metal industries to conserve energy and reduce emissions (Onu & Mbohwa, 2021b), the integration of manufacturing lean practices in furniture companies for sustainable production and improved operational performance (Miller et al., 2010), etc. The development of businesses, primarily small and medium-sized enterprises based on eco-industrial commitment, draws attention to improving old or traditional methods to actualize positive resolve for sustainable development (Dong et al., 2016). The abovementioned factors have been demonstrated in China (Zeng et al., 2017), linking external pressure to positively impacting sustainability implementation and performance. Researchers have also investigated implementing sustainability practices through strategies that promote conservative manufacturing (Despeisse et al., 2012). The present paper focuses on sub-Saharan Africa and uses selected industrial cases to ascertain the extent of the practice of sustainable production proactive measures to sustainable development from the industrial manufacturing perspective.

3. Methodology

In the present study, we examine nine companies, three selected from Nigeria, South Africa, and Uganda, to measure the level of adherence to sustainability practices and assess the impact of the concept's development and implementation in the industrial manufacturing sector. A short video teaching sustainable production principle was shared among the management staff of each company participating in the study, and it was intended to be distributed to the employees of the firms for educational purposes. This way, workers have knowledge of the subject matter and insight into the questionnaires, which they soon receive via emails, web services, and hard copies (Ageron et al., 2012). The data was specifically collected from manufacturing firms in the metal, plastic, and wood industries that were identified as actively engaging in sustainable operations. These firms were selected from the countries mentioned and are detailed in Table 4.1.

This helped the researcher to learn about successes in quality assurance and socio-environmental risk abatement. The open-ended questions were based on the sustainable production principles of simple agreed or disagreed responses and short word phrases to provide insight into the following five sustainable production principles. (1) product and production effectiveness, (2) waste management and the release of harmful or toxic substances, (3) conservation or conversion of materials and energy, (4) implementation of new practices or emerging technologies amidst challenges, and finally, (5) employee safety and satisfaction with the work conditions during manufacturing operations. The researcher visited at least one company from each field (metal, plastic, and wood) in the three countries from August 2019 to February 2020, and hands-on observation of companies' manufacturing activities was closely invigilated.

Although the sustainable production principles learned about did not cover the economics and income propensity

Table 4.1 Sample overview of the manufacturing sectors in the study

Sectors	Category of manufacturing									Total
	Metal (M)		Plastic (P)				Wood (W)			
	Ms	Mn	Mu	Ps	Pn	Pu	Ws	Wn	Wu	
South Africa	X			X			X			41.4
Nigeria		X			X			X		32.5
Uganda			X			X			X	26.1
% of Sample										100%

of manufacturing processes and operations, the technicality and sensitivity of sharing such information (financial and security) were crucial to most companies. However, most corporations are yet to have an economic framework upon which practitioners can appraise their sustainability practices and processes. The researcher carefully selected companies with more than fifty employees and a maximum workforce not exceeding two hundred fifty in all three categories of the sample group. A total of 157 participants provided helpful feedback in all nine companies that represented the percentage values for the sample categories shown in table 1, which also indicated the input from the participants within the focused manufacturing sectors.

To analyze the feedback, excellent, strong, good, limited, and weak measurement responses (75- 100%, 65-75%, 55-65%, 45-55%, and below 45%, respectively) were adopted to score on the drivers of sustainability practice and initiatives. However, for clarity purposes in the present report, the results, which are described in the subsequent section (Table 2), are used as follows: high '≠' (above 75%), moderate 'ü' (45-75%), low 'Ø' (below 45%) and not sure ' - ' to represent responses, based on level of satisfaction or agreement on a sustainable production implementation.

4. Results

The survey outcome is presented in five sections as empirical juxtapositions with the growing trend in sustainable production principles, shown in Table 4.2. The underlining principles are expressed among top managers and practitioners/experts interested in SME development in Africa to test sustainability practices and the success rates within the countries (three) of selection, thus representing the South, West, and Eastern African regions.

4.1 Product Characteristics and Production Effectiveness.

The series of organizational practices and operational processes during product development, design, and manufacture is an essential consideration to support the sustainable production target of a company (Peter et al., 2023a). However, in most cases, governmental interventions through policies and monitoring strategies may discourage product versatility (Onu, Pradhan, et al., 2023). Activities ranging from the elimination of waste generation, reuse or recycling, and companies' interest in consistently upgrading operations— maintenance services, with improvement in product raw material selection—result in optimal energy utilization and minimal emissions(Onu, Mbohwa, et al., 2023). Respondents report satisfaction and motivation towards work when socio-environmental concerns are eased, with the assurance of sufficient training, and while using the

necessary enabling technology. An average of 40% of the respondents affirm that the concept of sustainability or the message behind its definition is new; 80% of the participants expressed awareness of product recycling and the use of non-toxic or biodegradable materials. The remaining 20% hadn't any clue about the concepts. However, all participants agree that those above, backed by standardization, are the most effective sustainable production practices implemented among all three companies across the sample selection. This finding is supported by research (Ikumapayi et al., 2019; Peter et al., 2023b).

4.2 Waste Management and the Release of Harmful or Toxic Substances

Sustainable development and environmental preservation goals focus on proper waste disposal practices. Most companies are not interested in the take-back, reuse, or recycling option, especially metal manufacturing companies. Wood and plastics are more interested in and involved in the practice as a proposal for waste reduction and form only 58% of the companies willing to consider product return by consumers. Emphasis on waste prevention (Rahman et al., 2014; Saboo et al., 2014) comes before its reuse or recycling and are all sustainable practices that ensure raw materials handling, up to the by-product utilization in a "no waste" operational scenario that extends to product life cycle or serviceability. 80% of the respondents submit that all material resources sourced for production are wholly utilized during manufacturing, leaving no waste due to enabling and supporting technologies that support compact designs. Another perspective on waste management, which concerns the supply of ecological and ergonomic products, underpins the sustainability adherence practices by suppliers (environmentally friendly resources, processes, and products) to improve operations. However, only 28% of the respondents find this approach achievable for SMEs with little or no bargaining power over global suppliers of their raw materials (Moeuf et al., 2016). Regardless, all the participants support available governmental legislature that can influence suppliers' position on sustainable production through restrictions on using harmful materials and chemicals in non-conservative burning processes.

4.3 Conservation and Conversion of Materials and Energy

It is observed how respondents gave very little concern to energy efficiency practices in the metal manufacturing companies in all three countries selected. An average of 65% of the respondents within the metal, plastic, and wood manufacturing industries confirm the resourcefulness of their by- products in the systems/operations life cycle. Nonetheless, the survey record shows less than 50 percent consider, as part

Table 4.2 Sample overview of the manufacturing sectors in the study

Sustainable production principles	Sample Representation	Product characteristics and production effectiveness	Waste management and the release of harmful or toxic substances	Conservation/ conversion of materials and energy	Implementation of new practices or emerging technologies amidst challenges to improve operations	Employee safety and satisfaction of the work conditions during manufacturing operations consumption strategy
Presence of nascent enabling systems/ tools that support sustainability	M_1	↑	↑	↓	↑	↑
	P_1	↓	↑	↑	↑	↑
	W_1	✓	✓	↑	↑	↑
Investments and models that promote sustainability for socio-environmental successes	M_2	↑	✓	✓	↑	↑
	P_2	↑	↑	↑	↑	↑
	W_2	✓	↑	↑	✓	↑
Available external or Governmental legislature that promotes sustainable manufacturing processes	M_3	↑	✓	✓	↑	↑
	P_3	↓	↑	✓	↑	↑
	W_3	↓	↑	✓	↑	↑
Sustainability adherence practices by suppliers (environmentally friendly resources/process/product) to improve operations	M_4	↑	↑	↑	↑	↑
	P_4	↑	↑	↑	✓	↑
	W_4	✓	✓	↑	↑	↑
Remanufacturing initiatives and customers' freedom to return products (disposed/unwanted) to maintain the product cycle and sustainable	M_5	↓	✓	↓	✓	–
	P_5	✓ ↑		↑	↓	–
	W_5	↑	↑	↑	↓	–
Reduced wastes initiatives; using non-hazardous, bio-recyclable materials	M_6	✓	✓ ↑		↓	↑
	P_6	✓ ↑		↓	↑	↑
	W_6	✓ ↑		✓	↑	↑
Robust design and use of advanced materials as an energy efficiency strategy to meet sustainable	M_7	↑	↑	↑	↑	↑
	P_7	✓	↓	↑	↑	↑
	W_7	✓	✓	↑	↑	↑
Absence of negative work and environmental concerns for health and social satisfaction	M_8	↑	✓	↑		✓ ↑
	P_8	↑	✓	↓		✓ ↑
	W_8	↑	✓	✓		✓ ↑
Increased staff awareness and acknowledgment of sustainable operations to promote diversity during	M_9	↑	↑	↑		✓ ↑
	P_9	↑	↑	↑		✓ ↑
	W_9	↑	✓	↑		✓ ↑
Standardization compliance and professional practices	M_{10}	↑	↑	↑	↑	↑
	P_{10}	↑	↓	↑	↑	↑
	W_{10}	↑	↓	↑	✓	↑
Controlled pollution of wastewater & chemicals/gas, noise vibration, etc., for improved socio-environmental performance	M_{11}	↓	↑	↓	↑	↑
	P_{11}	↑	↓	↑	↑	↑
	W_{11}	↑	✓	↑	↑	↑

of their operations scheme, remanufacturing initiatives or the ability of customers to return used or unwanted products to maintain the product cycle as a sustainable consumption strategy. Also, 74% confirm their awareness of processes designed to maximize materials used during manufacturing operations in their organizations, resulting in reduced work and environmental concerns and improved health and social satisfaction through controlled pollution initiatives and energy conservation practices (energy savings).

Further consideration of this sustainable principle requested participants' opinions on renewable sources due to energy-efficient and non-hazardous materials and to meet the energy demands of the companies. Still, only 65% affirm the renewable sources strategy that finds use in the different processes for their manufacturing operation.

4.4 Implementation of New Practices or Emerging Technologies Amidst Challenges

Seven of nine companies hold firm reservations concerning nascent enabling systems and tools that support sustainability despite poor governmental policies supporting sustainable manufacturing processes in Africa. This comparison is drawn with counterpart nations like the American states, Asia-China, and other Arabian countries, where sustainability adherence practices by both suppliers and manufacturers have been incentivized to improve operations and lead to sustainable development. From the production perspective, investments in sustainable technologies such as energy-efficient heat exchangers, carbon capture, and liquid and gaseous waste treatment plants are pivotal for sustainable operations that promote diversity in manufacturing processes and socio- environmental success. 60% of the respondents do not agree that the cost of technology is too expensive compared to the economic benefits. In comparison, 50% of all the companies argue that the lack of staff awareness and acknowledgment of sustainability practices has left the manufacturing industry in a comatose state (Onu et al., 2023).

5. Conclusion

Sustainable production efforts are still in the early stages of implementation in Africa. Manufacturers are not sufficiently required to take part in sustainability initiatives by the region's governments. However, recent advances in portable telecommunication devices position consumers to pressure suppliers and manufacturers to become proactive in the sustainable development campaign. Sustainable strategies are potential drivers towards sustainable production actualization for SMEs in sub-Saharan Africa. The government's role must span awareness campaigns, subsidies, tax, training, and audit/monitoring issues among small and large firms. Stakeholders

can learn about the barriers to sustainability implementation practices in this study.

REFERENCES

1. Ageron, B., Gunasekaran, A., & Spalanzani, A. (2012). Sustainable supply management: An empirical study. *International Journal of Production Economics*. https://doi.org/10.1016/j.ijpe.2011.04.007
2. Bocken, N. M. P., Rana, P., & Short, S. W. (2015). Value mapping for sustainable business thinking. *Journal of Industrial and Production Engineering*. https://doi.org/10.1080/21681015.2014.1000399
3. Bocken, N. M. P., Short, S. W., Rana, P., & Evans, S. (2014). A literature and practice review to develop sustainable business model archetypes. In *Journal of Cleaner Production*. https://doi.org/10.1016/j.jclepro.2013.11.039
4. Despeisse, M., Mbaye, F., Ball, P. D., & Levers, A. (2012). The emergence of sustainable manufacturing practices. *Production Planning and Control*. https://doi.org/10.1080/09537287.2011.555425
5. Dong, L., Fujita, T., Dai, M., Geng, Y., Ren, J., Fujii, M., Wang, Y., & Ohnishi, S. (2016). Towards preventative eco-industrial development: An industrial and urban symbiosis case in one typical industrial city in China. *Journal of Cleaner Production*. https://doi.org/10.1016/j.jclepro.2015.05.015
6. Ikumapayi, O. M., Akinlabi, E. T., Onu, P., Akinlabi, S. A., & Agarana, M. C. (2019). A Generalized Model for Automation Cost Estimating Systems (ACES) for Sustainable Manufacturing. *Journal of Physics: Conference Series*, 1378(3). https://doi.org/10.1088/1742-6596/1378/3/032043
7. Joung, C. B., Carrell, J., Sarkar, P., & Feng, S. C. (2013). Categorization of indicators for sustainable manufacturing. *Ecological Indicators*. https://doi.org/10.1016/j.ecolind.2012.05.030
8. Lifset, R., & Graedel, T. E. (2015). Industrial Ecology. In *International Encyclopedia of the Social & Behavioral Sciences: Second Edition*. https://doi.org/10.1016/B978-0-08-097086-8.91023-7
9. Lindsey, T. C. (2011). Sustainable principles: Common values for achieving sustainability. *Journal of Cleaner Production*. https://doi.org/10.1016/j.jclepro.2010.10.014
10. Machado, C. G., Pinheiro de Lima, E., Gouvea da Costa, S. E., Angelis, J. J., & Mattioda, R. A. (2017). Framing maturity based on sustainable operations management principles. *International Journal of Production Economics*. https://doi.org/10.1016/j.ijpe.2017.01.020
11. Miller, G., Pawloski, J., & Standridge, C. (2010). A case study of lean, sustainable manufacturing. *Journal of Industrial Engineering and Management*. https://doi.org/10.3926/jiem.2010.v3n1.p11-32
12. Moeuf, A., Tamayo, S., Lamouri, S., Pellerin, R., & Lelievre, A. (2016). Strengs and weaknesses of small and medium sized enterprises regarding the implementation of lean manufacturing. *IFAC- PapersOnLine*. https://doi.org/10.1016/j.ifacol.2016.07.552

13. OCDE. (2014). The State of Play on Extended Producer Responsibility (EPR): Opportunities and Challenges. *Global Forum on Environment: Promoting Sustainable Materials Management through Extended Producer Responsibility (EPR)*. https://doi.org/10.1787/9789264189867-en

14. Onu, P., & Mbohwa, C. (2021a). Industry 4.0 opportunities in manufacturing SMEs: Sustainability outlook. *Materials Today: Proceedings*. https://doi.org/10.1016/j.matpr.2020.12.095

15. Onu, P., & Mbohwa, C. (2021b). Reimagining the future: Techno innovation advancement in manufacturing. *Materials Today: Proceedings*. https://doi.org/10.1016/j.matpr.2020.12.100

16. Onu, P., Mbohwa, C., & Pradhan, A. (2023). Artificial intelligence-based IoT-enabled biogas production. *IEEE-2023 International Conference on Control, Automation and Diagnosis, ICCAD'23*. https://doi.org/10.1109/ICCAD57653.2023.101523 49

17. Onu, P., Pradhan, A., & Mbohwa, C. (2023). Potential to use Metaverse for future teaching and learning. *Education and Information Technologies, Springer Nature*. https://doi.org/10.1007/s10639- 023- 12167-9

18. Onu, P., Pradhan, A., & Mbohwa, C. (2023). The potential of industry 4.0 for renewable energy and materials development – The case of multinational energy companies . *Heliyon* . https://doi.org/10.1016/j.heliyon.2023.e20547

19. Peter, O., & Mbohwa, C. (2019). Industrial energy conservation initiative and prospect for sustainable manufacturing. *Procedia Manufacturing*. https://doi.org/10.1016/j.promfg.2019.05.077

20. Peter, O., Pradhan, A., & Mbohwa, C. (2023a). Industrial internet of things (IIoT): opportunities, challenges, and requirements in manufacturing businesses in emerging economies. *Procedia Computer Science, 217*, 856–865. https://doi.org/10.1016/j.procs.2022.12.282

21. Peter, O., Pradhan, A., & Mbohwa, C. (2023b). Industry 4.0 concepts within the sub–Saharan African SME manufacturing sector. *Procedia Computer Science, 217*, 846–855. https://doi.org/10.1016/j.procs.2022.12.281

22. Rahman, N. A. A., Sharif, S. M., & Esa, M. M. (2014). Lean Manufacturing Case Study with Kanban System Implementation. *Procedia Economics and Finance*. https://doi.org/10.1016/s2212-5671(13)00232-3

23. Rajeev, A., Pati, R. K., Padhi, S. S., & Govindan, K. (2017). Evolution of sustainability in supply chain management: A literature review. In *Journal of Cleaner Production*. https://doi.org/10.1016/j.jclepro.2017.05.026

24. Saboo, A., Reyes, J. A. G., Er, A., & Kumar, V. (2014). A VSM improvement-based approach for lean operations in an Indian manufacturing SME. *International Journal of Lean Enterprise Research*. https://doi.org/10.1504/ijler.2014.062281

25. Wu, L., Subramanian, N., Abdulrahman, M. D., Liu, C., Lai, K. hung, & Pawar, K. S. (2015). The impact of integrated practices of lean, green, and social management systems on firm sustainability performance-evidence from Chinese fashion auto- parts suppliers. *Sustainability (Switzerland)*. https://doi.org/10.3390/su7043838

26. Zeng, H., Chen, X., Xiao, X., & Zhou, Z. (2017). Institutional pressures, sustainable supply chain management, and circular economy capability: Empirical evidence from Chinese eco-industrial park firms. *Journal of Cleaner Production*. https://doi.org/10.1016/j.jclepro.2016.10.093

Note: All the tables in this chapter were compiled by the author.

Sustainable Materials Processing and Manufacturing – Lin Zhu et al. (eds)
© 2024 Taylor & Francis Group, London, ISBN 978-1-032-88599-5

Parameter Optimisation and Cost Analysis of Lavender Oil Production using Steam Distillation

Erin Reece Flavell[1], Liam Lai[2], Promise Mashatole[3] & Kevin Graham Harding[4]
School of Chemical and Metallurgical Engineering, University of the Witwatersrand, South Africa

ABSTRACT: Due to the increasing demand for essential oils as a natural ingredient in the cosmetic, pharmaceutical, perfume, and aromatherapy industries, this paper endeavours to determine optimal parameters for the extraction of lavender oil and explore the commercial viability of small-scale lavender oil production in a South African context. A total of 14 steam distillations were carried out using steam distillation times of 30-, 60- and 90 minutes on a native South African variant of the plant – *Lavandula x intermedia*, more colloquially known as 'Margaret Roberts' lavender. To test the efficacy of different distillation times, as well as the economic potential of using 'Margaret Roberts' lavender as a source of lavender oil, oil quality, and yield were analysed using GC-MS for oils from both fresh and aged lavender stems. It was discovered that fresh lavender had a maximum yield of 1.13% at a distillation time of 60 minutes, while aged lavender, stored for 1-2 weeks, had a maximum yield of 0.66 % at a distillation time of 60 minutes. Low or absent concentrations of linalool in all cases suggest that 'Margaret Roberts' lavender is less suitable for use in cosmetic and perfume production than conventional lavender variants such as Grosso and English lavender, and is better suited for cleaning products and detergents. Cost analysis indicates profits as high as 905.06 ZAR per 20 mL are projected if the plant is cultivated on site and the hydrosol resulting from each extraction is offered as an additional product, supporting the potential financial viability of the venture.

KEYWORDS: Essential oils, Extraction, *Lavandula x intermedia*, Oil yield, Chemical composition, Distillation time

1. Introduction

Essential oils are hydrophobic liquids extracted from a variety of different plants in the form of concentrated volatile compounds. They are known for their medicinal and therapeutic applications and have found considerable popularity in the fields of aromatherapy and naturopathy. (Kar et al., 2018)

'Quality', in this case, will be measured according to oil composition, with different chemical compounds imbuing different qualities to the various essential oils, such as pleasant aromas or anti-microbial activity.

Lavender oil is one of the most popular and profitable essential oils in the realm of aromatherapy, cosmetics, and dermatology. Alongside its pleasant aroma, lavender oil has

also been found to possess antibacterial, anti-depressive, antioxidant, anti-inflammatory, and sedative properties, hence its common application in industries such as cosmetics, food and beverage, and aromatherapy. (Cardia et al., 2021; Cavanagh & Wilkinson, 2002) Primary constituents of interest in lavender include linalool, linalyl acetate, 1,8-cineole, and camphor, with the ratio of these constituents varying dependent on the extraction method and the genetic makeup of the plant. (Cavanagh & Wilkinson, 2002)

The species of lavender most commonly used as a source of lavender oil are *Lavandula angustifolia* (English lavender) and *Lavandula × intermedia* (a hybrid of English lavender and Portuguese lavender), where *Lavandula × intermedia* typically yields more oil, but of lower quality than oil of the *Lavandula angustifolia* variety. (Wainer et al., 2022)

[1]1843629@students.wits.ac.za, [2]2088538@students.wits.ac.za, [3]2090898@students.wits.ac.za, [4]kevin.harding@wits.ac.za

DOI: 10.1201/9781003538646-5

In South Africa, the Grosso variety is mostly used for their higher essential oil extraction quantities; however, they only flower between December to February which limits the time in which they can be harvested, stored, and dried for oil extraction. (Lavender SA, 2016)

The national and global market for essential oils has increased within the last few years, with a global CAGR projected at 7.5% from 2020 to 2027. For a developing country such as South Africa, partially replacing imported essential oils with those that are locally produced would play a significant role in stimulating the country's economy. (Govindasamy et al., 2013)

Since the Grosso variety does not flower annually, it is harder to rely on them to consistently produce lavender oil on a commercial scale. The Margaret Roberts variety is a South African bred variant of the *Lavandula x intermedia* type; it is a hybrid between True English Lavender and Spike Lavender which can flower all year round. (Lavender SA, 2016) This report will endeavour to ascertain whether the Margaret Roberts species is a viable source of lavender oil in terms of chemical composition and oil yield.

Essential oils are extracted using a variety of methods depending on the physical and chemical characteristics of the plant material. (Burt, 2004) Distillation, the most common method, is comprised of three different types – namely hydro-distillation, combined water- and steam distillation, and direct steam distillation. Of these methods, direct steam distillation is the most used, worldwide. (Talati, 2017). While this method has the advantage of preventing thermal degradation of the oil constituents, extensive research is necessary to adapt this method to producing oil of higher qualities, while also reducing the distillation time and energy consumption. (Filly et al., 2016; Talati, 2017)

Gas chromatography–mass spectroscopy (GC-MS) combines the separation properties of gas chromatography with the detection features of mass spectrometry to determine the presence of different constituents within a sample and is commonly applied in various scenarios such as environmental monitoring, forensic cases, pharmaceutical applications, and food- and essential oils analysis. (Chauhan et al., 2014) In the case of essential oils analysis, GC-MS is capable of detecting the occurrence of compounds such as esters, alcohols, terpenes, and aldehydes; this information can then be used to determine the quality of the oils produced. (Chauhan et al., 2014)

This report aims to compare the feasibility of extracting lavender oil from aged lavender flowers versus fresh lavender flowers by distilling the oil at varying distillation times, with varying water/plant ratios. Cost analysis and theoretical scale-up were then considered based on optimized yield values and GC-MS analysis was applied to both the fresh- and aged lavender oils.

2. Material and Methods

2.1 Plant Material

The plant used for the extraction experiments was 'Margaret Roberts' lavender, classified officially as *Lavandula × intermedia*. Lavender stems were purchased from LavenderSA in Pretoria and were separated into two groups. The 'aged' stems were stored in open containers in fresh water, away from direct sunlight, for 1 - 2 weeks before being used for extraction. The second group – the 'fresh' stems – were stems that were deflowered and utilized within a day of collection from suppliers. Upon experimentation, the plants were deflowered manually, with the lavender spikes being weighed after removal from the stems.

2.2 Steam Distillation Extraction

Steam distillation was selected as the extraction method for the following experiments, as this method makes up 93% of all essential oils extractions and is the most popular method of lavender oil extraction to be applied on a commercial scale. (Masango, 2005) The glassware used for the steam distillation extraction were as follows:

- Round bottom flask
- Two-neck flask with openings at the top and bottom (still)
- Liebig condenser
- Separating funnel
- Two connecting bridges

First, distilled water was added to the round bottom flask and brought to a boil. A control of 600 mL distilled water was used for each experiment, and the water was boiled at a temperature of 104 °C by a heating mantle used on its maximum power of 220 V. A total of 14 experiments were run – six runs with aged lavender and eight runs with fresh lavender. The distillation times were controlled at 30-, 60- and 90 minutes and the plant weight in the still varied between 60 g and 80 g, with experiment 14 containing 40 g of plant material. For analysis, the GC-MS Shimadzu QP2010 Ultra machine model was used, with hexane as the solvent and a helium carrier gas.

Analysis of chemical constituents present in the oils extracted from the Margaret Roberts lavender was completed using Gas Chromatography-Mass Spectrometry, more specifically the Shimadzu GC-MS-QP2010 Ultra model which was provided by the University of Witwatersrand.

Table 5.1 Total experiments with their respective times and masses

Experiment number	Time (min)	Mass of flowers (g)
Experiment 1	30	60
Experiment 2	30	60
Experiment 3	60	60
Experiment 4	60	60
Experiment 5	90	60
Experiment 6	30	80
Experiment 7	60	60
Experiment 8	60	60
Experiment 9	30	60
Experiment 10	90	60
Experiment 11	60	60
Experiment 12	60	80
Experiment 13	90	80
Experiment 14	60	40

3. Results

3.1 Oil Yield Analysis

Experiments 1 – 6 were done with aged lavender, whilst experiments 7 – 14 were done with fresh lavender; in both cases, distillation time was varied between 30 min, 60 min, and 90 min, with yield calculated as a percentage of the oil mass weighed after distillation over the plant mass weighed before distillation.

Analysing the experiments using 60g aged flowers of the Margaret Roberts variety, analysis shows that experiment 4, at a distillation time of 60 min, yielded the highest oil percentage of 1.73% which is 197.4% greater than the maximum yield at a distillation time of 30 min, and a 346.3% greater than the yield at 90 min. However, it should be noted that this point of maximum yield is aberrant when compared to the other aged lavender yields and should be considered with scepticism. The next highest yield was the analysis on 60g fresh flowers at a distillation time of 30 min, with an oil yield percentage of 1.13% (experiment 4), which was 65.2% greater than a distillation time of 60 min when the maximum yield at this time was considered, and 72.7% greater than at 90 min.

While a 60 min distillation of aged lavender did produce the highest yield of lavender oil overall, it has already been established that this point appears aberrant in terms of Fig. 5.1, where the trend suggests relatively stable oil yields for aged lavender, irrespective of distillation periods. Disregarding this point, the maximum oil yields for fresh lavender trend higher than those for aged lavender across all distillation times – this agrees much more closely with established literature. (Kazaz et al., 2009)

Therefore, a yield of 1.13% when fresh lavender is distilled for 30 minutes can be taken as the highest yield achieved, with fresh lavender generally outperforming aged lavender, and shorter extraction periods emerging as superior to longer times. Overall, however, these values are significantly lower than those obtained by Zheljazkov, who determined the effect of steam distillation time on *Lavandula angustifolia*. Their peak yield was 6.8%, obtained at 60 minutes of distillation, suggesting that 'Margaret Roberts' lavender has a lower yield than commercially extracted lavender. (Zielinski, 2022)

3.2 Chemical Composition Analysis

Lavender oil quality has been judged according to the presence of linalool, 1,8-cineole, camphor, caryophyllene, alpha-pinene, and beta-pinene in the oil samples. Literature

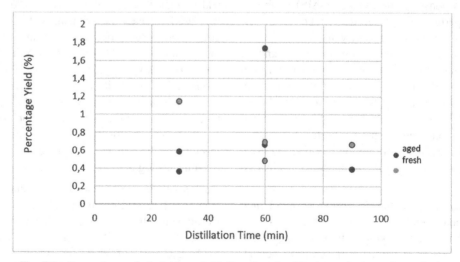

Fig. 5.1 Percentage of oil yield vs distillation time for 60g lavender sample analysis

states that these components are usually present in lower percentages but could peak at 40%, in some cases. (Beale et al., 2017; Blažeković et al., 2018; Kasai & Kubot, 2018) Compounds were identified using GC-MS analysis, which picked up about 40 compounds for the aged lavender samples and not more than 15 compounds for the fresh lavender samples. Experiment 14 had inconclusive results, with no common components in the sample.

It should also be noted that the standard deviation associated with the GC-MS data was high and the lack of consistency in oil composition suggests careful control of experimental parameters such as water temperature and time between harvesting and experimentation may be required to ensure quality remains stable.

Fresh Lavender Oil Analysis

Analysing the chemical composition of the oil extracted from the fresh Margaret Roberts flowers, the compounds varied from experiment to experiment with ranges of cineole (11.14%-45.64%), alpha-pinene (0%-29.79%), beta-pinene (9.43%-30.79%), caryophyllene (0%-7.28%) and camphor (0%-25.03%), as well as 0.27% linalool and 1.15% ocimene, which were only found in the analysis of one experiment amongst eight.

Concentrations of linalool, the main chemical compound responsible for the sweet and distinctive lavender fragrance, were low, with the highest percentage being 0.27% in experiment 13. The presence of linalyl acetate was also found to be negligible across all 8 experiments, indicating that the oil contained a higher camphor and cineole composition – this is in line with established literature, which suggests that steam-distilled lavender oil has higher camphor content than other extraction methods. (Wainer et al., 2022)

A high camphor content and low linalool concentration in all oil samples indicate that Margaret Roberts lavender oil would be better for soaps and detergents as opposed to perfumery and cosmetics, as it would smell pungently of mint, and have hints of pine as well, due to the significant presence of alpha-pinene and beta-pinene. (Sadasivuni et al., 2016)

Aged Lavender Oil Analysis

Analysing the aged Margaret Roberts oil chemical composition, the compounds mentioned above varied from experiment to experiment with ranges of cineole (12.75% - 26.45%), linalool (1.02%-5.65%), alpha-pinene (0%-2.39%), beta-pinene (0%-7.77%), caryophyllene (9.42%-33.44%), and camphor (0%-8.75%), with 2.94% ocimene in only one experiment amongst six. Alpha-bisabolol was also present, reaching a maximum of 10.48% in experiment 1.

The presence of linalool was low once again in the aged oils, with high cineole concentrations which, at its maximum, was four times that of the highest linalool recorded.

Table 5.2 Chemical composition ranges for Spike lavender, as well as the fresh- and old Margaret Roberts extracts

Compound	Literature	Fresh (Margaret Roberts)	Aged (Margaret Roberts)
Camphor (%)	10-20	0.25	0-9
Caryophyllene (%)		0-7	9-34
Cineole (%)	20-30	11-46	12-27
Linalool (%)	40-50	0-0.3	1-6
Ocimene (%)		0-1.2	0-3
Alpha-pinene (%)		6-30	0-3
Beta-pinene (%)		9-31	0-8

Comparing Aged and Fresh Lavender Compositions

The chemical compositions of the fresh- and aged Margaret Roberts lavender oil can be compared with each other, as well as to that of Spike lavender as taken from literature; this can be seen in Fig. 5.1. (Essential Oil Crops, 2009)

In the case of other compounds such as camphor, cineole, and pinene, the greater concentrations in fresh lavender oil when compared to aged lavender oil can be explained by evaporation, oxidation, and uncontrolled changes in the oil during storage periods. (Najafian, 2016)

The higher presence of pinene in the fresh analysis compared to the old analysis indicates that the overall smell of the fresh Margaret Roberts is more 'pine-like' than that of the aged Margaret Roberts. Additionally, lower concentrations in aged lavender as opposed to fresh lavender suggest degradation of 1,8-cineole with time, a finding which agreed with established literature. (Zheljazkov et al., 2013)

Linalool was not detected in any of the fresh lavender samples except for experiment 13, which was composed of 0.27% of linalool, whereas commercial lavender oil has linalool content ranging from 25% - 38%. (Beale et al., 2017) High ratios of camphor to linalool indicate that none of the samples were of the same quality as commercial lavender, and likely could not be used in high-value cosmetic products and perfumes.

The camphor content can be assumed to degrade with time, as seen through the lower concentrations in the aged lavender oil as opposed to the fresh samples. Oils with higher camphor content are commercially regarded as low quality, with commercial lavender oil typically containing less than 1.2% of camphor. (Giray, 2019)

The fresh lavender oil samples had caryophyllene concentrations ranging from 0.38% – 7.28%, whilst popular *Lavandula angustifolia* and *Lavandula latifolia* varieties typically have concentrations peaking at 2.8% and 1.9%, respectively. (Mori et al., 2016; Salido et al., 2011) An increase in concentration is observed for the aged plants when compared to the fresh samples, peaking at 33.44%. This compound is known to have sedative, antioxidant, and anti-inflammatory effects. (Franciosi, 2016)

If the value of the samples is based primarily on linalool and camphor contents with high-linalool and low-camphor being deemed as more desirable, aged lavender emerges as a clear winner. However, regardless of whether fresh- or aged lavender is used, the Margaret Roberts oils will be outperformed by True Lavender in this regard, making the Margaret Roberts oils an inherently subpar alternative. However, if the oil is marketed particularly for use in detergents, cleaning supplies, and medicinal purposes and is valued accordingly, oils that are high in camphor, cineole, and pinene become more desirable. In this case, fresh lavender oils emerge as superior, producing greater yields and more attractive chemical compositions than their aged counterparts for the production of cleaning products and medicines.

4. Cost Analysis

If steam distillation was to be applied in the process, production of lavender oil alone would not be particularly profitable. However, two products could essentially be produced simultaneously as the wastewater collected at the end of the process, known as hydrosol, becomes infused with the aroma of the essential oil during the extraction, producing a pleasant-smelling water capable of being sold as an additional product. This could provide a supplementary source of income.

Based on general prices in the existing market, a basis of a 20 mL product of lavender oil will be considered for this economic analysis; it is generally sold for between 100 ZAR and 250 ZAR for a 20 mL product with hydrosol sold for approximately 150 ZAR/L. Thus, for the sake of these calculations, the products on offer will be assumed to be 20 mL of lavender oil for 175 ZAR and 1L of hydrosol (ie: 'lavender water') for 150 ZAR. Lavender stems have been costed at 115 ZAR for 1000 stems, the electricity required for the operation of the heating mantle has been costed at 2.558 ZAR/kWh, and the collective water required for evaporation into steam, as well as use in the condenser, has been priced at 19.78 ZAR/kL, assuming 10-15 kL total usage per month. (City of Johannesburg Water and Sewer Tariffs for 2022/2023, 2022; Garden Mecca, 2022; GlobalPetrolPrices.com, 2022)

The number of runs required to produce 20 mL was calculated using the density of lavender oil, reported as 0.895 g/mL. (The Good Scents Company, 2021) For experiment 9, 0.6802g of oil was produced, calculated as 0.76 mL

according to Equation 1. Therefore, 26.32 runs (rounded to 27) are required to produce 20 mL of product with each run being 30 min long and producing 110 mL of hydrosol. In total, 13.5 hours of distillation will be required per 20 mL of lavender oil produced.

Since a 220V heating mantel was utilized and a type N 16 A power socket was assumed, the required kilowatt hours have been calculated as 47.52 kWh according to the equation below. (World Standards, 2022)

$$\text{Power (kWh)} = \frac{\begin{array}{c}\text{heating mantle voltage (V)} \times \text{current (A)} \times \\ \text{distillation time (hours)} \times \text{required runs}\end{array}}{1000}$$

The flow rate from an average South African water faucet has a maximum flow of 12 L/min; because the condenser used only a light flow, 3 L/min was taken as a sensible flow rate for purposes of calculating the cost of condenser water. (Strauss, 2022). With 27 runs at 30 min each, giving 810 min in total, 2430 L of water is calculated to be used in the condenser. With 600 mL used per run, 16.2 L of water is used to make steam. Thus 2446.2 L of water in total is used to produce 20 mL of lavender oil.

To determine the economic feasibility of extracting Margaret Roberts lavender oil, the overall costs for producing a specified quantity of oil based on the steam distillation experiments conducted have been analysed. In the case of cultivating lavender instead of buying flowers, purchasing costs have been excluded from the calculations.

Operating at a yield of 1.13%, the total production profits per 20 mL of lavender oil produced can be seen in Table 5.3. Offering hydrosol as a product increases profits exponentially, with a maximum profit margin of 905.06 ZAR per 20mL lavender oil sold when the lavender is cultivated and all hydrosol produced is sold. However, even without cultivation, a respectable profit of 310.06 ZAR can be made via the sale of hydrosol in addition to lavender oil. For the venture to be profitable, it can therefore be asserted that the sale of hydrosol as an ancillary product is essential – in the case of cultivation, offering hydrosol as an additional product increases profits by a gargantuan 17793.58%.

Table 5.3 Profit breakdown for different business models using experiment 9, with a yield of 1.13%

Profit (ZAR)	Conditions
310.60	Purchased lavender; hydrosol sold
905.06	Grown lavender; hydrosol sold
–589.94	Purchased lavender; no hydrosol sold
5.06	Grown lavender; no hydrosol sold

5. Conclusion

The aim of the project looked at determining the optimal distillation time for Margaret Roberts lavender oil extraction; it was found that for fresh flowers, an optimal distillation time of 30 min could be achieved, with a maximum oil yield of 1.13%. For aged Margaret Roberts, for which stems were collected and stored for a week, it was deemed that distillation times did not have a significant effect on the yield of lavender oil, with fresh lavender producing greater product yields overall.

The chemical composition analysis using GC-MS of both the old and fresh Margaret Roberts lavender oil indicated very low percentages of linalool, with a maximum of 5.65% from the aged oil analysis. Given the high composition of cineole, camphor, and alpha- and beta-pinene, the Margaret Roberts lavender has a more pungent, herbaceous fragrant, making it more suitable in industries such as medicine, cleaning agents, and detergents. It was deemed unable to compete with the likes of True Lavender in terms of perfumery and cosmetics.

The cost analysis performed showed that maximum profits of 905.06 ZAR can be obtained per 20mL of lavender oil produced if hydrosol is offered as an ancillary product and lavender is cultivated rather than purchased. Thus, offering lavender oil and its associated hydrosol both as products, growing the lavender oneself, and marketing the oils for the production of medicinal brews, detergents, and cleaning agents emerges as the optimal business model for the commercial production of Margaret Roberts lavender oil.

REFERENCES

1. Beale, D. J., Morrison, P. D., Karpe, A. V., & Dunn, M. S. (2017). Chemometric Analysis of Lavender Essential Oils Using Targeted and Untargeted GC-MS Acquired Data for the Rapid Identification and Characterization of Oil Quality. *Molecules 2017, Vol. 22, Page 1339, 22*(8), 1339. https://doi.org/10.3390/MOLECULES22081339

2. Blažeković, B., Yang, W., Wang, Y., Li, C., Kindl, M., Pepeljnjak, S., & Vladimir-Knežević, S. (2018). Chemical composition, antimicrobial and antioxidant activities of essential oils of Lavandula × intermedia 'Budrovka' and L. angustifolia cultivated in Croatia. *Industrial Crops and Products, 123*, 173–182. https://doi.org/10.1016/J.INDCROP.2018.06.041

3. Burt, S. (2004). Essential oils: Their antibacterial properties and potential applications in foods - A review. *International Journal of Food Microbiology, 94*(3), 223–253. https://doi.org/10.1016/j.ijfoodmicro.2004.03.022

4. Cardia, G. F. E., Silva-Comar, F. M. de S., Rocha, E. M. T. da, Silva-Filho, S. E., Zagotto, M., Uchida, N. S., Amaral, V. do, Bersani-Amado, C. A., & Cuman, R. K. N. (2021). Pharmacological, medicinal and toxicological properties of lavender essential oil: A review. *Research, Society and Development, 10*(5), e23310514933. https://doi.org/10.33448/rsd-v10i5.14933

5. Cavanagh, H. M. A., & Wilkinson, J. M. (2002). Biological activities of lavender essential oil. *Phytotherapy Research : PTR, 16*(4), 301–308. https://doi.org/10.1002/PTR.1103

6. Chauhan, A., Goyal, M. K., & Chauhan, P. (2014). GC-MS Technique and its Analytical Applications in Science and Technology. *Journal of Analytical & Bioanalytical Techniques 2014 5:6, 5*(6), 1–5. https://doi.org/10.4172/2155-9872.1000222

7. Essential Oil Crops. (2009). *Lavender Production*. Department of Agriculture, Forestry and Fisheries. https://www.yumpu.com/en/document/read/7272477/lavender-production-department-of-agriculture-forestry-and-

8. Filly, A., Fabiano-Tixier, A. S., Louis, C., Fernandez, X., & Chemat, F. (2016). Water as a green solvent combined with different techniques for extraction of essential oil from lavender flowers. *Comptes Rendus Chimie, 19*(6), 707–717. https://doi.org/10.1016/J.CRCI.2016.01.018

9. Franciosi, A. (2016). *Caryophyllene: Definition, Effects, And Benefits - Honest Marijuana*. Honest Marijuana. https://honestmarijuana.com/caryophyllene/

10. Garden Mecca. (2022). *Lavandula "Lavender" Margaret Roberts*. https://gardenmecca.co.za/products/Lavandula-'Hollandia'-Lavender-5-Liter-p490909221

11. Giray, F. H. (2019). An Analysis of World Lavender Oil Markets and Lessons for Turkey. *Https://Doi.Org/10.1080/0972060X.2019.1574612, 21*(6), 1612–1623. https://doi.org/10.1080/0972060X.2019.1574612

12. GlobalPetrolPrices.com. (2022). *South Africa electricity prices, March 2022* . https://www.globalpetrolprices.com/South-Africa/electricity_prices/

13. Govindasamy, R., Arumugam, S., & Simon, J. E. (2013). An assessment of the essential oil and aromatic plant industry with a focus on africa. *ACS Symposium Series, 1127*, 289–321. https://doi.org/10.1021/BK-2013-1127.CH018

14. *City of Johannesburg Water and Sewer Tariffs for 2022/2023*, (2022) (testimony of Johannesburg Water).

15. Kar, S., Gupta, P., & Gupta, J. (2018). Essential oils: Biological activity beyond aromatherapy. *Natural Product Sciences, 24*(3), 139–147. https://doi.org/10.20307/nps.2018.24.3.139

16. Kasai, H., & Kubot, Y. (2018). Analyses of Volatile Components of Lavender (Lavandula angustifolia HIDCOTE and Lavandula x intermedia GROSSO) as Influenced by Cultivar Type, Part, and Growth Season. *Yakugaku Zasshi : Journal of the Pharmaceutical Society of Japan, 138*(12), 1569–1577. https://doi.org/10.1248/YAKUSHI.18-00159

17. Kazaz, S., Erbaş, S., & Baydar, H. (2009). The effects of storage temperature and duration on essential oil content and composition oil rose (Rosa damascena Mill.). *Turkish Journal of Field Crops, 14*(2), 89–96.

18. Lavender SA. (2016). *Lavender Plants*. https://www.lavendersa.co.za/lavenderplants.html

19. Masango, P. (2005). Cleaner production of essential oils by steam distillation. *Journal of Cleaner Production, 13*(8), 833–839. https://doi.org/10.1016/J.JCLEPRO.2004.02.039

20. Mori, H. M., Kawanami, H., Kawahata, H., & Aoki, M. (2016). Wound healing potential of lavender oil by acceleration of granulation and wound contraction through induction of TGF-β in a rat model. *BMC Complementary and Alternative Medicine, 16*(1). https://doi.org/10.1186/S12906-016-1128-7

21. Najafian, S. (2016). The effect of time and temperature on the shelf life of essential oils of Lavandula officinalis. *Http://Dx.Doi.Org/10.1080/10412905.2016.1165743, 28*(5), 413–420. https://doi.org/10.1080/10412905.2016.1165743

22. Sadasivuni, K. K., Ponnamma, D., Kim, J., Cabibihan, J. J., & AlMaadeed, M. A. (2016). Biopolymer Composites in Electronics. *Biopolymer Composites in Electronics*, 1–521. https://doi.org/10.1016/C2014-0-04575-3

23. Salido, S., Altarejos, J., Nogueras, M., Sánchez, A., & Luque, P. (2011). Chemical Composition and Seasonal Variations of Spike Lavender Oil from Southern Spain. *Http://Dx.Doi.Org/10.1080/10412905.2004.9698698, 16*(3), 206–210. https://doi.org/10.1080/10412905.2004.9698698

24. Strauss, H. (2022). *South African Tap and Flow Rate Gap Analysis* (Issue January).

25. Talati, A. (2017). Extraction methods of natural essential oils. *AIRASE, The Association for the International Research of Aromatic Science and Education.* https://doi.org/10.13140/RG.2.2.18744.34564

26. The Good Scents Company. (2021). *Spike Lavender Oil, Spain.* TGSC Information System. http://www.thegoodscentscompany.com/data/es1584691.html

27. Wainer, J., Thomas, A., Chimhau, T., & Harding, K. G. (2022). Extraction of Essential Oils from Lavandula x intermedia "Margaret Roberts" Using Steam Distillation, Hydrodistillation, and Cellulase-Assisted Hydrodistillation: Experimentation and Cost Analysis. *Plants, 11*(24), 3479. https://doi.org/10.3390/PLANTS11243479

28. World Standards. (2022). *South Africa - Power plug, socket & mains voltage in South Africa.* Worldstandards.Eu. https://www.worldstandards.eu/electricity/plug-voltage-by-country/south-africa/

29. Zheljazkov, V. D., Cantrell, C. L., Astatkie, T., & Jeliazkova, E. (2013). Distillation time effect on lavender essential oil yield and composition. *Journal of Oleo Science, 62*(4), 195–199. https://doi.org/10.5650/JOS.62.195

30. Zielinski, E. (2022). *10 Best Essential Oils for Healing and How to Use Them!* Natural Living Family. https://naturallivingfamily.com/best-essential-oils/

Note: All the tables and figure in this chapter were compiled by the author.

Sustainable Materials Processing and Manufacturing – Lin Zhu et al. (eds)
© 2024 Taylor & Francis Group, London, ISBN 978-1-032-88599-5

Water Purification Using Freshwater Algae

Ketalya Reddy, Alma Snyman and Kevin Graham Harding*

School of Chemical and Metallurgical Engineering, University of the Witwatersrand, Johannesburg, South Africa

ABSTRACT: The focus of this work was to determine what conditions should be used to maximise water purification through algae growth. In addition, this study determined the effect of changing the process parameters on algae growth, investigated what impurities there were before and after water purification and provided an optimum solution for water treatment by algae purification. The experiments were carried out as two separate tests, Test 1 and Test 2, to determine the process parameters, temperature and carbon dioxide concentration, to see the effects they have on the nutrient uptake of algae for water purification. Ion Chromatography (IC) and Chemical Oxygen Demand (COD) are employed to analyse the samples. The findings from this indicates that algae can significantly purify wastewater through nutrient uptake. The rate of phosphate, chloride and sulfate removal, as well as COD reduction, were all affected when the temperature and carbon dioxide flow rates were varied. The values for temperature and percentage of flow that produced an optimum solution for water purification by algal growth were 30°C and 100%, respectively. These parameters can be used to design an optimum water purification process using algal growth as an alternative to other water treatment options, returns.

KEYWORDS: Biorefinery, Culture, Environmental impact, Nutrients, Wastewater

1. Introduction

The use of algal growth for water purification has been shown to significantly purify water (Sen et al., 2013). This experiment examines how to optimize the algae development process. It has become clear that doing so will increase the effectiveness of water filtration.

The ideal algae species should possess the following qualities (Brar et al., 2022): a high photo-conversion efficiency with quick and steady growth in the presence of pollutants; high lipid content and significant biofuel by-products; high CO2 assimilation capacity and minimal nutrient requirements; tolerance to temperature change and self-flocculating ability for simple cell harvesting. When looking at the ideal algae qualities, this can be incorporated into the growth of algae and how different factors such as temperature and carbon dioxide concentration would affect this growth. The aim of this work was to determine what the process parameters are to maximise water purification by algal growth by looking at Emmerentia Dam water. This in turn can aid in the understanding of how to use these findings and incorporate it into situations where water needs to be purified naturally. The parameters can also show the effects of too much algal growth in natural environments under similar conditions. The problem statement was to determine the effect of changing the process parameters of algae growth, investigate what impurities are present in the water before and after purification and to provide an optimum solution for water treatment by algal purification. The analysis of this will be done using COD and anion analysis using ion chromatography.

2. Literature Review

Further looking at the impact temperature would have on the growth of algae would help in understanding how this can be

---

*Corresponding author: kevin.harding@gmail.com

DOI: 10.1201/9781003538646-6

used to find an optimal growth rate for algae to grow as well as reduce the amount of nutrients found in the water. The growth rate of algae is extremely dependent on the temperature of the growth environment. A higher temperature is usually associated with an increased growth rate with the optimal temperature ranging between 25°C to 35°C depending on the species of algae (Ahmad et al., 2020). A higher temperature increases the rate of the photosynthetic reaction which leads to faster nutrient uptake and algal growth.

The development rate of algae is greatly influenced by the carbon dioxide present, which is used in the photosynthesis process. According to research done in 2018 (Tang et al., 2018), adding CO_2 to an algae-bioreactor enhanced the algal growth by 35% since it lowered the pH of the system, which is ideal for growth. A summary of the algal growth and maximal biomass generated at a specific CO_2 concentration was provided in the study conducted by (S. P. Singh & Singh, 2014) It was shown that the amount of biomass and lipids in microalgal species increased as CO_2 concentration rises (S. P. Singh & Singh, 2014).

As discussed, algae growth is affected by temperature and carbon dioxide concentration. However, algal growth is also impacted by the nutrients found in wastewater, particularly nitrogen, phosphorous, and carbon. An increase in the rate of algal development would result from the concentration of these nutrients being higher (Chen et al., 2011), thus by changing the temperature and carbon dioxide concentration, the nutrients found in the water is affected.

As the growth of algae is linked strongly with water purification, studies have been done to further prove the impact algae has on the nutrients present in wastewater after algae treatment. (Bogan et al., 1960) were the ones who originally proposed and researched the intensive growth and subsequent harvesting of the algal biomass as a strategy for eliminating wastewater-borne nutrients. (Oswald & Golueke, 1966) conducted additional research on it and advocated using high-rate algal treatment to remove the potential for algae development in wastewater. A large-scale South African study on the removal of industrial nitrogenous wastes using high-rate algal ponds, as reported by (Altona et al., 2005) found that a multi-stage algal system is necessary to exert the full removal potential of nitrogen through algal biomass incorporation and algal harvesting. From these studies it has been proven that algae have a positive effect on the purification of wastewater.

In addition to temperature and carbon dioxide concentration, algal growth and nutrient uptake are influenced by a complex interaction of physical parameters, including pH, light intensity and biotic factors. It is anticipated that higher algal densities will result in better growth and greater nutrient removal efficiency. High algal density, however, would result in self-shading, an accumulation of auto-inhibitors,

and a decline in photosynthetic efficiency (Abdel-Raouf et al., 2012). Hence, finding the correct ratio of algae density is important to purify water without resulting in self-shading.

The analyses that are used were COD and anion analysis. Indirect measurement of contaminants (organics) in a water sample is done using COD analysis. It is a crucial factor in determining the quality of water (SciMed, 2022). The COD levels found in surface water resources normally range from 20 mg/L or less in clean waters to more than 200 mg/L in waters that are receiving effluents (Jain & Singh, 2003). For analyzing the chemistry of water, ion chromatography is utilized. Major cations including lithium, sodium, ammonium, potassium, calcium, and magnesium as well as major anions like fluoride, chloride, nitrate, nitrite, and sulfate may all be measured in the parts-per-billion (ppb) range using ion chromatographs(Weiss, 2004).

3. Methodology

The methodology can be seen as running two separate tests that investigate two different parameters. Test 1 will investigate the effect of carbon dioxide on algal growth and how the biomass aids in the purification of water while Test 2 investigates the effect of temperature on algal growth and its effects on water. Daylight was the light source used.

3.1 Materials

The material listings can be seen in Table 6.1 where each Test required separate materials.

Table 6.1 The materials needed for Test 1 (carbon dioxide concentration varied) and Test 2 (temperature varied)

Test 1: Effects of carbon dioxide concentration	Test 2: Effects of temperature
• 1L fresh water algae culture • 5L water from a local dam (Emmerentia Dam) • CO_2 Cylinder	• 100ml fresh water algae culture • 500ml water from a local dam (Emmerentia Dam) • Heating mantels

3.2 Method

Test 1

Analysis was done on the dam water collected initially. Test 1 was performed in a large column that continuously pumped carbon dioxide into the algae-water mixture maintaining the 5:1 ratio of water to algae (Fig. 6.1). This test is done to test how the carbon dioxide concentration affects the growth of algae and its ability to purify water. The amount of carbon dioxide going into each column is based on the position of the valve opening with approximately 100% meaning the valve is fully opened (Table 6.2).

Table 6.2 Test 1 experiment variables*

Experiment	1	2	3	4	6
Valve opening	0%	25%	50%	75%	100%

* The valve openings depict the how open the valve was where 100% meant the valve was fully open and 0% meant the valve was fully closed

Fig. 6.1 The experimental set up of Test 1. The algae were placed in 5 large columns that contained dam water

Test 2

Test 2 uses the temperature as the independent variable and tests how this parameter effects the growth of algae and the purity of water. Test 2 was done in the space of two weeks using four conical flasks and heating mantels in addition to four stopper to ensure that the water does not evaporate once heated. 500 mL of local dam water was placed in a conical flask and set aside as the control (Fig. 6.2). 500 mL of local dam water was placed into each conical flask along with 100 mL of freshwater algae. The temperature of each conical flask was varied, using a heating mantel (Table 6.3).

Table 6.3 Test 2 showing the temperatures of each of the conical flasks*

Experiment	6	7	8	9	10
Temperature (°C)	20 (Standard room temperature)	25	30	35	40

* The standard room temperature is at 20 °C and the temperature was increased in intervals of 5 °C after that for each experiment.

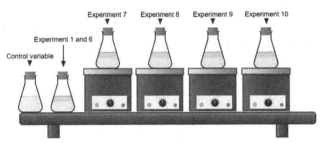

Fig. 6.2 Test 1 Experimental set-up

3.3 Analysis

The analysis that took place used parameters that could evaluate the quality of the water. The analysis used were;

Anion analysis using ion chromatography: Initially the samples for the Ion Chromatography (IC) were prepared in advance. The water that was collected as samples from the tests was purified using Nylon Syringe filters that were of pore size 0.45μm. This was done to rid excess solids as only liquids can be processed through the machine. In addition, a dilution step was added where the sample was diluted by 5 thus had a dilution factor of 5 as the samples originally had high concentrations.

COD: COD quantifies the amount of DO that is consumed under regulated circumstances during the oxidation of organic material and inorganic substances like ammonia or nitrite. In order to test for COD, the water sample was digested for two hours at 150°C with potassium dichromate and sulfuric acid in a sealed vial. The vials were then read by a spectrophotometer and results are given in mg/L. The chemical oxygen demand was used to see the nutrient removal of the overall experiment as seen in (Guldhe et al., 2017)

The percentage removal:

$$\frac{\text{inital concentration} - \text{final concentration}}{\text{initial concentration}} \times 100$$

4. Results

4.1 Chemical Oxygen Demand

The chemical oxygen demand (COD) was measured through a period of time, in this case 21 days. The interval times taken were at the beginning of the experiment (Day 1), the middle (Day 11) and the end (Day 21) to see how the COD varied throughout the experiment. The COD decreased in the control from 1500 mg/l to around 400 mg/l by the 21st day.

Test 1 is shown in Fig. 6.3 which shows how the carbon dioxide concentration affects the growth of algae and the purity of the water. The COD increased in when the valve was fully closed from 246 mg/L to 339 mg/L to 307 mg/L. The COD was similar when the valve was 25% open where it started close to 1137 mg/L and increased to 1395 mg/L. The COD when the valve was 50% open decreased overall from 806 mg/L to 704 mg/L.

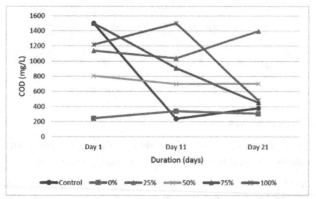

Fig. 6.3 The COD was taken for each experiment in Test 1

This trend from when the valve was 50% open followed through to when the valve was 75% open which decreased exponentially from 1500 mg/L to 452 mg/L (Fig. 6.3). Although when the valve was 100% open had increased in the middle of the test to 1500 mg/L, it ended in a decreased value of 482 mg/L.

Test 2 is also shown in Fig. 6.4, which represents Experiment 6 to Experiment 10, where the temperature is varied. The COD increased at 20°C from 246 mg/L to 339 mg/L to 307 mg/L. When the temperature was at 25°C, the COD started at 275 mg/L and by the middle of Test 2 went to a low of 132 mg/L and then by the end of the test went up to 291 mg/L.

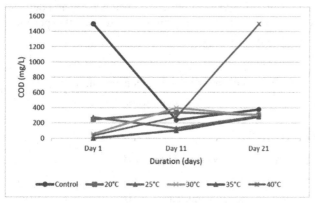

Fig. 6.4 The COD was taken for each experiment in Test 2

When the temperature was at 30°C (Fig. 6.4), the COD showed a trend whereby it started at 56 mg/L and increased to 398 mg/L then decreased to 299 mg/L. At 35°C, the COD started at 0.05 mg/L and increased to 101 mg/L by the middle of Test 2 and increased slightly at the end to 292 mg/L. At the start when the temperature was 40°C the COD sat at 35 mg/L and showed an increasing trend where at the middle of the experiment the COD was 280 mg/L and finally went further

up to 1500 mg/L.

Anion analysis using Ion Chromatography

Using anion analysis to see what occurred when the carbon dioxide concentration changed by looking at the concentrations of phosphate, chloride and sulfate, what can be seen is that the control for the phosphate concentration stayed in a similar range except for one large value at day 15 to 17 that showed an increase from 624.1 mg/L back down to 265.5 mg/L (Fig. 6.5a). When the valve was open to 50% there was a large increase in the middle of the experiment at day 11 as the phosphate concentration went from 353.4 mg/L to 1005 mg/L. However, overall, the concentration of phosphate from beginning to end when the valve was open to 50% went from 535.2 mg/L at the beginning of the experiment to 168.8 mg/L at the end. This was followed through when the valve was open to 25% where there was an increase at day 11 from 338.3 mg/L to 959.5 mg/L showing a peak in Fig. 6.5a) at day 11 but also experienced am overall decrease in the concentration of phosphate from 501.6 mg/L to 257.6 mg/L. The same trend was seen when the valve was opened to 100% a there was an increase on day 11 from 297.4 mg/L to 893.6 mg/L but this experiment also experienced an overall decrease from 530.8 mg/l to 244.7 mg/L.

The chloride concentration seen in (Fig. 6.5b) shows a large peak when the valve is open to 50% on day 11 going from 353.39 mg/L to 1005.1 mg/L, however from beginning of the experiment to the end of the experiment the chloride concentration decreased from 535.22 mg/L to 168.77 mg/L. Another two peaks are seen when the valve is open to 100% on day 11 there was an increase from 297.41 mg/L to 893.64 mg/L and on day 19 where there was an increase from 443.83 mg/L to 1100.9 mg/L. However, as seen when the valve was open to 50%, when the valve was open to 100% there was a decrease from beginning to end from 530.78 mg/L to 244.72mg/L. When the valve was open to 0%, 25% and 75% the same trend followed where there was an overall decrease in chlorine concentration from beginning to end. When the valve was 0% open the chlorine concentration decreased from 69.23 mg/L to 51.21 mg/L while at 25% valve opening the chorine concentration decreased from 85.92 mg/L to 68.32 mg/L. There was a larger decrease when the valve was open to 75% as the chlorine concentration went from 467.92 mg/L to 170.4 mg/L which is 0.36 times smaller than the beginning value.

The sulphate concentrations shown in Fig. 6.5c) show an overall increase in all the sulphate concentration values from beginning to end. A large peak can be seen when the valve was open to 0% on day 15 from 81.29 mg/L to 269.3 mg/L. In addition to this the control experienced a large decrease in sulphate concentration from beginning to end from 227.3 mg/L to 73.24 mg/L. Looking at the values when the valve

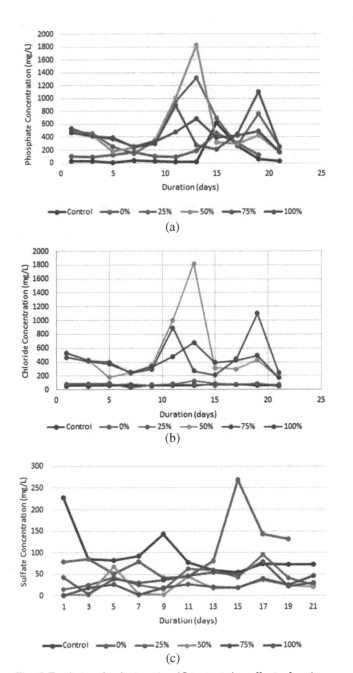

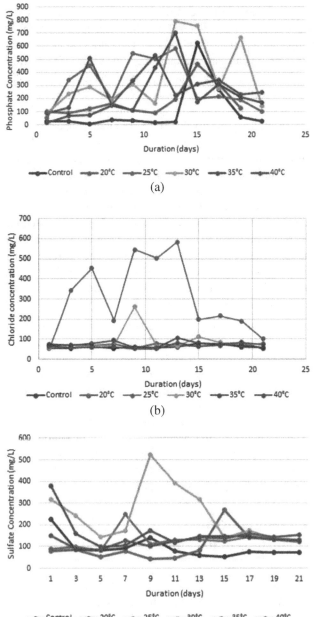

There were sporadic peaks throughout the duration of Test 2 for the phosphate concentrations (Fig. 6.6a). The largest peak was seen at 30°C at day 13 and day 15 of 789.2°C and 751.6°C, respectively. Looking at the peaks the largest peak for 35°C was seen on day 11 going from 435 mg/L to 703.4 mg/. For 20°C the highest peak was at day 15 of 462.7 mg/L while the highest for 25°C was at day 13 of 583.2 mg/L. The highest peak for when the temperature was at 40°C Day 11 of 529.7 mg/L. What can also be seen is that the overall phosphate concentration from beginning to end increased. At

Fig. 6.5 Anion Analysis using IC to test the effect of carbon dioxide on algae growth and water purification

was open to 25% there was an increase from beginning to end with the end value being 1.6 times bigger than the beginning value of 15.91 mg/L. When the valve was open to 50% there was an exponential increase in the sulfate concentration from beginning to end going from 1.7 mg/L to 20.77 mg/L. At 75% valve opening another increase can be seen from 1.2 mg/L to 46.12 mg/L from beginning to end. When the valve was open to 100% the smallest sulphate concentration increase was seen where the end value was 0.7 times bigger than the beginning value of 42.85 mg/L.

Fig. 6.6 Anion Analysis using IC to test the effect of temperature on algae growth and water purification

20°C the concentration increased the most from a beginning value of 101.4 mg/L to an end value of 128.6 mg/L. From 25°C to 35°C all the phosphate concentrations increased whereby the end value of 25°C was 0.5 times bigger than the beginning, the end value of 30°C was 0.4 times bigger than the beginning and at 35°C a smallest increase where the end value was 0.1 times bigger than the beginning value of 17.14 mg/L. At 40°C there was an overall decrease in phosphate concentration where the beginning value was 92.1 mg/L to an end value of 246.6 mg/L.

When looking at the chloride concentrations there is one set of data that stands out from the rest which is when the temperature is at 25°C (Fig. 6.6b). The values for the chlorine concentration all start at around the same values ranging from 50-60 mg/L however, chlorine experienced an exponential increase with three large peaks occurring at day 5, day 9 and day 11 with values of 452.99 mg/L, 544.02 mg/L and 583.16 mg/L, respectively. The only other temperature that experienced a peak was at 30°C on day 9 of 261.1 mg/L. For the other temperatures a trend is noticed where the values stayed more or less similar. Looking at an overall trend from beginning to end to see whether the chlorine concentrations increased or decreased shows that the chlorine concentrations increased when the temperature was at 25°C, 30°C and 40°C whereas a decrease in chlorine concentration was seen when the temperature was at 20°C and 35°C. The decrease when the temperature was at 20°C was from 69.23 mg/L to 51.21 mg/L while the decrease when the temperature was at 25°C was from 74.35mg/L to 57.92 mg/L.

Looking at the sulphate concentration when the temperature was at 20°C, 25°C and 40°C there was an increase in sulphate concentration from beginning to end while when the temperate was at 30°C and 35°C the sulphate concentration decreased from beginning to end (Fig. 6.6c). A large peak is seen when the temperature was at 30°C for the sulphate concentrations on day 9 going from 173.5 g/L to 524.5 mg/L. At 30°C however, the overall decrease from beginning to end was from 317.1 mg/L to 132.4 mg/L while when the temperature was at 35°C the decrease was from 380.5 mg/L at the beginning to 128.8 mg/L at the end.

5. Discussion

5.1 Analysis of the Effect of Carbon Dioxide Concentration

The overall trends that can be seen is that there are minimal chloride concentrations for the control, when the valve is fully closed and when the valve is open to 25%. In addition to this all the chloride concentrations showed an overall decrease from beginning to end while all phosphate concentrations showed the same trend except when the valve

was fully closed. What is interesting to note is that sulfate had an inverse trend whereby all the sulfate concentrations at the beginning of the test are much lower than that at the end except when the valve was fully opened which showed a decrease in the overall sulfate concentration, however the sulfate concentrations are all below 250 mg/L meaning that they meet clean water standards(Jain & Singh, 2003).

The nutrient removal efficiencies depend upon the initial concentration of nutrients in the wastewater and the microalgal strains used (Guldhe et al., 2017). Albeit saying this when looking at the COD values for the effect of carbon dioxide concentration there is no percentage removal when the valve was open to 0 and 25% in terms of the amount of nutrients seen in the COD analysis. However, COD was only taken at the beginning, middle and end of the experiment. Thus, the reasoning behind the COD increasing exponentially could be due to an increase in a specific anion concentration. There was an increase in sulphate concentrations from beginning to end with the valve opened to 0% increasing by 65% for the sulphate concentration which coincides with an increased COD of 24%. When the valve was open to 25% there was an overall 56% increase in the sulphate concentration and this showed in the COD with an increase of 22%. According to (Rinzema & Lettinga, 2008), looking at the COD/sulfate ratio, if the ratio is less than 0.67 it would mean that there are insufficient nutrients in the wastewater for the complete reduction of sulphate. Looking at the values there is sufficient nutrients as all the COD/sulfate ratios exceed 0.67. The best value for the ratio found in Jeong et al., 2008 was at 11.6 COD/sulfate ratio, where the optimum methane production rate was decreased by 60%. The largest ratio being at 25% valve opening of 56.1 and the smallest being when the valve was open to 0% of 1.9. Thus, the complete removal of organic matter would only occur under the conditions of sulfate reduction which was achieved for all valve openings and allows for methanogenesis to occur simultaneously with the sulfate reduction (Rinzema & Lettinga, 2008).

The removal efficiencies found in (Zhang et al., 2013), were 40.8% for COD, 15.8% for nitrogen and 49.9% for phosphate. Comparing this to the effect of carbon dioxide concentration found, a percentage removal of 70% and 60% for when the valve was open to 75% and 100%, respectively. While the phosphate percentage removal was 63% and 53% for when the valve was open to 75% and 100%, respectively. This means that comparing the results from this study to the one from (Zhang et al., 2013), showed a better efficiency in the removal of phosphates as well as the COD reduction for when the valve was open to 75% and 100%. In addition to this another reason for this high nutrient absorption when the carbon dioxide concentration is increased could be due to the carbon dioxides effect in the photosynthesis process which would have led to growth in the algae due to the continuous supply as suggested by (Guerrero-Cabrera et al., 2014). In addition to this the COD/ sulfate ratio was bigger when the valve was open to 100% compared to when the valve was open to 75% meaning better sulfate reduction and methanogenesis would occur when the valve is open to 100% (Rinzema & Lettinga, 2008).

5.2 Analysis of the Effect of Temperature

Increasing the temperature can lead to an increase in the quantity of ammonia to volatize as well as phosphate to precipitate which can show in the COD for the effect of temperature where there is no percentage removal in terms of the amount of nutrients seen in the COD analysis (Guerrero-Cabrera et al., 2014) . However, when looking at this in hand with the COD/sulfate ratio, all the values are above 0.67 which indicates ample sulphate reduction as well as methanogenesis. The values for the COD/Sulfate ratio were from 2.2 to 9.7 where the highest value was at 40°C (Rinzema & Lettinga, 2008). In addition to this looking at the COD at the end of the test, 40°C had the largest COD of 1500 mg/L which coincides with an increase in phosphate concentration of 167% thus showing that the increased temperature increased the amount of phosphate to precipitate as mentioned by (Guerrero-Cabrera et al., 2014). The only temperature that showed a percentage removal was at 20°C which could be a result of physisorption or the enhancement of the self-diffusion coefficient from increasing the temperature.

Phosphate concentration increase was the highest when the temperature was at 35°C and 40°C while the lowest increases in phosphate concentration were at 30°C and 20°C. As previously stated, pH and dissolved oxygen play a role in phosphate concentration as well as increasing temperature (Guldhe et al., 2017). What is shown it that the higher temperatures at 35°C and 40°C have larger increases in phosphate concentrations instead of percentage removals. For the chloride concentration, the only temperatures that showed a percentage removal were at 20°C and 35°C with percentage removals of 26% and 22%, respectively. For the sulphate concentrations, percentage removals are seen for 30°C and 35°C of 58% and 66%, respectively. According to (Ahmad et al., 2020), the optimum temperature would range from 25°C to 35°C, citing that the higher temperature would increase the photosynthetic reaction and lead to a faster nutrient uptake. However, from the results of the experiments run testing the effect of temperature, 35°C would not be an optimum value to use and 20°C would not be in this bracket. Thus, 30°C would be the optimum temperature according to literature and the proven results that showed a high percentage removal of sulphates and chlorides.

5.3 Applicability of Results

The applicability of this study is vast and somewhat inexpensive depending on the application of the results. The fresh water algae are a proven feedstock for biofuels and numerous other products used in nutraceuticals and the therapeutic industry as well being grown using the wastewater for biomass generation ad nutrient remediation (Rawat et al., 2011). The algae biomass grown is rich in lipids, carbohydrates and proteins, this can be utilized for biofuel generation and for feed applications (B. Singh et al., 2015). Alternatively, this alga can be used for value-added products such as pigments in terms of natural food colouring (Suganya et al., 2016). In addition to this the algae used in this study can be added to fish farm water which supports better growth of the algae and leads to high lip contents. This would be then substituted for purchased nutrients that are needed for biodiesel production and can aid in eliminating costs (Enwereuzoh et al., 2021).

Another use of algae grown in this study for water purification can be at the Sasol pant in Secunda, Mpumalanga. Sasol has not met any of their Green House Gas (GHG) emissions reduction goals with an increase in emissions in the year 2020 and 2021(Paul, 2021). Algae has the ability to capture carbon dioxide, as seen in this study, could aid in reducing GHG emissions at the Sasol plant in Secunda. This would be done by introducing algae pond next to the plant when the carbon dioxide produced in the pant can be transported to the pond and allow the algae to grow.

According to a review done on "Integrating micro-algae into wastewater treatment" (Mohsenpour et al., 2021), it was seen that integrating algae into an alternative biological wastewater treatment option is technologically and environmentally feasibly. The review discussed the micro-algae section of the plant be regarded as an installation cost with the rest of the micro-algae system having little to no operation cost. Implementing these findings into the study, the optimum carbon dioxide concentration and temperature for algae growth for water purification can be used in a wastewater treatment plant. However, unlike the studies suggestion to use the temperatures of the surrounding area, it would be better to build a reactor that increases the temperature to 30°C as this was the optimum temperature for water purification. The reactor can contain the immobilized algae-system which would eliminate the cost associated with separating algal biomass from treated water before discharge and use a 100% valve opening for the carbon dioxide concentration (Christenson & Sims, 2012). However, further investigation would need to be done on the light utilisation and how this would affect the temperature and carbon dioxide concentrations.

6. Conclusion

There are minimal changes in chloride concentrations for the control when the valve is totally closed and when the valve is open to 25%, according to the overall trends that can be seen. Additionally, except for when the valve was entirely closed, all chloride concentrations showed a general drop from start to finish, but all phosphate concentrations exhibited the same tendency. What's noteworthy is that, save from when the valve was fully opened, which indicated a drop in the total sulfate concentration, all of the sulfate concentrations at the start of the test are significantly lower than those at the conclusion.

The only temperature that displayed a percentage elimination according to COD was at 20°C, which may have been due to physisorption or the temperature-induced increase in the self-diffusion coefficient. However, research suggests that the ideal temperature should be between 25°C and 35°C. According to the findings of the experiments conducted to determine the impact of temperature, 20°C would not fall within this range and 35°C would not be an ideal amount to employ. According to the research and tested results that demonstrated a high percentage of sulphates and chlorides elimination, 30°C would therefore be the ideal temperature.

These findings are applicable to the production of feedstock for biofuels, a wide range of medicinal and nutraceutical goods, as well as plants grown with wastewater for biomass generation and nutrient remediation. This is in addition to wastewater treatment plants using an immobilized algae system to employ algae growth for water purification.

To conclude what can be seen from this study is that algae has significantly purified wastewater through nutrient uptake. The use of these findings ranges from biofuel production to uses in wastewater treatment plants. The effect of too much algae can be seen when the temperatures were at 35°C and 40°C which led to a large increase in phosphate concentrations. The effects of changing the process parameters of temperature and carbon dioxide concentrations impacted the rate of phosphate, chloride and sulfate removal, in addition to the COD reduction. Thus, the values for temperature and carbon dioxide concentration that gives an optimum solution for water treatment by algal purification is 30°C and 100% valve opening, respectively.

7. Recommendations

Algae has proven to be effective in some instances, however, in most of the experiments, it seemed more algae was grown than there was water to clean. The algae that were grown can be used for a multitude of bigger projects such as using it to grow spirulina through the use of the cyanobacteria in algae.

Algae can be used to create algae oil which can further create biodiesel through a transesterification process. Algae can also be used to make natural food colouring. Using these findings, this optimal temperature and carbon dioxide concentration can be implemented in a wastewater treatment plan. The conditions can be implemented into a reactor after which the water can be filtered out through microfilters. In terms of using, it to purify water for future projects, a different ratio of water to algae can be used as well as an additional process parameter of light intensity

REFERENCES

1. Abdel-Raouf, N., Al-Homaidan, A. A., & Ibraheem, I. B. M. (2012). Microalgae and wastewater treatment. *Saudi Journal of Biological Sciences*, *19*(3), 257–275. https://doi.org/10.1016/J.SJBS.2012.04.005
2. Ahmad, S., Kothari, R., Shankarayan, R., & Tyagi, V. v. (2020). Temperature dependent morphological changes on algal growth and cell surface with dairy industry wastewater: an experimental investigation. *3 Biotech*, *10*(1). https://doi.org/10.1007/S13205-019-2008-X
3. Altona, R. E., Bosman,), Breyer-Menke, C.), & Lever, N. A. (2005). *Disposal of wastewater from Modderfontein Factory: review of the biological nitrogen removal systems.*
4. Bogan, R. H., Albertson, O. E., & Pluntze, J. C. (1960). Use of Algae in Removing Phosphorus From Sewage. *Journal of the Sanitary Engineering Division*, *86*(5), 1–20. https://doi.org/10.1061/JSEDAI.0000297
5. Brar, P. K., Örmeci, B., & Dhir, A. (2022). Algae: A cohesive tool for biodiesel production alongwith wastewater treatment. In *Sustainable Chemistry and Pharmacy* (Vol. 28). Elsevier B.V. https://doi.org/10.1016/j.scp.2022.100730
6. Chen, M., Tang, H., Ma, H., Holland, T. C., Ng, K. Y. S., & Salley, S. O. (2011). Effect of nutrients on growth and lipid accumulation in the green algae Dunaliella tertiolecta. *Bioresource Technology*, *102*(2), 1649–1655. https://doi.org/10.1016/J.BIORTECH.2010.09.062
7. Christenson, L. B., & Sims, R. C. (2012). Rotating algal biofilm reactor and spool harvester for wastewater treatment with biofuels by-products. *Biotechnology and Bioengineering*, *109*(7), 1674–1684. https://doi.org/10.1002/BIT.24451
8. Enwereuzoh, U., Harding, K., & Low, M. (2021). Microalgae cultivation using nutrients in fish farm effluent for biodiesel production. *South African Journal of Chemical Engineering*, *37*, 46–52. https://doi.org/10.1016/J.SAJCE.2021.03.007
9. Guerrero-Cabrera, L., Rueda, J. A., García-Lozano, H., & Navarro, A. K. (2014). Cultivation of Monoraphidium sp., Chlorella sp. and Scenedesmus sp. algae in Batch culture using Nile tilapia effluent. *Bioresource Technology*, *161*, 455–460. https://doi.org/10.1016/J.BIORTECH.2014.03.127
10. Guldhe, A., Ansari, F. A., Singh, P., & Bux, F. (2017). Heterotrophic cultivation of microalgae using aquaculture wastewater: A biorefinery concept for biomass production and nutrient remediation. *Ecological Engineering*, *99*, 47–53. https://doi.org/10.1016/J.ECOLENG.2016.11.013

11. Jain, S. K., & Singh, V. P. (2003). Water Quality Modeling. *Developments in Water Science*, *51*(C), 743–786. https://doi.org/10.1016/S0167-5648(03)80067-9

12. Jeong, T. Y., Cha, G. C., Seo, Y. C., Jeon, C., & Choi, S. S. (2008). Effect of COD/sulfate ratios on batch anaerobic digestion using waste activated sludge. *Journal of Industrial and Engineering Chemistry*, *14*(5), 693–697. https://doi.org/10.1016/J.JIEC.2008.05.006

13. Mohsenpour, S. F., Hennige, S., Willoughby, N., Adeloye, A., & Gutierrez, T. (2021). Integrating micro-algae into wastewater treatment: A review. *Science of The Total Environment*, *752*, 142168. https://doi.org/10.1016/J.SCITOTENV.2020.142168

14. Oswald, W. J., & Golueke, C. G. (1966). Eutrophication Trends in the United States: A Problem? on JSTOR. *Water Pollution Control*, 964–975. https://www.jstor.org/stable/25035572

15. Paul, D. (2021). *Carbon criminal Sasol shows no real signs of reforming dirty operations – _Centre for Environmental Rights*. https://cer.org.za/news/carbon-criminal-sasol-shows-no-real-signs-of-reforming-dirty-operations

16. Rawat, I., Ranjith Kumar, R., Mutanda, T., & Bux, F. (2011). Dual role of microalgae: Phycoremediation of domestic wastewater and biomass production for sustainable biofuels production. *Applied Energy*, *88*(10), 3411–3424. https://doi.org/10.1016/J.APENERGY.2010.11.025

17. Rinzema, A., & Lettinga, G. (2008). The effect of sulphide on the anaerobic degradation of propionate. *Http://Dx.Doi.Org/10.1080/09593338809384544*, *9*(2), 83–88. https://doi.org/10.1080/09593338809384544

18. SciMed. (2022). *What is chemical oxygen demand (COD)?* https://www.scimed.co.uk/education/what-is-chemical-oxygen-demand-cod/

19. Sen, B., Tahir, M., Sonmez, F., Turan Kocer, M. A., & Canpolat, O. (2013). Relationship of Algae to Water Pollution and Waste Water Treatment. *Water Treatment*. https://doi.org/10.5772/51927

20. Singh, B., Guldh, A., Singh, P., Rawat, I., Bux, F., & Singh, A. (2015). Sustainable production of biofuels from microalgae using a biorefinary approach. *Applied Environmental Biotechnology: Present Scenario and Future Trends*, 115–128. https://doi.org/10.1007/978-81-322-2123-4_8/COVER

21. Singh, S. P., & Singh, P. (2014). Effect of CO2 concentration on algal growth: A review. *Renewable and Sustainable Energy Reviews*, *38*, 172–179. https://doi.org/10.1016/J.RSER.2014.05.043

22. Suganya, T., Varman, M., Masjuki, H. H., & Renganathan, S. (2016). Macroalgae and microalgae as a potential source for commercial applications along with biofuels production: A biorefinery approach. *Renewable and Sustainable Energy Reviews*, *55*, 909–941. https://doi.org/10.1016/J.RSER.2015.11.026

23. Tang, T., Wan, P., & Hu, Z. (2018). CO_2 Bubbling to Improve Algal Growth, Nutrient Removal, and Membrane Performance in an Algal Membrane Bioreactor. *Water Environment Research : A Research* Publication of the Water Environment Federation, *90*(7), 650–658. https://doi.org/10.2175/106143017X15131012153121

24. Weiss, J. (2004). Handbook of Ion Chromatography - Volume 1 - Third Edition. *Book*.

25. Zhang, T. Y., Wu, Y. H., Zhu, S. feng, Li, F. M., & Hu, H. Y. (2013). Isolation and heterotrophic cultivation of mixotrophic microalgae strains for domestic wastewater treatment and lipid production under dark condition. *Bioresource Technology*, *149*, 586–589. https://doi.org/10.1016/J.BIORTECH.2013.09.106

Note: All the figures and tables in this chapter were compiled by the author.

Sustainable Materials Processing and Manufacturing – Lin Zhu et al. (eds)
© 2024 Taylor & Francis Group, London, ISBN 978-1-032-88599-5

Drying of Biomass in a Multistage Auger Pyrolysis Reactor

Verlin Govender, Lulama Furumela, Bombeleni Zitha, Kevin Graham Harding*

School of Chemical and Metallurgical Engineering, University of the Witwatersrand, Johannesburg, South Africa

ABSTRACT: For the conversion of organic material into products that are rich in energy, pyrolysis is a thermochemical process that is effective and environmentally safe. Three portions of these products are separated: liquid bio-oil, solid biochar, and non-condensable gases. The production of bio-oil, a type of biofuel, is often more economical, especially when pyrolysis technologies are used. A small-scale auger reactor is one of the simplest technologies used. The auger reactor consists of multiple stages to make one unit however the focus will be the feed preparation of sawdust. Preparation affects the bio-oil characterization therefore efficient preparation is imperative. The design, construction, and operation of a functional drying unit. The link between the auger's rotating speed and the type of sawdust is used to analyze the feeding system. Obtaining the optimal residence time when drying three types of sawdust (Syringa, Poplar and Acacia). Determining the optimal drying temperature of sawdust at temperature between 80°C -150°C. Drying can be heated using either the flue gas from the direct-use combustor or another source of process heat. The source of heating for this experiment was a heating tape attached to the auger. The objective is to determine the moisture content percent of sawdust before and after the experiment using mass difference and TGA analysis at different temperatures. The optimum drying time ranged from 100°C to 120°C. It was noted that the type of sawdust had a greater influence on the moisture content and the residence time as compared to heating temperature. The efficiency of the auger reactor was greatly influenced by particle size.

KEYWORDS: Drying, Moisture content, Pyrolysis, Residence time, Thermogravimetric analysis

1. Introduction

The transition to cleaner energy sources is now required on a global scale. Reduced climate change is the primary objective. The use of fossil fuels is one of the main causes of global warming. With rising greenhouse gas emissions and rising solid waste from linked industries, such as automakers, increased use of these fuels creates major problems. Because of the high price of energy globally, there has never been a greater need for energy sources that are more environmentally friendly (Ahmed et al., 2020). Alternative energy sources to fossil fuels including coal, petroleum, and natural gas include biomass, wind, solar, and tidal energy.

One of the most promising renewable energy sources is biomass. Among all renewable resources, biomass is appealing because it is a plentiful by-product of forestry that can be processed into biofuels, bio-based products, and chemicals using a variety of processes. It can produce "biofuels," like ethanol, biodiesel, and renewable gasoline. In addition to lowering greenhouse gas emissions, biomass is also a considerably more affordable solution. This is because some of the crops used can be grown locally without the requirement for exports. An example is ethanol production. There are several different types of biomass feedstocks that can be used. Forest residue, food waste materials and agricultural waste are among the processes available. A by-product of the furniture industry, sawdust is created when wood is shaved, trimmed, cut, and ground to prepare it for furniture production. Sawdust can be used as a feedstock for energy recovery operations to create products with value

*Corresponding author: kevin.harding@wits.ac.za

DOI: 10.1201/9781003538646-7

additions, which may help to overcome challenges with its traditional combustion and usage (Ahmed et al., 2020). More than 2 million m3 sawdust are produced annually by the world's forestry industry (Mwango and Kambole, 2019). Typically, this sawdust is discarded or left to rot on the forest floors. Through the application of pyrolysis, the calorific value of this sawdust can be removed.

Pyrolysis is the thermal breakdown of organic material in an inert atmosphere at temperatures between 400°C and 600°C in the absence of oxygen to produce biochar, biooil and biogases. Product yields and attributes will vary depending on the biomass feedstock, pyrolysis process, and operation parameters (Brassard et al., 2017). The ultimate products desired will frequently determine which pyrolysis process is preferred over others. There are three types of pyrolysis: 1) conventional/slow pyrolysis, 2) fast pyrolysis, and 3) ultra-fast/flash pyrolysis. The solid substance is often modified using slow pyrolysis to reduce the amount of oil produced. The number of gases and oil produced is maximized during fast and ultra-quick (flash) pyrolysis. Pyrolysis can occur in a variety of reactors. The batch, auger, and fluidized bed reactors are the most technologically and economically desirable reactors for pyrolysis (Campuzano, Brown, and Martnez, 2019). Because it can move a range of bulk materials, the auger reactor is perfect. The auger screw or conveyor mechanism allows sawdust to be transported along the reaction pathway in a larger size distribution. Additionally, it enables convenient feed and release points along the auger. A hopper for storing biomass and a screw feeder that allows material to flow into the reactor typically make up the feeding system for an auger reactor (Brown, 2009).

To achieve efficient pyrolysis and produce quality biofuels drying becomes important in eliminating the moisture content. Drying, which comes first in the process of biomass gasification and pyrolysis, is crucial for the stability of industrial output as well as for how much preheating is needed throughout the process. Decreasing the water content in the biomass will reduce the amount of energy required to increase the feedstock temperature to the process temperature with a higher ramping rate. From lab to industrial scale, numerous researchers have investigated the drying process for biomass. The particle size examined in the literature can range from a large piece of wood with a diameter of 1 mm to 10 mm to as fine as crushed particles. The drying medium can be air, nitrogen, or even superheated steam generated from biomass leftovers. When a raw material is obtained, it typically contains 40% to 50% water. The water content can range from 6% to 8% after drying, which is adequate for industrial use.(Li & Yin, 2019) When a substance is heated, moisture is initially removed, followed by pyrolysis reactions, and finally any leftover thermal processes. This paper focuses mainly on the first stage of pyrolysis between the temperatures 80-150°C using fully functional benchtop-scale auger reactor specifically designed for that purpose.

2. Materials and Method

2.1 Construction and Design

The reactor's design was influenced by a working benchtop-scale auger and an analysis of various design factors from related reactors found in the literature. A single screw design was found to be more practical considering the previous restrictions, despite the twin-screw reactor's overall superior functionality. The construction materials were readily available at the workshop hence no additional budget was included. The 13 mm auger screw that was used had a diameter of 2cm. The dimensions of this screw served as the basis for the reactor's design. The inner reaction tube and the product separation T-bar were all built using galvanized steel plumbing pipes. A hopper was constructed using funnel and attached to the reaction tube. The reactor's only electrical component which is the motor came from various appliances. The workshop purchased the motor that drives the screw.

2.2 Experimental Procedure

Sawdust preparation

The electronic sieve shaker, model ES 200, is set up with screens of sizes 1180, 850, 400, 300, 212, 125, and 106 (all in microns), with the highest screen size at the top and the smaller ones descending until the pan is at the bottom. After that, the device is run for 10 minutes with the representative sample in the top screen. This was done for all the three types of sawdust (Acacia, Syringa and Poplar). To remove big and small particles that might have encouraged additional deposition onto the auger and hence clogging, both of which would hinder the flow through the inner tube, sawdust is sieved between 212-300µm by scraping the dust over a screen. All experiments with sawdust discussed from this point forward used this screened sample. The weight of the sawdust on each screen is then measured using a sensitive scale with a precision of 5 significant numbers. The sawdust weighed at approximately 1.7g for all the experimental runs that were about to take place.

Auger reactor settings

The temperature controller was set to a required temperature between 80-150°C converted to Fahrenheits to go in with units used for the device. After adjusting the temperature, a minimum of five minutes was given between each temperature change to allow the temperature to settle inside the auger. The motor is switched on and set to a rotational speed of 3.5, 4.5 and 6.5rpm.

Experiments and analysis using mass difference

The measured saw dust is placed into the hopper. The experimental runs were 72 with 24 experiments for each speed. Residence time was recorded using a stopwatch, this is the time it takes for sawdust to start coming out from the auger after it has been placed in the hopper. The sides of the feed tube must be repeatedly banged with a metal rod to simulate the vibrating action that a regular hopper would have to assure steady flow. The dried sawdust was collected and weighed at 5 significant figures using a sensitive scale. The final mass of sawdust and moisture content were calculated for all three sawdust types.

Experiments and analysis using TGA

10 mg of dried sawdust from the auger reactor was placed into the TGA. This was done three times (Acacia, Poplar, Syringa). The TGA temperature ranged from 15-900°C. The procedure took over for at least 2 hours until the next sample could be fitted in. The settings for the TGA are explained further in Part 2: Thermogravimetric analysis.

3. Results

3.1 Part 1: Mass Difference Analysis

The drying curves in Fig. 7.1, range from 80 to 150°C. Syringa sawdust could be dried from 7.158% to 1.902% moisture content in 30 seconds at a drying temperature of 150°C. 30 seconds at 140°C, from 7.373% to 2.042% within 30 seconds at 130°C, from 7.811% to 2.314%. From 9% to 2.261% at 120 °C in 30 seconds. Within 30 seconds at 110°C, from 7.373% to 2.042%. From 7.0% to 1.598% at 100°C in 30 seconds. 30 seconds at 90°C, from 9.672% to 2.795%. 30 seconds at 80°C, from 9.934% to 2.795%. Syringa's ideal residence duration was 30 seconds at 120 °C and 4,04% moisture content. Between 150°C and 80°C, the

average drying rate was 0.175%/sec, 0.178%/sec, 0.183%/sec, 0.225%/sec, 0.178%/sec, 0.180%/sec, 0.229%/sec, and finally 0.238%/sec. The moisture is evaluated as 5.80 percent in the proximate and ultimate analysis of syringa sawdust from literature (Chukwuneke et al., 2019). Because mahogany is the closest species to syringa, for which data was unavailable, those values were taken from that species. Fixed carbon content is 9.5%, ash content is 1.24 percent, and volatile matter is 79.11 percent. Equation (1) yields a determined moisture content at the ideal temperature of 4.04%, which is similar to the number found in the literature with a one percent error. We calculated the ash concentration to be 4.21% using equation (2); this difference may be the result of equipment failures. The fixed carbon, which depends on volatile matter, could not be further determined because the computed volatile matter differed from that in the literature. This may be the case since the syringa values were estimated rather than the actual ones. Then, these values are validated using the TGA analysis.

The drying curves in Fig. 7.2, range from 80 to 150°C. Poplar sawdust could be dried from 11.015% to 1.5713% moisture content in 20 seconds at a drying temperature of 150°C. 20 seconds pass between 11.4367% and 2.723% at 140°C. Within 20 seconds at 130°C, from 11.758% to 3.345%. Within 20 seconds at 120°C, from 9.120% to 1.107%. Within 30 seconds at 110°C, from 13.628% to 1.039%. 20 seconds at 100 °C, from 14.008% to 4.377%. Within 20 seconds at 90°C, from 14.512% to 4.710 percent. 20 seconds at 80 °C, from 15.399% to 5.283%. Poplar's optimum residence duration was 20 seconds at 110 °C and 4.87% moisture content. Between 150°C and 80°C, the average drying rate was 0.472%/sec, 0.436%/sec, 0.420%/sec, 0.401%/sec, 0.629%/sec, 0.481%/sec, and finally 0.5058%/sec. According to the literature (Li & Yin, 2019), the moisture content of poplar sawdust is treated as 6 percent and 40 percent of the mass

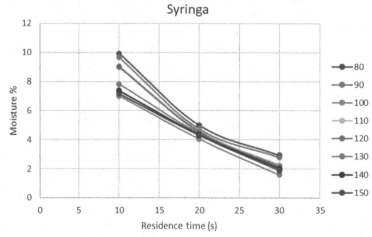

Fig. 7.1 Syringa, moisture content at different temperatures in degrees Celsius

Poplar

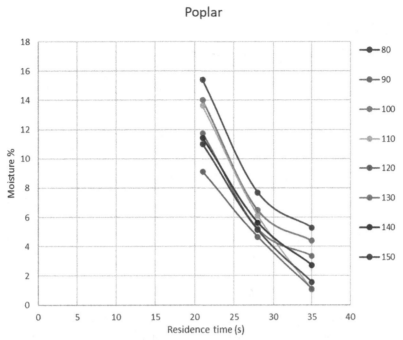

Fig. 7.2   Poplar, moisture content at different temperatures in degrees Celsius

of dry biomass, respectively. 9.5 percent of the carbon is fixed, 0.5 percent is ash, and 90 percent is volatile. Equation (1)'s result of 4.87% for the calculated moisture content at the ideal temperature is nearly identical to the value found in the literature with a small variation. We calculated the ash concentration to be 5.11% using equation (2); this difference could be the result of equipment overheating. The fixed carbon, which depends on volatile matter, could not be further determined because the computed volatile matter differed from that in the literature. The adhesion and cohesion forces that were present during the experiment may be to blame for this. Then, these values are validated using the TGA analysis.

The drying curves in Fig. 7.3, range from 80 to 150°C. Acacia sawdust may be dried from 5.690% to 3.588% moisture content in 12 seconds at a drying temperature of 150°C. From 5.718% to 3.631% in 12 seconds at 140°C. From 5.819% to 3.648% in 12 seconds at 130°C. From 4.971% to 3.633% at 120°C in 12 seconds. From 4.881% to 3.526% in 12 seconds at 110°C. Within 12 seconds at 100°C, from 5.931% to 3.843%. 20 seconds at 90°C, from 5.975% to 3.931%. At 80°C, the range is 12 seconds from 6.050% to 4.153%. Acacia's optimum residence duration was 12 seconds at 100°C and 3.96% moisture content. From 150°C to 80°C, the average drying rate was 0.175%/sec, 0.173%/sec, 0.181%/

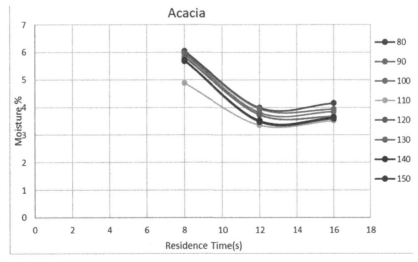

Fig. 7.3   Acacia, moisture content at different temperatures in degrees celsius

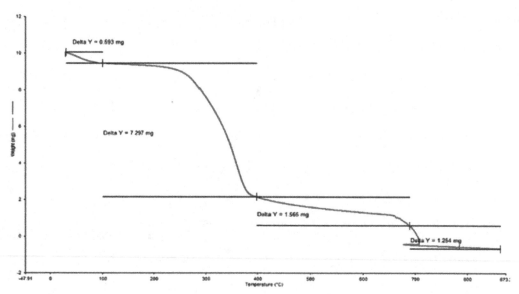

Fig. 7.4 Poplar TGA analysis

sec, 0.112%/sec, 0.113%/sec, 0.174%/sec, 0.170%/sec, and finally 0.158%/sec. The moisture is evaluated as 3.79 percent in the immediate and comprehensive study of acacia sawdust from literature (Márquez-Montesino et al., 2015). 19.21 percent of the carbon is fixed, 4.01 percent of the carbon is ash, and 76.77 percent of the carbon is volatile. Even though it was somewhat higher, equation (1)'s calculated moisture content at the ideal temperature was 3.96%, which is the number that is the most comparable among the three types of sawdust employed. Using equation (2), we calculated the ash content to be 4.13%, which correlates to the 4.01% value reported in the literature. The fixed carbon, which depends on volatile matter, could not be further determined because the computed volatile matter differed from that in the literature. The unknown values are verified using TGA analysis.

Drying is a crucial step in fast pyrolysis because of the short residence period; it typically takes place at room temperature or up to 150 °C. The graphs in Fig.s 7.5, 7.6, and 7.7 show that the ideal temperature did not rise over a maximum of 150°C but instead fluctuated from 100°C to 120°C. These ideal drying temperatures are effective for most pyrolysis types, notably fast pyrolysis. In comparison to Poplar, Acacia and Syringa had an average drying rate that was lower and similar, ranging from 0.10%/sec to 0.25%/sec. This finding might be explained by the sawdust's compositional characteristics.

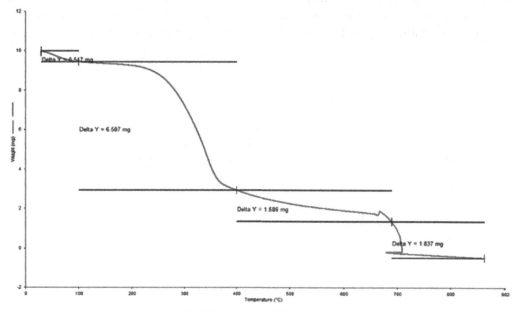

Fig. 7.5 Syringa TGA analysis

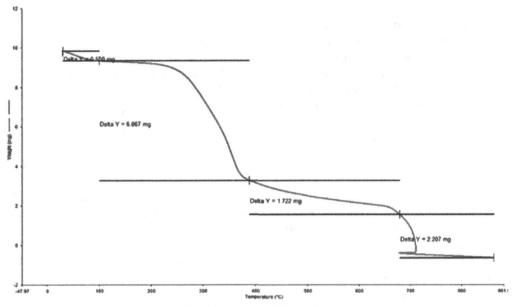

Fig. 7.6 Acacia TGA analysis

Compared to the other two varieties of sawdust, Poplar demonstrated stronger cohesive forces. This impacted the analysis of the experiment. The gas phase residence time was maintained at 28 s in most runs that have undergone studying. To study the transient pyrolysis behaviour, some tests were run at shorter residence times (SRT) of 4 and 15 seconds (Newalkar et al., 2014). For each type of sawdust in our investigation, the residence time was 12, 20, or 30 seconds, which is within the average range.

3.2 Part 2: Thermogravametric Analysis

TGA analysis was carried out in a modular pattern, using a mechanical device, the STA 6000. The sample was heated to 900°C and time, temperature, and weight data were recorded during the heating period. The non-isothermal experiments were performed in atmospheric pressure under nitrogen or oxygen environment with a flow rate of 20mL/min from room temperature to 900 °C. The temperature program is as follows: from 30 to 110 °C, gas is switched to nitrogen; from 110 to 700°C, gas is switched to oxygen; and finally, gas is switched to oxygen until it reaches 900°C. A heating rate of 10 °C/min was chosen as the study variable. The starting weight of the sample was between 10 to 10.5 mg, with particle sizes ranging from 212 to 300µ m. A computer that worked together with the equipment continuously recorded weight losses that occurred in response to temperature increases. All of the experiments in this study were duplicated twice, with an uncertainty of less than 1%.

According to Fig. 7.4, the drying process has three stages. Moisture evaporation from ambient temperature to 110°C was attributed for the initial stage (5.93% weight loss).

The second stage is characterized by a significant weight loss between 200 and 405 °C and a sharp decrease in the weight of the poplar sawdust; this stage may be related to the decomposition of hemicellulose, whereas the maximum value (occurred at 361°C) is related to the maximum decomposition rate of cellulose, a significant component of wood. About 83% of the total weight dissolved quickly during the second stage. This value corresponds to the volatile matter of 90% mentioned in literature. It is common knowledge that cellulose decomposes at a range of 325–375°C, hemicelluloses at 225–350°C, and lignin at 250–500°C. The final stage (405-900°C) involves the continued cracking of poplar sawdust leftovers because of lignin degradation. For cellulose, similar patterns in mass loss rates were noted. At this point, there was just a small loss of weight; at a slower rate, 11.99% of the entire weight was cracked. Finally, 12.54% of the initial mass of the poplar sawdust sample was preserved as a solid residue (carbonaceous residues within inorganic solid particles).

Syringa has moisture content of 5.47% and thermal degradation starts at about 120°C. For the proximate analysis, Fig. 7.5 shows the TGA profile of sawdust drying, devolatilization, subsequent char production, and ultimately char oxidation. The sample's moisture loss is represented by the first weight loss, which occurs at about 120° C. Moisture content can be lowered by up to 5% of the sample weight at temperatures below 120°C. Devolatilization and pyrolysis of primarily organic materials are responsible for the second weight drop those results from raising the temperature to 900° C. While the maximum value (occurred at 3720°C) is related to the maximum decomposition rate of cellulose. Hemicelluloses reportedly breakdown more quickly than cellulose and lignin

(Becidan et al., 2007). Celluloses and lignin began to break down above 200°C and produce additional volatiles up to 400°C. Beyond 400 °C, the degradation rate slows down in line with the breakdown of lignin's constituent elements. At 900°C, all the volatiles evolved, leaving only the char. Up to 77% of the initial weight of the sawdust sample is the yield of the volatile substance in this stage. According to the literature cited above, the volatile matter in the mass difference calculations is 79.11%, which is in line with the amount shown on the graph.

Acacia has moisture content of 5% and thermal degradation starts at about 100°C.

The drying process involves three steps, as shown in Fig. 7.6. For the initial stage (5% weight loss), moisture evaporation from ambient temperature to 100°C was cited as the cause. While the maximum value (occurred at 392°C) is related to the maximum decomposition rate of cellulose, a significant component of wood, the second stage is characterized by a significant weight loss between 220 and 405°C and a sharp decrease in the weight of the poplar sawdust. This stage may be related to the decomposition of hemicellulose. During the second stage, almost 73.25% of the entire weight swiftly disappeared. All the volatile substances developed at 900°C, leaving only the char. The yield of the volatile component at this step can reach up to 75% of the original weight of the sawdust sample. Finally, 22.07% of the initial mass of the poplar sawdust sample was preserved as a solid residue (carbonaceous residues within inorganic solid particles). The literature figure for the volatile matter was 76.77%, which is consistent with the actual value of 75%.

3.3 Factors Contributing to the Next Stages of Pyrolysis

Particle size

Findings show that biomass particle size can significantly affect the timing of devolatilization as well as the yields of species. By reducing the particle size, the yields of the volatiles were decreased. This was noted because for all the three types of sawdust the values from literature were higher than the ones, we obtained in the TGA. The particle size we employed was the smallest size out of the sieving sizes unlike the pellets that are typically used used in other experiments. A fine powder from the size (212-300μ m). Particle form also has an impact on product yields and composition. Several study teams investigated how biomass particle size affected the pyrolysis procedure and expenses. Their findings showed that as particle size increases, more char and gas are produced while the yield of bio-oil decreases. Additionally, after a certain point, an increase in particle size has little effect on the products' yield. What is more intriguing is that when particle size rises, water production yield increases. (Bennadji

et al 2019) used TGA and a bench-scale tubular reactor to investigate the impact of particle size on product yields. The next stages of pyrolysis will be positively impacted because our particle size was kept constant and at the smallest size feasible, leading to the production of high bio-oil content with less gas and char.

Composition of biomass

The composition of the biomass feedstock should be considered when trying to increase the yield of a certain product because the physio-chemical characteristics of each component differ depending on the kind of biomass. Using biomass that contains cellulose and hemicellulose is preferred for producing biochar and high yields of biooil. Additionally, lignin would aid in the production of dense and viscous bio-oil and is more challenging to pyrolyze than the cellulose component. A biomass is of high quality if it contains 20–30% of the bulk in hemicellulose. We determined that Acacia had hemicellulose content of 35.16 percent, cellulose content of 32.75 percent, and lignin content of 16.81 percent out of the three types of biomasses we chose. For poplar, cellulose was 42.20 percent, lignin was 20.95 percent, and hemicellulose was 16.60 percent. Hemicellulose makes up 16.80 percent of syringa, cellulose makes up 48.50 percent, and lignin makes up 15.30 percent (Pranoto et al., 2020). Acacia will provide the highest output of bio-oil since its hemicellulose content is within the necessary range. Since all the sawdust components are highly preferred for high bio-oil yield, the next stages of pyrolysis will result in the best outcomes.

4. Conclusion

The type of sawdust used has an impact on the residence time. In comparison to heating temperature, the type of sawdust has a bigger impact on moisture content. The rate of the devolatilization processes increased along with the temperature. While the TGA's average ideal residence time was at 5%, the mass difference calculations' average optimum residence time was at 4% moisture content. There was just a 1% variance, which indicates that the moisture content calculations were consistent. The equipment and operating conditions may have resulted in such. The discrepancy is tolerable and supports our findings. The optimum drying time ranged from 100°C,110°C, 120°C at residence times of 12,20 and 30 seconds. Both the optimum residence time and optimum drying temperature were at acceptable ranges. The purpose was to assess the moisture content of the three types of sawdust using the mass difference, however further proximate and ultimate analysis was done to gather more information and basis of comparison. Using the mass difference further calculations were not made due to lack of information. However, we were able to compute it further through the TGA analysis, volatile matter and ash was calculated. These values together with the moisture content were correlated and contrasted with those reported in the literature. It is suggested that the sawdust particle size should be (212-300m) or smaller and particle characteristics such as adhesion and cohesion should be reviewed first to prevent clogging of the auger reactor. Preferably sawdust with less cohesion forces will be best suited to operate in the auger reactor.

REFERENCES

1. Ahmed, A., Abu Bakar, M. S., Sukri, R. S., Hussain, M., Farooq, A., Moogi, S., & Park, Y. K. (2020). Sawdust pyrolysis from the furniture industry in an auger pyrolysis reactor system for biochar and bio-oil production. Energy Conversion and Management, 226. https://doi.org/10.1016/j.enconman.2020.113502
2. Brassard, P., Godbout, S., & Raghavan, V. (2017). Pyrolysis in auger reactors for biochar and bio-oil production: A review. In Biosystems Engineering (Vol. 161, pp. 80–92). Academic Press. https://doi.org/10.1016/j.biosystemseng.2017.06.020
3. Brown, J. N., Brown, R. C., Heindel, T. J., & Raman, D. R. (2009). Development of a lab-scale auger reactor for biomass fast pyrolysis and process optimization using response surface methodology.
4. Campuzano, F., Brown, R. C., & Martínez, J. D. (2019). Auger reactors for pyrolysis of biomass and wastes. In Renewable and Sustainable Energy Reviews (Vol. 102, pp. 372–409). Elsevier Ltd. https://doi.org/10.1016/j.rser.2018.12.014
5. Chukwuneke, J. L., Ewulonu, M. C., Chukwujike, I. C., & Okolie, P. C. (2019). Physico-chemical analysis of pyrolyzed bio-oil from swietenia macrophylla (mahogany) wood. Heliyon, 5(6). https://doi.org/10.1016/j.heliyon.2019.e01790
6. Li, X., & Yin, C. (2019). A drying model for thermally large biomass particle pyrolysis. Energy Procedia, 158, 1294–1302. https://doi.org/10.1016/j.egypro.2019.01.322
7. Márquez-Montesino, F., Correa-Méndez, F., Glauco-Sánchez, C., Zanzi-Vigouroux, R., Rutiaga-Quiñones, J. G., & Aguiar-Trujillo, L. (2015). Pyrolytic degradation studies of acacia mangium wood. BioResources, 10(1), 1825–1844. https://doi.org/10.15376/biores.10.1.1825-1844
8. Mwango, A. and Kambole, C. (2019) "Engineering Characteristics and Potential Increased Utilisation of Sawdust Composites in Construction—A Review," Journal of Building Construction and Planning Research, 07(03), pp. 59–88. doi:10.4236/JBCPR.2019.73005.
9. Li, X., & Yin, C. (2019). A drying model for thermally large biomass particle pyrolysis. Energy Procedia, 158, 1294–1302. https://doi.org/10.1016/j.egypro.2019.01.322
10. Newalkar, G., Iisa, K., Damico, A. D., Sievers, C., & Agrawal, P. (2014). Effect of temperature, pressure, and residence time on pyrolysis of pine in an entrained flow reactor. Energy and Fuels, 28(8), 5144–5157. https://doi.org/10.1021/ef5009715
11. Pranoto, P., Nugrahaningtyas, K. D., & Putri, R. N. O. (2020). Study of final temperature and heating rate variation to pyrolysis of Acacia (Acacia mangium W.) wood waste. IOP Conference Series: Materials Science and Engineering, 959(1). https://doi.org/10.1088/1757-899X/959/1/012012

Note: All the figures in this chapter were compiled by the author.

Sustainable Materials Processing and Manufacturing – Lin Zhu et al. (eds)
© 2024 Taylor & Francis Group, London, ISBN 978-1-032-88599-5

Design, Prototyping and Testing of Biodegradable Sanitary Pads

Ashna Ramasur[1], Kauthar Hassan[2], Prebantha Moodley[3] and Kevin Harding[4]
School of Chemical and Metallurgical Engineering, University of the Witwatersrand, Johannesburg, South Africa

ABSTRACT: Conventional sanitary pads contain harmful plastics and toxins; therefore, the need arises to develop a low-cost biodegradable alternative. An investigation was carried out with the aim of producing competent disposable sanitary pad prototypes that are both low-cost and biodegradable. Two different prototypes were produced. The bottom layer was developed by producing and testing a gelatine bioplastic, embedded corn starch bioplastic, and a stretchy corn starch bioplastic. The tests proved that the embedded bioplastic was the most suitable for use. Wood pulp fluff, cellulose sheets and organic cotton was used to form the core of prototype 1. The same components, except the cellulose sheet, was included in the core of prototype 2. A bamboo nappy liner was used as the top sheet for both prototypes. A biodegradability test showed that the embedded bioplastic had the largest mass reduction of 52% over time, while the organic cotton had the lowest mass reduction of 13%. Testing the prototypes proved that prototype 2 was better performing overall, with an absorption speed of 4.32 s, a maximum capacity of 63 ml, and a moisture retention of 87.62%. Prototype 2 was R2 cheaper than prototype 1, at a cost of R6.26. Both prototypes were very costly but met part of the aim as they were fully biodegradable and competent. Investigations involving scaling-up production and obtaining material in bulk would assist with a reduction in costs.

KEYWORDS: Biodegradable, Bioplastic, Feminine Hygiene, Menstruation, Sanitary pad

1. Introduction

Menstruation begins when females are around 11 years of age. It occurs on a 21–28-day cycle and has a duration of between 3 and 7 days [5]. During this period, the lining of the uterus is shed and discharged as menstrual blood if the female is not impregnated. The average amount of blood lost during the period is around 35 ml [5]. It is for this reason that sanitary pads are required, as they allow the blood to be collected while allowing the female to continue with daily activities.

Majority of the sanitary pad products on the market contain dioxins, petrochemicals, and volatile organic compounds, that are harmful to both the environment and to the individuals who make use of them [1]. The plastics used within the layers of the pads are not biodegradable, and they therefore take up space in landfill sites. They also pose as a threat to the environment and individuals working at such a site, since they release harmful toxins over time. As it stands, two factors constitute the lack of access to feminine hygiene products, one of which is financial barriers [5]. The existing sanitary pads are costly and therefore not easily accessible to individuals from all backgrounds.

1.1 Problem Statement and Aim

Due to the harm that these products cause, and the high cost, the need arises to investigate the development of a low-cost biodegradable sanitary pad alternative. This was investigated with the aim of developing competent disposable sanitary pad prototypes, composed of both low-cost and biodegradable materials. This was to be achieved through the objective of using readily available and affordable material to produce two different prototypes, and to then test them to determine their effectiveness.

[1]21604012@students.wits.ac.za, [2]18514434@students.wits.ac.za, [3]Prebantha.moodley@wits.ac.za, [4]kevin.harding@wits.ac.za

DOI: 10.1201/9781003538646-8

1.2 Literature Review

Some of the feminine hygiene products that exist on the market are tampons, menstrual cups, menstrual underwear, reusable sanitary pads, and disposable sanitary pads. In a study, a questionnaire showed that in a group of females from varying financial backgrounds and age groups, 96% preferred the use of disposable sanitary pads [3]. This was supported by a study in which 81% of a group of females between the ages of 26 and 40 years old preferred the use of disposable pads during the daytime [2].

The conventional products contain components such as polypropylene in the top sheet, and super absorbent polymers in the core. These are non-biodegradable plastic components that can result in the pad taking between 500 and 800 years to fully decompose in a landfill site [3]. Furthermore, according to a study on feminine hygiene products and waste management, approximately 10 grams of greenhouse gases are released during the production of a disposable sanitary pad [3]. A biodegradable alternative is therefore of importance.

The basic structure of a disposable biodegradable sanitary pad can be seen in Fig. 8.1.

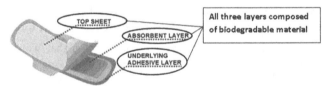

Fig. 8.1   Basic structure of a biodegradable sanitary pad

The top layer needs to be composed of materials that allow the fluid to be transferred to the core, while providing comfort. Bamboo nappy liners are suitable for such a layer as they contain bamboo fibres and organic cotton in a non-woven structure, which allows fluid to pass through the liner in the top sheet of nappies. The core material would need to be composed of fibres that are highly absorbent and affordable such as cellulose fibres, which is essentially wood pulp fluff obtained from pulp sheets and organic cotton. The bottom layer can be composed of a bioplastic which is formed from components such as gelatine and corn starch. Variants would need to be produced to obtain a layer that is impermeable to fluid since it needs to hold the contents of the pad and the fluid absorbed by it, while preventing leakage [4].

Reliable tests for the pads are the absorption speed test, maximum capacity test, and moisture retention test [1]. The absorption speed test assists with determining how fast the fibres absorb fluid. The maximum capacity test determines if the pad can hold the required volume of solution in accordance with technical specifications. The moisture retention test determines whether the pad would rewet the skin. A biodegradability test assists with determining the biodegradability of the sanitary pad, and the structural integrity.

2. Materials and Methods

2.1 Materials

The materials and major equipment that was utilized for the project are listed in Table 8.1, Table 8.2 and Table 8.3.

Table 8.1   Materials and equipment for bioplastic production and preliminary testing

Materials:	Major equipment:
• Corn starch • Glycerol • 5% Vinegar • Distilled water • Bamboo liner • Gelatine	• 1000 ml beaker • Stirring rod • Scale • Silicon sheets • Laboratory hot plate • Plastic tray • Thermometer • Texture analyser

Table 8.2   Materials and equipment for prototype production

Materials:	Major equipment:
• Organic cotton balls • Cellulose sheets • Wood pulp sheets • Bamboo liner • Corn starch bioplastic embedded with bamboo liner	• Pestel and mortar • Stainless steel tray • Cardboard mould • Biomass mill • Grass shredder • Industrial hammer mill

Table 8.3   Materials and equipment for component and prototype testing

Materials:	Major equipment:
• NaCl (Table salt) • Distilled water • Blue food colouring • Filter paper • A sample of each component used to produce the prototypes • Compost soil	• Thermometer • 60 ml syringe • 500 ml beaker • 1000 ml beaker • Scale • 700 g weight • Texture analyser • Stainless steel plate • Laboratory hot plate

2.2 Methods

The methods were divided in the order of completion of work in the laboratory.

Bioplastic production and preliminary testing

Two types of bioplastics were produced for testing purposes, and a third bioplastic sample was obtained from a biodegradable plastic research project.

The gelatine bioplastic was produced dissolving 8 mL of glycerol into 1000 ml of distilled water. 360 ml of the solution was poured into a 1000 ml beaker and heated to a temperature of 90°C, while gradually stirring in 6.95 g of gelatine. It was then poured in a tray and kept at room temperature for 1 week. A transparent sheet of plastic was formed.

The embedded corn starch bioplastic was produced by dissolving 95 g of corn starch into 600 ml of distilled water. 50 ml of 5 % vinegar and 80 ml of glycerol were then stirred into the mixture, and it was heated while continuously stirring until it was thick and translucent. It was spread into a thin layer on a silicon sheet and embedded with a bamboo liner and was left to dry for 24 to 48 hours.

A stretchy corn starch bioplastic was produced using the same method used for the previous corn starch bioplastic (before embedding it with the bamboo liner). However, this bioplastic was produced with different ratios of the components. 60 g of corn starch, 50 ml of glycerol, 40 ml of vinegar, and 400 ml of water was used.

All three samples were tested by observation for stickiness, brittleness, ease of solubility, and flexibility. They were also tested for tensile strength using a texture analyser within a limit of 0-80% strain. The most suitable sample was then chosen as the bottom layer for both prototypes.

Prototype production

Wood pulp sheets were passed through a grass shredder and then through a biomass mill, using two different screen sizes, to obtain two variations of wood pulp fluff. A sample of pulp fluff produced by an industrial hammer mill was also obtained from industry. The best sample was chosen for use in producing the core of the prototypes with a cardboard mould. The core was placed on the centre of the chosen bioplastic sheet. A bamboo liner was placed on the core, and the three layers were sealed together at the edges of the core using an impulse plastic heat sealer and a clothing iron. The order of the layers can be seen in Fig. 8.2. The pad was then cut into a conventional shape with dimensions as shown in Fig. 8.3.

Prototype 1	Prototype 2
Layer 1: Bamboo liner top layer	**Layer 1**: Bamboo liner top layer
Layer 2: Wood pulp fluff, cellulose sheet & organic cotton middle layer	**Layer 2**: Wood pulp fluff & organic cotton middle layer
Layer 3: Bioplastic bottom layer	**Layer 3**: Bioplastic bottom layer

Fig. 8.2 Order of the layers in the prototypes

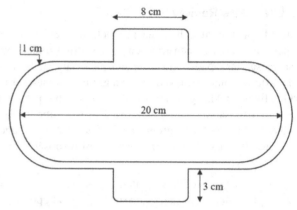

Fig. 8.3 Prototype dimensions

Component and prototype testing

A biodegradability test involved burying a sample of each material used to produce the prototypes in compost soil at room temperature. They were removed and weighed after 24 hours as the "Day 1" weight, to account for moisture uptake from the soil. The six samples used were the pulp fluff, organic cotton, cellulose sheet, embedded corn starch bioplastic, gelatine bioplastic, and bamboo liner. The samples were then buried again, and were reweighed weekly, over a span of 4 weeks, to determine their mass reduction over time.

The remaining tests required a liquid solution that would mimic menstrual blood. This was produced by mixing 164 g of salt in 896 ml of water and heating the mixture to 35°C. Blue food colouring was added to make it easier for observation. Five pad types were used for the tests, these included the two prototypes developed, two types of biodegradable pads on the market (Brand 1 and Brand 2), and one non-biodegradable pad on the market (Brand 3). The tests were triplicated for each pad type.

An absorbency speed test involved drawing 8 ml of the solution in a 10 ml syringe and transferring it to a 60 ml syringe with the plunger removed, and the front end blocked. The pad was then placed above the back of the 60 mL syringe, and the pad and syringe were inverted together. The time taken for the fluid to be fully absorbed was recorded.

A maximum capacity test involved filling a tray with 600 ml of the solution and fully immersing the pad into the solution for 1 minute, then removing and holding it sideways for 1 minute allowing for excess solution to run off. The pad was then reweighed to determine the maximum capacity. The following equations were used:

Mass of fluid absorbed = Mass of wet pad – Mass of dry pad [1]

Volume of fluid absorbed = Mass of fluid absorbed/ Density of fluid [2]

A rewet test was performed by recording the dry weight of the pad, then discharging 20 ml of the blood substitute solution along the pad at 2ml/s. The pad was reweighed, and filter paper was placed onto the pad. A 700 g weight was placed on the filter paper and removed after 15 minutes. The pad was reweighed once more to determine how much moisture was retained. The following equations were used:

$$\text{Mass of fluid lost} = \text{Wet weight} - \text{Weight after 700g removal} \quad [3]$$

$$\text{Volume of fluid lost} = \text{Mass of fluid lost}/\text{Density of fluid} \quad [4]$$

$$\text{Fluid retained} = 20\ \text{ml} - \text{volume of fluid lost} \quad [5]$$

3. Results and Discussion

3.1 Bioplastic Production and Preliminary Testing

The bioplastics are shown in Fig. 8.4. Sample 1 is the gelatine bioplastic, sample 2 is the embedded corn starch bioplastic, and sample 3 is the stretchy corn starch bioplastic.

The ease of solubility was tested by placing a sample in warm saline solution at 40°C. The results for the preliminary testing are shown in Table 8.4, and the stress versus strain curves are shown in Fig. 8.5, where the stress (y-axis) is measured in MPa and the strain is measured in percentage.

The gelatine bioplastic had the highest tensile strength and broke at a percent strain of 13.23%. A higher tensile strength would be preferred. However, Table 4 shows that the gelatine bioplastic is not impermeable to fluid as it dissolved easily;

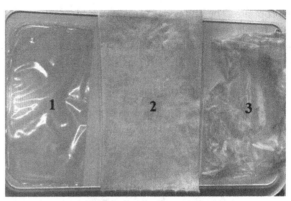

Fig. 8.4 Bioplastics obtained

Table 8.4 Preliminary bioplastic testing results

Bioplastic sample	Tensile strength (MPa)	Flexible	Brittle	Sticky	Easily soluble
Gelatine based bioplastic	7.67	X	✓	X	✓
Embedded corn starch bioplastic	2.65	✓	X	X	X
Stretchy corn starch bioplastic	0.73	✓	X	✓	X

it is also not flexible and is sticky and brittle, which are undesirable traits. This bioplastic was therefore deemed inappropriate. The stretchy corn starch bioplastic had the lowest tensile strength and broke at the lowest percent strain (12.9 %) when compared to the other two bioplastics, as shown in Fig. 8.5 (c). It was also sticky and was therefore

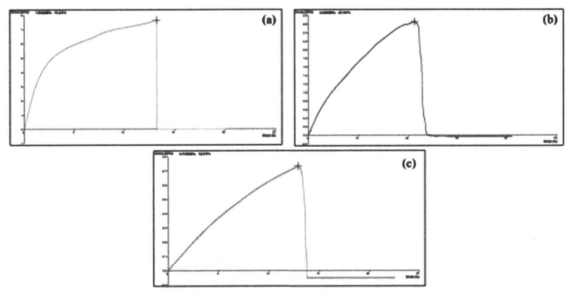

Fig. 8.5 (a) Stress vs strain curve (gelatine bioplastic), (b) Stress vs strain curve (embedded corn starch bioplastic), (c) Stress vs strain curve (stretchy corn starch bioplastic)

inappropriate. The embedded corn starch bioplastic was the most suitable for use as the bottom layer with a higher tensile strength than the stretchy corn starch plastic, breaking at the highest percent strain (21.31 %), as shown in Fig. 5 (b).

3.2 Prototype Production

The types of wood pulp fluff that were formed from the pulp sheets processing are shown in Fig. 8.6.

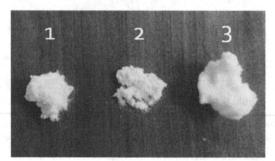

Fig. 8.6 Wood pulp fluff samples obtained

Sample 3 in Fig. 8.6 was obtained from an industrial hammer mill had a texture similar to that of organic cotton. A 6 mm biomass mill screen yielded a fluff that contained small solid pieces of pulp sheet (sample 1). The pulp fluff from a 4 mm screen yielded a sample that was a powder (sample 2). A powder is not appropriate for use in the sanitary pad core the particles would pose a danger to the skin and reproductive system. The sample obtained from the industrial hammer mill (sample 3) proved to be the best type of fluff for use in the core. It possessed properties similar to that of the fluff used in the core of brand 1. The cores that were formed for each prototype can be seen in Fig. 8.7:

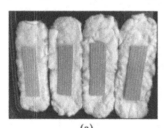
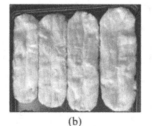

(a)   (b)

Fig. 8.7 (a) Prototype 1 core, (b) Prototype 2 core

The only difference between the two cores produced is the cellulose sheet in the core of prototype 1. This sheet was added with the aim of determining whether the extra component would increase the absorbency and maximum capacity of the prototype. The two prototypes are shown in Fig. 8.8.

Fig. 8.8 Prototypes formed

The extra cellulose core in prototype 1 was placed under the layer of organic cotton. The prototype on the left side of Fig. 8.8 is prototype 1, and the prototype on the right side is prototype 2. The pattern that can be seen on both prototypes is a result of a paper embossing machine. The patterns acted as fluid divergent channels, guiding fluid away from the wings and onto the core of the prototype.

3.3 Component and Prototype Testing Results

The biodegradability test results showed that the component weights on day 1 were much higher than day 0 due to the moisture uptake from the soil. The masses recorded on day 0 and day 1, and over the 4-week period can be seen in Table 8.5. The gelatine bioplastic was also included in the test to determine how long it would take for the plastic to degrade, so that further investigations can be carried out related to it. No results were obtained for this component as it broke apart and became sticky after one day of the test and could therefore not be weighed.

Table 8.5 Mass of each component over time

Component	Dry weight (Day 0) (g)	Day 1 (g)	Week 1 (g)	Week 2 (g)	Week 3 (g)	Week 4 (g)
Cellulose sheet	0.22	0.34	0.24	0.24	0.24	0.24
Wood pulp fluff	0.71	0.98	0.73	0.71	0.68	0.66
Bamboo liner	0.14	0.23	0.15	0.15	0.15	0.15
Organic cotton	0.62	0.68	0.68	0.63	0.62	0.60
Embedded corn starch bioplastic	0.71	0.86	0.43	0.42	0.42	0.41

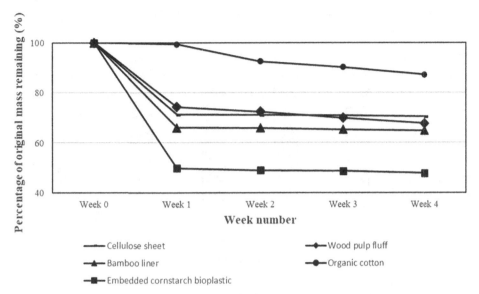

Fig. 8.9 Percentage of original mass remaining over time

The percentage of the original mass of each component remaining throughout the period of the test was plotted and can be seen in Fig. 8.9.

The component with the largest mass reduction was the embedded corn starch bioplastic with it's mass increasing by approximately 0.15 g after a day. After one week it was reduced to approximately 48% of it's original mass. The outer layers of the plastic disintegrated after a week and the bioplastic was reduced to a hard thin layer of bamboo liner, which slowly degraded over the rest of the test period. The organic cotton experienced the lowest mass reduction over the test period, as it only decreased to around 87% of it's original mass at the end of week 4. The bamboo liner and cellulose sheet continued to degrade very slowly. The bamboo liner reduced to 65% of its original mass, and the cellulose sheet reduced to 70% of its original mass at the end of week 4. The wood pulp fluff was reduced to 68% of it's original mass over the test period and experienced almost a linear reduction in mass after week 1. From these results, it could be deduced that the embedded corn starch bioplastic would be the fastest degrading component of the pad, as it would be in direct contact with soil and the external environment since it forms the bottom layer.

The absorption speed test results were obtained for each pad type. The testing was performed in triplicate. The results from each test run and the average amount of time taken for the solution to be absorbed for each pad type are shown in Table 8.6. The standard deviation of the runs was also calculated, to determine how much the values deviated from the average.

Table 8.6 Absorption speed for each pad type

Pad type	Absorption speed (s)			Average absorption speed (s)	Standard deviation (s)
	Run 1	Run 2	Run 3		
Prototype 1	6.47	4.90	7.26	6.21	1.20
Prototype 2	4.79	3.77	4.39	4.32	0.51
Brand 1	9.04	8.94	9.14	9.04	0.10
Brand 2	3.48	3.28	4.33	3.70	0.56
Brand 3	3.76	3.85	3.28	3.63	0.31

Brand 3 (non-biodegradable pad), was the best performing with an absorption speed of 3.63 seconds. This is due to the super absorbent polymers within the core. Prototype 2 had a faster absorption speed than prototype 1. Both prototypes performed better than Brand 1. The lower absorption speed for prototype 1 is a result of the extra cellulose sheet in the core. Prototype 2 was comparable to brand 2 in terms of it's absorption speed, and would therefore be a better prototype in terms of the speed at which fluid is drawn. Fluid was taken up faster by prototype 2 in comparison to prototype 1. Prototype 1 had the highest standard deviation, which means the results for the runs had a high variability. This could be a result of human error such as a time delay or a difference in the masses of the pads used for each run.

The maximum capacity test was also performed in triplicate. The volume of solution absorbed by the pad was calculated by use of Equation [1] and [2] as shown in the method section. The calculated density of the fluid was approximately 1.18 g/ml. A bar graph showing the average volume of solution absorbed by each pad type can be seen in Fig. 8.10.

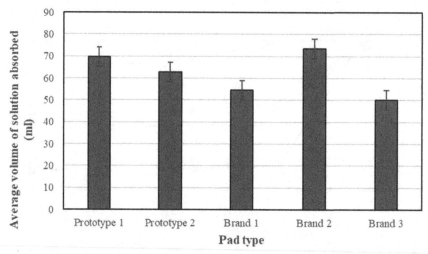

Fig. 8.10 Average volume of fluid absorbed by each pad

Table 8.7 Values for the calculation of the volume of fluid retained

Pad type	Average mass of fluid lost (g)	Average volume of fluid lost (ml)	Average volume of fluid retained (ml)	Average % moisture retained
Prototype 1	3.12	2.64	17.36	86.78
Prototype 2	2.92	2.48	17.52	87.62
Brand 1	4.36	3.70	16.30	81.51
Brand 2	3.10	2.63	17.37	86.86
Brand 3	0.70	0.60	19.40	97.02

Brand 2 was the best performing. It held around 74 ml. Prototype 1 was the second best performing, as it held around 70 ml. Prototype 1 performed better than prototype 2 due to the cellulose core. Both prototypes performed better than both brand 1 and brand 3. Brand 1 held much less fluid than the rest of the pads when it was allowed to run off. Brand 3 had a slower uptake of the fluid through the core of the pad once it was immersed, and therefore did not take up as much fluid as the rest of the pads during the 1 minute. Brand 2 performed better than the 2 prototypes as it had a more compact core, which allowed for more dispersion of the fluid. The prototype's cores were not as compact, fluid therefore reached the bottom layer faster. The test proved that having a biodegradable non-woven top sheet is more advantageous than having a polypropylene top sheet. Both prototypes were able to hold a minimum of 15-20 ml as required by technical specifications for sanitary pads.

The moisture retention test was also performed in triplicate using Equation [3] as shown in the method section. The volume of fluid lost was then determined using the density of the solution using Equation [4]. The average volume of fluid retained was determined using Equation [5], and the percentage of moisture retained could then be determined. The results from the test are shown in Table 8.7.

The results from the moisture retention test, as shown in Table 8.7, prove that brand 3 was the best performing with 97% moisture retained, while brand 1 had the lowest performance, retaining only 82% moisture. Prototype 2 performed slightly better than prototype 1. The slight difference in performance between the prototypes could once again be due to the cellulose sheet in prototype 1. Prototype 1 and brand 2 had similar results, both retaining around 87% of moisture. This made prototype 1 seemingly appropriate, even though prototype 2 performed slightly better. Selecting the prototype with a high moisture retention is important to ensure no rewetting and leaking.

3.4 Costing the Prototypes

The costs associated with the embedded bioplastic sheets are shown in Table 8.8, which shows the cost of each component used per sheet of bioplastic.

The bioplastic was very costly, at approximately R4.50 per pad. This is due to the high cost of glycerol. Costs associated with the prototypes were determined and shown in Table 8.9.

Table 8.8 Embedded bioplastic costing

Component	Cost per sheet (R)
Glycerol	2.24
Vinegar	0.13
Corn starch	1.03
Bamboo liner	1.10
Total	**4.50**

Table 8.9 Prototype 1 costing

Component	Cost per pad (R)	Cost per pad (R)
Wood pulp fluff	0.06	0.06
Organic cotton	0.60	0.60
Cellulose sheet	2.34	-
Bamboo liner	1.10	1.10
Embedded bioplastic	4.50	4.50
Total	**8.60**	**6.26**

The most expensive component in both the prototypes was the embedded bioplastic. Prototype 1 costs approximately R8.60 which is around R2 more than prototype 2, which costs R6.26. One of the major components constituting a high cost in prototype 1 is the cellulose sheet.

Both prototypes are expensive compared to the brands that they were compared to, which cost around R30 for a pack of 10 pads, and therefore a maximum of R3 each. Prototype 2 is a better choice for a low-cost sanitary pad, it does however need a cost reduction to meet the costs of pads on the market.

4. Conclusion and Recommendations

4.1 Conclusion

The prototypes met part of the aim as they were competent and fully biodegradable. They were however very costly in comparison to other brands. The objectives of using readily available and affordable materials had limitations as these materials were of high cost. Prototype 1 performed better than prototype 2 in the maximum capacity test which proved that it is more absorbent, but prototypes held a maximum capacity more than the required amount according to technical specifications for sanitary pads. Both the prototypes performed better than brand 1 (a biodegradable brand), and which made them seem more absorbent and able to absorb fluid faster than brand 1. The prototypes were also able to retain a higher percentage of moisture than brand 1. Prototype 1 would take longer to fully degrade than prototype 2. The

organic cotton component would take the longest to fully degrade. The two prototypes were successfully produced and tested as part of the objectives, providing insight as to which prototype would be most suitable as a low-cost biodegradable sanitary pad. Prototype 2 was the best performing overall.

4.2 Recommendations

Recommendations for further investigations related to this project may include but are not limited to:

* The development of a biodegradable adhesive for the bottom layer to stick to garments would be advantageous.
* Purchasing material in bulk would reduce the costs.
* The absorption speed test can be carried out using a more accurate piece of equipment instead of the syringe.
* The maximum capacity test could be improved by placing the pad in a centrifuge.

Acknowledgements

I would like to thank my supervisor, Prof. Kevin Harding, and my co-supervisor, Mrs. Prebantha Moodley, for their guidance. I would also like to thank the School of Chemical and Metallurgical Engineering for providing the laboratory space and workshop equipment required. I also thank my research partner, Kauthar Hassan, for her contribution.

REFERENCES

1. Barman, A., Katkar, P.M. and Asagekar, S.D. (2017) 'Development of Eco-friendly Herbal Finished Sanitary Napkin', IJIRST-International Journal for Innovative Research in Science & Technologyl, 4. Available at: www.ijirst.org.
2. Parent, C. et al. (2022) 'Menstrual hygiene products: A practice evaluation', Journal of Gynecology Obstetrics and Human Reproduction, 51(1). Available at: https://doi.org/10.1016/j.jogoh.2021.102261.
3. Parthasarathy, S. et al. (2022) 'Menstrual hygiene and waste management: The survey results', Materials Today: Proceedings [Preprint]. Available at: https://doi.org/10.1016/j.matpr.2022.05.531.
4. Pohlmann, M. (2016) Design and Materials Selection: analysis of similar sanitary pads for daily use, Journal of Engineering Research and Application www.ijera.com. Available at: www.ijera.com.
5. Shibly, Md.M.H. et al. (2021) 'Development of biopolymer-based menstrual pad and quality analysis against commercial merchandise', Bulletin of the National Research Centre, 45(1). Available at: https://doi.org/10.1186/s42269-021-00504-2.

Note: All the figures and tables in this chapter were compiled by the author.

Sustainable Materials Processing and Manufacturing – Lin Zhu et al. (eds)
© 2024 Taylor & Francis Group, London, ISBN 978-1-032-88599-5

Assessment of Recycling Plastic Bottle Waste Considering Public Behavior and Attitude: Case Study Ibadan, Nigeria

Johnson A. Oyewale, Lagouge K. Tartibu

Department of Mechanical and Industrial Engineering Technology, University of Johannesburg, Johannesburg, 2028, South Africa

Imhade P. Okokpujie*

Department of Mechanical and Industrial Engineering Technology, University of Johannesburg, Johannesburg, 2028, South Africa

Department of Mechanical and Mechatronics Engineering, Afe Babalola University, Ado 360001, Ekiti State, Nigeria

ABSTRACT: Plastic pollution is one of the most dangerous challenges and pressing environmental issues confronting Ibadan and the rest of the world. Ibadan, the state capital of Oyo State in Nigeria, is the focus of the study. Data were collected from 605 individuals via questionnaire administration using a random sampling technique based on the socioeconomic characteristics of residents with balanced demographics. Plastic bottles, whose usage in this part of the world is unavoidable, have become an untamed, unmanaged beast due to behaviors and attitudes towards their disposal for recycling. The study was conducted for two months (10 January–15 March 2022) on a public survey of plastic bottle waste recycling. The study aims to provide an updated survey of public behavior and attitudes towards the uses, disposals, and recycling of plastic bottle waste in the city of Ibadan, Nigeria. Of the various categories of solid waste most generated by people, about 75% of the populace identified PBW as their most generated solid waste. The survey reveals that post-consumers of products do not recycle more than 80% of the plastic bottle waste used in Ibadan in plastic bottles. This results from poor sensitization in the recycling system, which leads to poor recycling outcomes. The study concludes that a well-structured return network must be implemented to deliver sufficient, convenient, and efficient recycling of plastic bottle waste.

KEYWORDS: Plastic pollution, Plastic bottle wastes (PBW), Recycling, Solid waste, Population growth

1. Introduction

Solid waste is a non-liquid and non-gaseous product of human activities that are regarded as useless (Dung, Mankilik and Ozoji, 2017), (J et al., 2019), and (Mussa and Suryabhagavan, 2021). There are significant categories of solid waste when considering the possible risks of environmental contamination [4] as described by the integrated solid waste management system (United Nations Economic and Social Commission for Asia and the Pacific, 2002). Thermoplastic resins are commonly used in different applications ranging from soft drinks and water bottles to furniture, food packaging, vehicles, medical supplies, and electronic goods. Commonly used thermoplastic resins are in different applications ranging from soft drinks and water bottles, furniture, food packaging, vehicles, medical supplies, and electronic goods. Over the past decades, plastic bottles have gained more market value and continue to replace glass bottles in the packaging industry. Presently, plastic pollution is the world's main challenge in waste management. When considering the potential risks of environmental contamination, many solid waste falls into two categories (Proshad et al., 2017). To create an effective plastics management framework, primary goal was to create a preliminary inventory of plastics in Nigeria. Searching

*Corresponding author: ip.okokpujie@abuad.edu.ng

DOI: 10.1201/9781003538646-9

contemporary literature and the UN Comtrade database for import data of various polymer categories and significant product categories containing plastic using harmonized system (HS) codes to calculate the percentage of plastic in these goods, algebraic equations were constructed. Between 1996 and 2014, imports of basic plastics into Nigeria totalled about 14,200,000 tons. Total plastic imports of 3,420,000 tons were made up of 5,545,700 tons of component imports and 3,420,000 tons of finished goods. Over six years, almost 194,000 tons of plastic toys were imported. 17,620,000 tons of plastic are imported in total, including as raw materials, and finished goods. 23,400,000 tons of imported plastic freshly made plastic, and plastic parts entered the technological environment (Babayemi *et al.*, 2018).

The massive inflow of plastic and other polymers into Nigerian technology has significant effects on waste management, resource recovery, marine litter, and pollution. Less than 12% of the garbage produced because of the massive influx of plastics into Nigerian technology is recycled. This essential waste and resource category needs to be managed sustainably. Reuse, recycling, waste conversion to energy, and proper plastic control policy frameworks are examples of potential mitigating methods for waste plastic (Yalwaji, John-Nwagwu and Sogbanmu, 2022). Gradually, plastics are becoming part of our lives, and they are becoming indispensable because of their many properties, such as low density, strength, durability, robustness, and low cost (Mwanza and Mbohwa, 2017) (Ncube *et al.*, 2021). In developing countries in Africa, about 85% of waste is improperly disposed of (Adebayo Bello and bin Ismail, 2016). Nonetheless, the problem is often aggravated by poor or inadequate sustainable management practices, leaving developing African countries facing a multitude of environmental and health problems (Ferronato and Torretta, 2019). As the population increases, consumption of plastic-aided goods also increases. Oyo-state comprises 16 districts with an estimated population of over 6,000,000 (est. 2020 population) and >3,577,605 in the urban areas, which ranks it the 3rd largest city in Nigeria and 17th in Africa (Oyebode, 2022).

Population growth in most big cities is becoming unbearable. Unplanned and rapid urbanization has contributed immensely to overwhelming growth in the municipalities (Mwanza and Mbohwa, 2017). Consequently, individuals' solid waste increases, subjecting the environment and people to dangers. Recycling is suggested as an essential option in the solid waste management hierarchy to reduce the spread and impacts posed by end-of-life (EoL) and the end of use (EoU) post-consumer plastic bottle wastes (Ncube *et al.*, 2021) (Matter, Dietschi and Zurbrügg, 2013). Currently, there is a need for recycling, recovery, and management of plastic waste (Singh *et al.*, 2017). Increasing awareness of plastic pollution is giving rise to plastic recycling and innovations to address plastic

challenges, leading to new markets, jobs, and manufacturing opportunities in the future (Kosior and Mitchell, 2020).

Attitude is a valence response toward performing behavior (Oguge, Oremo and Adhiambo, 2021). (Khan, Ahmed and Najmi, 2019) (Botetzagias, Dima and Malesios, 2015) conducted studies based on the theory of planned behavior, TPB, and confirmed that awareness of consequences and convenience are the primary drivers of returning or recycling intention. A subsequent review conducted by [16] also suggested that while individuals are aware of the adverse health and environmental impacts of plastic consumption, their consumption habits, benefits of plastic use, and situational factors often slow their willingness to make their own choices to reduce plastic consumption. The proper management of waste in urban areas is seen as a result of the good behavior of the people and the government (Olukanni, Pius-Imue and Joseph, 2020) (Debrah, Vidal and Dinis, 2021). If effectively managed, it contributes significantly to various developments and reforms in the municipality. The use of plastic bottles for soft drinks and bottled water in this part of the world became predominantly popular towards the end of the 1990s and since then has grown to a level gradually eliminating the use of returnable glass bottles for soft drinks (Ferrara, De Feo and Picone, 2021) (UNCTAD, 2022). The uncared attitudes towards disposing of these bottles have left the streets and roads littered with these plastic bottle wastes (Grobler, Schenck and Chitaka, 2022) (Mihai *et al.*, 2022). Inadequate sensitization by the waste management authorities to let people know the adverse effect these plastic wastes introduce to the environment and human health makes it more impossible to intercept indiscriminate disposals of plastic bottles (Alabi *et al.*, 2019).

This study presents an analysis of the attitude and behavior of people towards the usage, disposal, and recycling of plastic bottle wastes within the study area. The study aims at reporting the present situation and suggesting a possible solution of a well-structured return network to be put in place to deliver sufficient, convenient, and efficient recycling of plastic bottle wastes. The specific objectives of the study include the to know the level of awareness about solid waste management in Ibadan. Identify current practices of plastic bottle waste disposal with the appraised residents' access and willingness to waste facilities near them. And to encourage residents to imbibe a recycling culture of plastic bottle waste.

2. Materials and Methods

The area of study is Ibadan, the capital city of Oyo state, in the southwestern part of Nigeria, about 130 km inland northwest of Lagos and 530 km southwest of Abuja, the federal capital. Ibadan is a prominent transit point between the coastal region and areas in the underdeveloped parts of Nigeria. The city

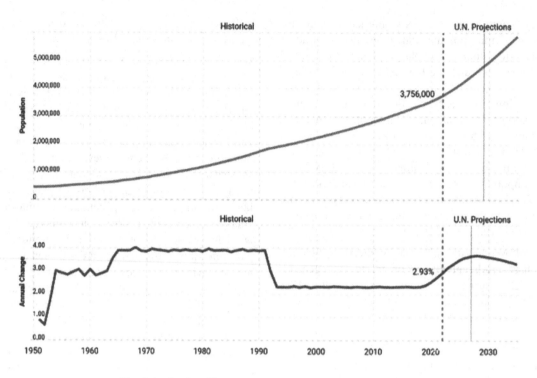

Fig. 9.1 Ibadan, Nigeria metro area population 1950-2022

Source: World Population Prospects 2022, 2022

is the largest in Nigeria and has a total area of 3080 km^2. The economic activities of Ibadan include agriculture, trade, handicrafts, manufacturing, and service industries. It is an important commercial center; virtually every street and corridor in the traditional core and the inner suburb of the city is a market square. The current population (Fig. 9.1) of Ibadan in 2022 is 3,756,000, a 2.93% increase from 2021, which was 3,649,000 (Awosanya *et al.*, 2022) (Adewoyin, Chukwu and Sanni, 2018). The selected area of study is Egbeda. Egbeda, located in the city of Ibadan is a district in Oyo state. It is bounded by 7° 20'.43"– 7° 22'.55" N latitudes and 3° 46' 4 " – 3° 58'.2" E longitudes. This study area has not had many spatial variations of topographic features, as the elevation of the area is 219.2 Meters (719.2 Feet) (Fig. 9.2). The population distribution of the city and the land use map serve as a basis for estimating waste generation in Ibadan. The waste generation rate in Ibadan was calculated from the 15 percent rate of street refuse at 0.6 kilograms per capita per day (Table 9.1) (Adeosun *et al.*, 2015).

There has been a significant implication of the population growth rate in Ibadan on solid waste generation (Moruf, Oluwasinaayomi and Mubarak, 2020). With increasing population and area, industrialization and urbanization are also increasing, waste generation has always been a major environmental problem (Ogundele, Rapheal and Abiodun, 2018) (Packaging and Group, 2020). The questionnaire used to collect the necessary information was well structured to address balanced demographics of the mixed language (English, Yoruba, Igbo, and Hausa, etc.) speaking people from the city of Ibadan between the age of 18 and above. Aside from the distribution of printed questionnaires, information was sought by one-one with individuals to get sufficient information further.

The methodology and analysis approach followed the approach used by the Hong Kong Public Opinion Research Institute (Fig. 9.3) (Packaging and Group, 2020), where a total number of 743 surveys were made, and 605 of those surveys were eventually validated for analysis. This figure showed a response rate of 81%, which is an appreciable response to present an accurate picture of the public behavior and attitude toward plastic bottle waste disposal and recycling. The survey was carried out over two months (10th January – 15th March 2022).

Table 9.1   Rate of waste generation in Ibadan

Waste	The rate in kg per capita per day
Domestic waste	0.5
Street waste	0.1
Total waste	0.6

Source: Olusa, Enisan & Adebisi. 2020

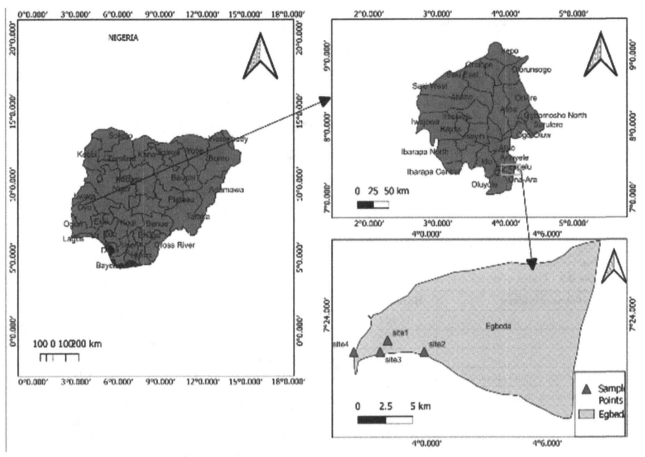

Fig. 9.2 Location map of the study area

Source: Author's compilation

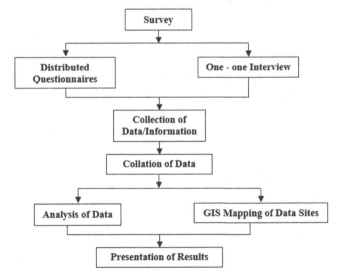

Fig. 9.3 Methodology framework of the study

Source: Author's compilation

3. Results and Discussions

The number of solid wastes considered for the survey generated in Ibadan was estimated and presented in Table 9.2 below. The study results give the average tidy sum of the generated solid waste from the respondents. It was discovered that plastic bags and bottles constitute the highest waste (38%). Table 9.2 and Fig. 9.4 show that plastic bottles are the most generated waste, with most of the plastic waste disposed of on the go, i.e., thrown away as people move on the streets after consuming products in plastic bottles.

Table 9.2 Responses on waste were primarily generated from respondents

Solid waste materials	Responses on most generated wastes	% on responses.
Paper & carton	147	24%
Plastic bags/bottles	232	38%
Glass	7	1%
Tins/cans	46	8%
Fiber bags	67	11%
Others	108	18%

Source: Author's compilation

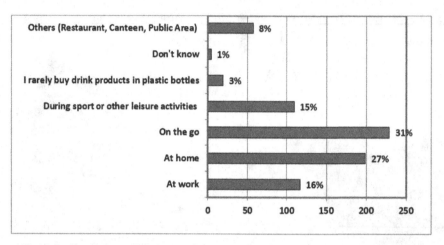

Fig. 9.4 Percentage distribution from points of disposal of plastic bottle waste

Source: Author's compilation

Table 9.3 Points of disposal of plastic bottles

Points of disposal	No respondents
At work	117
At home	199
On the go	229
During sports or other leisure activities	109
I rarely buy drink products in plastic bottles	19
Don't know	4
Others (Restaurants, Canteen, Public Area)	57

Source: Author's compilation

The study establishes different conditions based on individual awareness and attitudes toward waste disposal in the study area. Very close to 80% of the correspondent indicated that almost none of the plastic bottle waste is dropped off at various collection centers to be recycled. Only 6% of the respondents responded that they rarely recycle or hardly recycle plastic bottle waste after each use (Table 9.4).

Table 9.4 Status of recycling of plastic bottles.

Conditions of recycling	No of respondents
I recycle nearly all the plastic bottles I consume	38
I do not recycle any or almost none of the plastic bottles I consume	472
I recycle less than half of the plastic bottles I consume	93
I recycle the majority of the plastic bottles I consume	18
I hardly buy any drinks in plastic bottles	19
Don't know	87

Source: Author's compilation

Recycling these plastic wastes is a severe challenge in the city of Ibadan. It has been found that around 65% of the plastic waste generated is not recycled; this is shown in Table 9.3 and Fig. 9.4 below. Another critical point is the matter of convenience and trust; to encourage plastic waste recycling significantly, individuals need to develop a serious returning culture of this plastic waste. It was discovered in the study that the highest percentage of 37% of the respondents, preferred to return plastic waste near where they live, and 16% chose to return plastic waste on the go. This number represents more than half of individuals to return their used plastic waste; if this could encourage, an appreciable volume of plastic waste would be taken off the streets for recycling and reuse.

In another case, finding a convenient collection center is a hindrance individuals face to returning plastic waste; as a result, disposal of plastic waste is done anywhere. 47% of respondents indicated finding a convenient collection center is a problem, while 16% declared that holding to my empty bottles is inconvenient. Figure 9.5 shows why they rarely or never recycle plastic bottles. The returning culture and recycling of plastic waste could be encouraged when post-consumers are motivated; the most significant motivation is that individuals want to conserve resources and reduce the amount of waste going to landfills.

4. Conclusion

This study mainly used a simple randomized questionnaire as a tool for identifying the effect of individual behavior and attitude in the selected study area of the Ibadan metropolis. The behavior and attitudes of post-consumers toward the disposal and recycling of plastic waste were studied. Various questions were answered that helped in achieving the set objectives. The findings revealed that because plastic waste is abundant, waste management is not properly managed by

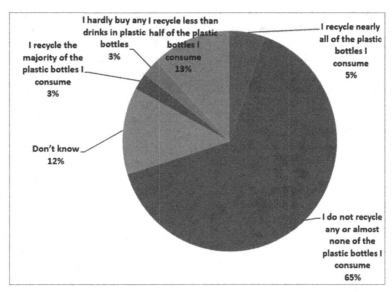

Fig. 9.5   Percentage of recycling of plastic bottles

Source: Author's compilation

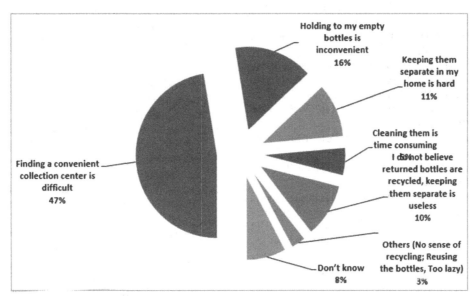

Fig. 9.6   Reason for rarely or never recycling your plastic bottles

Source: Author's compilation

efficiently recycling plastic waste. However, respondents have given positive responses that could enhance the proper management of the plastic waste channelled through recycling. As a result, these major solutions were proposed to address the issue of illegal disposal of post-consumer plastic waste on Ibadan's streets.

i. A well-structured return network must be implemented to deliver proper, convenient, and efficient recycling.

ii. Convenience in terms of location triggers return behavior and encourages a recycling culture.

iii. Plastic waste management education and sensitization, both formal and informal, encourages return behavior.

REFERENCES

1. Adebayo Bello, I. and bin Ismail, M.N. (2016) 'Solid Waste Management in Africa: A Review', *International Journal of Waste Resources*, 6(2). Available at: https://doi.org/10.4172/2252-5211.1000216.

2. Adeosun, O.J. *et al.* (2015) 'Assessment of Waste Management Practices on Farms in Abeokuta Environ , Ogun State', (November), pp. 98–105.

3. Adewoyin, Y., Chukwu, N.-N.A. and Sanni, L.M. (2018) 'Urbanization, Spatial Distribution of Healthcare Facilities and Inverse Care in Ibadan, Nigeria', *Ghana Journal of Geography*, 10(2), pp. 96–111. Available at: https://doi.org/10.4314/gjg.v10i2.7.

4. Alabi, O.A. *et al.* (2019) 'Public and Environmental Health Effects of Plastic Wastes Disposal: A Review', *J Toxicol Risk Assess*, 5, p. 21. Available at: https://doi.org/10.23937/2572.

6. Awosanya, E.J. *et al.* (2022) 'veterinary sciences Detection of Echinococcus granulosus sensu lato in Environmental Samples from Ibadan , Oyo State , South West Nigeria', pp. 1–9.

6. Babayemi, J.O. *et al.* (2018) 'Initial Inventory of Plastics Imports in Nigeria as a Basis for More Sustainable Management Policies', *Journal of Health and Pollution*, 8(18), pp. 1–15. Available at: https://doi.org/10.5696/2156-9614-8.18.1.

7. Botetzagias, I., Dima, A.F. and Malesios, C. (2015) 'Extending the Theory of Planned Behavior in the context of recycling: The role of moral norms and of demographic predictors', *Resources, Conservation and Recycling*, 95, pp. 58–67. Available at: https://doi.org/10.1016/j.resconrec.2014.12.004.

8. Debrah, J.K., Vidal, D.G. and Dinis, M.A.P. (2021) 'Raising awareness on solid waste management through formal education for sustainability: A developing countries evidence review', *Recycling*, 6(1), pp. 1–21. Available at: https://doi.org/10.3390/recycling6010006.

9. Dung, M.D., Mankilik, M. and Ozoji, B.E. (2017) 'Assessment of College Students' Knowledge and Attitudes Towards Solid Waste Management in North Central Zone of Nigeria', *Science Education International*, 28(2), pp. 141–146. Available at: https://doi.org/10.33828/sei.v28.i2.7.

10. Ferrara, C., De Feo, G. and Picone, V. (2021) 'Lca of glass versus pet mineral water bottles: An italian case study', *Recycling*, 6(3). Available at: https://doi.org/10.3390/recycling6030050.

11. Ferronato, N. and Torretta, V. (2019) 'Waste mismanagement in developing countries: A review of global issues', *International Journal of Environmental Research and Public Health*. MDPI AG. Available at: https://doi.org/10.3390/ijerph16061060.

12. Grobler, L., Schenck, R. and Chitaka, T.Y. (2022) 'Waste Management , Littering and Illegal Dumping : A Literature Review Waste Management , Littering and Illegal Dumping : A Literature Review Literature Review : Clean cities and towns : Understanding societal behaviour in order to reduce and divert waste', (June). Available at: https://doi.org/10.13140/RG.2.2.10256.07681.

13. J, I.I. *et al.* (2019) 'Current Status Of Solid Waste Management Strategies In Akure Municipality , Ondo State', 7(4), pp. 40–51.

14. Khan, F., Ahmed, W. and Najmi, A. (2019) 'Understanding consumers' behavior intentions towards dealing with the plastic waste: Perspective of a developing country', *Resources, Conservation and Recycling*, 142(September 2018), pp. 49–58. Available at: https://doi.org/10.1016/j.resconrec.2018.11.020.

15. Kosior, E. and Mitchell, J. (2020) *Current industry position on plastic production and recycling*, *Plastic Waste and Recycling: Environmental Impact, Societal Issues, Prevention, and Solutions*. Elsevier Inc. Available at: https://doi.org/10.1016/B978-0-12-817880-5.00006-2.

16. Matter, A., Dietschi, M. and Zurbrügg, C. (2013) 'Improving the informal recycling sector through segregation of waste in the household - The case of Dhaka Bangladesh', *Habitat International*, 38, pp. 150–156. Available at: https://doi.org/10.1016/j.habitatint.2012.06.001.

17. Mihai, F.C. *et al.* (2022) 'Plastic Pollution, Waste Management Issues, and Circular Economy Opportunities in Rural Communities', *Sustainability (Switzerland)*, 14(1). Available at: https://doi.org/10.3390/su14010020.

18. Moruf, A.A., Oluwasinaayomi, F.K. and Mubarak, O.L. (2020) 'Public-Private Partnership (PPP) in residential solid waste management in Ibadan: Challenges and opportunities', *Journal of Geography and Regional Planning*, 13(1), pp. 30–40. Available at: https://doi.org/10.5897/jgrp2019.0721.

19. Mussa, A. and Suryabhagavan, K. V. (2021) 'Solid waste dumping site selection using GIS-based multi-criteria spatial modeling: a case study in Logia town, Afar region, Ethiopia', *Geology, Ecology, and Landscapes*, 5(3), pp. 186–198. Available at: https://doi.org/10.1080/24749508.2019.1703311.

20. Mwanza, B.G. and Mbohwa, C. (2017) 'Drivers to Sustainable Plastic Solid Waste Recycling: A Review', *Procedia Manufacturing*, 8, pp. 649–656. Available at: https://doi.org/10.1016/j.promfg.2017.02.083.

21. Ncube, L.K. *et al.* (2021) 'An overview of plasticwaste generation and management in food packaging industries', *Recycling*, 6(1), pp. 1–25. Available at: https://doi.org/10.3390/recycling6010012.

22. Oguge, N., Oremo, F. and Adhiambo, S. (2021) 'Investigating the Knowledge and Attitudes towards Plastic Pollution among the Youth in Nairobi, Kenya', *Social Sciences*, 10(11), p. 408. Available at: https://doi.org/10.3390/socsci10110408.

23. Ogundele, O.M., Rapheal, O.M. and Abiodun, A.M. (2018) 'Effects of Municipal Waste Disposal Methods on Community Health in Ibadan - Nigeria', *Polytechnica*, 1(1–2), pp. 61–72. Available at: https://doi.org/10.1007/s41050-018-0008-y.

24. Olukanni, D.O., Pius-Imue, F.B. and Joseph, S.O. (2020) 'Public perception of solid waste management practices in Nigeria: Ogun state experience', *Recycling*, 5(2). Available at: https://doi.org/10.3390/recycling5020008.

25. Oyebode, M.O. (2022) 'An Interrogation of the Security , Peace and Development in some Selected Rural Communities of Oyo State', (September).

26. Packaging, S.B. and Group, W. (2020) 'SURVEY PLASTIC BOTTLE RECYCLING PUBLIC ATTITUDES AND BEHAVIOURS', (January).

27. Proshad, R. *et al.* (2017) 'Toxic effects of plastic on human health and environment : A consequences of health risk assessment in Bangladesh', *International Journal of Health*, 6(1), p. 1. Available at: https://doi.org/10.14419/ijh.v6i1.8655.

28. Singh, N. *et al.* (2017) 'Recycling of plastic solid waste: A state of art review and future applications', *Composites Part B: Engineering*, 115, pp. 409–422. Available at: https://doi.org/10.1016/j.compositesb.2016.09.013.

29. UNCTAD (2022) 'Substitutes for single-use plastics in sub-Saharan Africa and south Asia'.

30. United Nations Economic and Social Commission for Asia and the Pacific (2002) 'Chapter 8 Types of wastes', *United Nations ESCAP Library*, pp. 170–194. Available at: http://www.unescap.org/sites/default/files/CH08.PDF.

31. *World Population Prospects 2022* (2022).

32. Yalwaji, B., John-Nwagwu, H.O. and Sogbanmu, T.O. (2022) 'Plastic pollution in the environment in Nigeria: A rapid systematic review of the sources, distribution, research gaps and policy needs', *Scientific African*, 16, p. e01220. Available at: https://doi.org/10.1016/j.sciaf.2022.e01220.

Sustainable Materials Processing and Manufacturing – Lin Zhu et al. (eds)
© 2024 Taylor & Francis Group, London, ISBN 978-1-032-88599-5

Production and Biodegradation Testing of Bioplastics

Edwin Botha[1], Tokelo Chuene[2], Davena Mathobisa[3], Kevin Harding[4]

School of Chemical and Metallurgical Engineering, University of the Witwatersrand, Johannesburg, South Africa

ABSTRACT: Plastic is a valuable material, but its non-biodegradable nature has caused problems in the waste stream, polluting both land and water. With the introduction of biodegradable bioplastics, the negative environmental effects of conventional plastics are nullified. This research aimed to produce bioplastics from everyday materials and to evaluate their biodegradability in water, soil, and compost in two environments: room temperature ($\pm$ 31°C) and a controlled temperature (25°C) for five weeks. Four bioplastics were made and consisted of (1) starch, (2) starch and spirulina, (3) starch and gelatine, and (4) gelatine; glycerol was the plasticizer. The composition and properties of the bioplastics were tested using FTIR and XRD, their tensile strengths were measured, and the change in mass and physical appearance were also observed over the five weeks. From the FTIR and XRD readings, the starch and starch-spirulina bioplastics had the same chemical compositions, but their physical characteristics were different. The gelatine-starch bioplastic had the same physical properties as the starch-only bioplastic, and the gelatine-only bioplastic had a different chemical composition from all the other bioplastic types. The gelatine-based bioplastics completely disintegrated in all three mediums for both environments. The starch-based bioplastics disintegrated more slowly, and on average lost around 45–50% of their mass. SEM analysis of the starch-based bioplastics showed that the samples, in all three mediums and both environments, underwent degradation with distinct changes in their appearance and showed evidence of microbial activity.

KEYWORDS: Aerobic degradation, Technical standards, Thermosets, Thermoplastics, Plasticizers

1. Introduction

Plastic has been extensively used in both industrial and domestic sectors due to its versatility and its changeable and manipulable properties such as flexibility, heat resistance, and mechanical strength. Plastics are made from petroleum-based materials, which are non-biodegradable, non-renewable, and unsustainable and cause harm to the environments they end up in (Iñiguez et al., 2018). To address this issue, two solutions can be implemented: increasing recycling and reusing; or producing bio-plastics, which are biodegradable and sustainable (Harding et al., 2017). The objective of this study was to produce bioplastics from everyday materials, test their mechanical properties, and evaluate their biodegradability in water, soil, and compost over five weeks under controlled and uncontrolled temperature conditions.

The tensile strength of the bioplastics was measured with a universal tensile machine, and the compositions were studied using X-ray diffraction (XRD) and Fourier transform infrared spectroscopy (FTIR).

2. Literature Review

Plastics can be referred to as bioplastic if they are derived from plant material or are derived from materials that can biodegrade into their natural components (Harding et al., 2017). Bioplastics can be divided into 2 groups, biodegradable bioplastics, and non-biodegradable bioplastics.

Biodegradable bioplastics are produced from protein sources which include soy protein, milk protein, gelatine, and polysaccharides such as starch, chitosan and carboxymethyl

[1]1600069@students.wits.ac.za, [2]2112560@students.wits.ac.za, [3]2103767@students.wits.ac.za, [4]kevin.harding@wits.ac.za

DOI: 10.1201/9781003538646-10

cellulose (Suderman et al., 2018). These types of bioplastics include thermoplastic starch, polyhydroxy-alkenoates, polylactic acid, seaweed polysaccharide bioplastic, fungal mycelium-based bioplastics, bioplastics from shells and tree discard (Atiwesh et al., 2021).

Non-biodegradable bioplastics are usually produced from green resources such as biomass. The production process involves pre-treatment, hydrolysis, fermentation, and several steps of organic reactions. Non-biodegradable bioplastics include bio-polyethylene (bio-PE), bio-polypropylene (bio-PP), bio-polyethylene-terephthalate (bio-PET), bio-poly tri-methylene terephthalate (bio-PPT) and bio-polyamide (bio-PA) (Rahman & Bhoi, 2021).These plastics are usually known as synthetic plastics and need to be recycled to avoid plastic pollution.

The biodegradation of bioplastics allows them to be a better alternative to conventional plastics since it can biodegrade in basic environmental conditions such as heat, light, moisture, chemical conditions, and biological activity (Shah & Alshehrei, 2017). The microorganisms involved in the degradation of natural and synthetic plastics are bacteria, fungi and actinomycetes. Plastics are usually biodegraded aerobically in nature and anaerobically in sediments and landfills. Anaerobic degradation produces carbon dioxide, water, and methane while aerobic biodegradation produces carbon dioxide and water. Soil, water, marine and compost are the mediums for biodegradation (Emadian et al., 2017).

The methodologies for monitoring biodegradability can be divided into 4 groups according to their general operation. The methods are CO_2 measurements, spectroscopy, mass loss and visual analysis. The CO_2 measurements use equipment like cumulative measurement respirometry (CMR) and gravimetric measurement respirometry (GMR), and direct measurement respirometry (DMR). Spectroscopy includes Nuclear magnetic resonance (NMR), Attenuated total reflectance spectroscopy (ATR-FTIR) and near-infrared (NIR). (Ruggero et al., 2021)

3. Methodology

3.1 Materials

- Materials used included: gelatine, corn-starch, glycerol, white vinegar, and spirulina powder.
- Mediums for biodegradation: garden soil, compost and tap water.
- Equipment: baking trays, muffin tray and window squeegee

3.2 Sample Preparation

Three types of biodegradable plastics were produced. Gelatine-based bioplastic, corn starch-based bioplastic and bioplastic made from both corn starch and gelatine.

Gelatine-based bioplastic: A glycerol solution made of 4 ml glycerol and 100 ml water was placed on the stove and allowed to heat up. When the temperature reached 70°C, 6.75 g of gelatine was added and allowed to dissolve.

Corn starch-based bioplastic: 40 ml vinegar, 60 g of corn starch, 50 ml glycerol and 400 ml distilled water were added to a beaker and mixed. The mixture was then heated while being stirred.

Corn starch and spirulina-based bioplastic: The same procedure as the one for corn-starch-based bioplastic is used but spirulina is added here.

Corn starch and gelatine-based bioplastic: 60 g of corn starch, 40 ml vinegar, 50 ml glycerol and 400 ml distilled water mixture was heated and stirred on a hot plate. Once the mixture reached a temperature of 50 °C, 6.75 g of gelatine was added.

Once all mixtures thickened, it was poured and spread out into a pan.

3.3 Biodegradation

The samples were put in muffin trays and the cups were filled with either compost, soil, or water and placed in an environment with a controlled temperature (25°C) and a second uncontrolled environment (average 31°C).

3.4 Analysis

Mass loss: The bioplastic samples were allowed to biodegrade in both controlled and uncontrolled conditions. The mass of the samples was taken weekly for 5 weeks.

Tensile strength: The stress and strain of the 3 bioplastics produced were measured using a universal tensile machine. The samples were clamped and pulled measuring the stress and strain.

Scanning Electron Microscope (SEM): A scanning electron microscope was used to analyse the biodegradation of the bioplastic. The voltage was kept at 5.00 kV the magnification was varied between 124 X, 500 X and 1240 X. The samples were coated with carbon and gold palladium and mounted on an aluminium stub.

Fourier Transform Infrared spectroscopy (FTIR): FTIR spectra of all bioplastic samples were recorded using a PerkinElmer Spectrum Version 10.5.4 spectrometer. The spectrometer was operating in attenuated total reflectance (ATR) and was used to compare the chemical bonds and functional groups between the films. The frequency range of 450-4000 cm^{-1} was used.

X-ray diffraction (XRD): X-ray diffraction analysis was performed for gelatine-based, starch-based, and hybrid-based bioplastics. The X-ray patterns were obtained between a range of 5° and 40° (2θ). The step used was 0.028° with a step time of 92.5 s.

4. Results

4.1 FTIR Analysis

An FTIR analysis was conducted for the identification and comparison of the different bioplastics (Fig. 10.1). For the hybrid bioplastics, the peak observed at 3293.50 cm^{-1} and 2929.04 cm^{-1} are from corn starch and they are associated with O-H and – CH$_2$ stretching vibrations. The bands at 1648.06 cm^{-1} and 1412.2 cm^{-1} were associated with the O-H bonding of water and CH$_2$ groups (Tan et al., 2022). Usually, the region of saccharide bands covers the range 1180-953 cm^{-1}, thus the peaks at 1151. 52 cm^{-1}, 1105.39 cm^{-1} and 1077.66 cm^{-1} are associated with the stretching of vibration of C-O bonds in C-O-H groups while the peak at 1019.54 cm^{-1} is associated with C–O in C–O–C groups (Namazi & Dadkhah, 2010). The peaks for the starch-based bioplastic and the spirulina and starch-bioplastics the peaks are 3294.24 cm^{-1} and 3293.15 cm^{-1}, and 2926.21 cm^{-1} and 2927.23 cm^{-1} respectively. These are the same as the peaks seen in the hybrid bioplastic which were associated with the O-H and -CH$_2$ stretching vibrations. For the gelatine-based bioplastic, the peak 3298.67 cm^{-1} is associated with the vibrational stretching of -OH groups, at 2927.31 cm^{-1} it is associated with C-H stretching, at 1631.11 cm^{-1} is associated with C=O stretching while the peak at 1033.66 cm^{-1} is associated with C-O-H stretching (Mroczkowska et al., 2021).

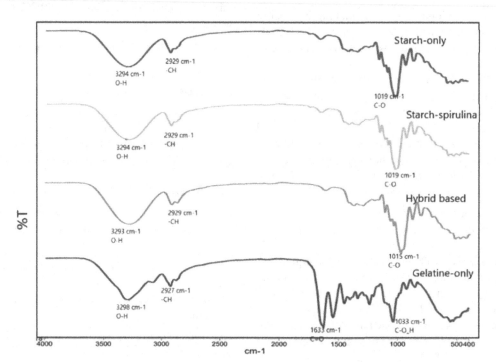

Fig. 10.1 FTIR spectra of gelatine-based, starch-based, hybrid based and starch and spirulina blend

4.2 XRD Analysis

Figure 10.2 shows the XRD profiles of gelatine, starch, and hybrid-based bioplastics. The diffraction peaks for starch-based bioplastics were at 20.05°, 23.10°, 26.05°, 28.05° and 35.0°. The bioplastic does not have the A-type crystalline structure of corn starch because the glycerol molecules replaced the intramolecular and intermolecular hydrogen bonds (O-H) (Tan et al., 2022). For gelatine-based bioplastics, the peaks are at 8.30, 23.05 and 34.05. The characteristic peaks are assigned to the triple-helical crystalline structure gelatine. The diffraction peak at 8.3 is directly proportional to the diameter of the triple helix structure of the gelatine (Peña et al., 2010). The intensity of the peak at 8 decreases when glycerol is added (Suderman et al., 2018). The hybrid plastic has diffraction at 25.50 and 35.50. This is a mixture of gelatine and corn starch and thus has 2 different types of structures coming into contact together with glycerol. The physicochemical properties of the bioplastics are different.

4.3 Tensile Strength

The elongation of the starch and gelatine-only bioplastics is 13.25%. When the two were mixed to produce a hybrid bioplastic, the elongation increased to 21.85%. Gelatine-based bioplastic had the highest tensile strength at 7.67 MPa,

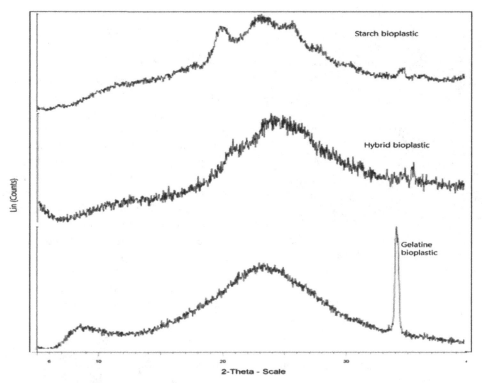

Fig. 10.2 XRD profiles of gelatin, starch, and hybrid-based bioplastics

hybrid bioplastic followed at 0.89 MPa and starch bioplastic was last at 0.86 MPa before failure.

4.4 Mass Loss

Gelatin: For the gelatine samples in uncontrolled temperature conditions, the samples in the water disappeared within the first week. The mass of the sample in the soil increased and then the sample disappeared, while for the sample placed in compost, the mass initially increased in the first week, but then started decreasing after week one.

For the controlled environment, the samples in compost and water disappeared within the first week while the mass of the sample in soil decreased until week 2 and then the sample disappeared. All samples completely disintegrated after the five-week period.

Starch-based bioplastic: For the controlled environment, the mass of the samples increased in the first week because they absorbed the water/moisture and then the mass started decreasing after the first week. For the uncontrolled environment, the samples placed in water and soil initially gained weight before a weight reduction could be seen from week 2 onwards. The samples placed in compost started losing mass immediately. After the five-weeks, the total mass loss for all samples were 54 % and 44 % respectively.

Hybrid-based bioplastic: The hybrid samples placed in the controlled environment all gained weight in the first week.

From week 2, the masses of samples placed in soil and compost. started to decrease while the sample placed in the water broke down into pieces and was gelatinized. For the samples in the uncontrolled environment, only the sample in water gained weight in the first week before decreasing. The mass of the samples placed in soil and compost decreased immediately. After the five-weeks, the total mass loss for all samples were 72 % and 52 % respectively.

4.5 SEM Analysis

SEM analysis was performed on the same scale to monitor what happened during the biodegradation period. The samples were analysed weekly to observe the changes on the surface.

Room conditions

Figure 10.3 shows pictures taken weekly through SEM to monitor surface changes of the samples. The first pictures on each row represent the samples before biodegradation where the surface was smooth. For the samples that were allowed to biodegrade in water, it was observed that as weeks passed by the surface started developing fibres and changed from smooth to rough. For the sample in compost, there were pieces of compost and fibres on the surface of the samples.

The fibres were evidence of the presence of fungi on the surface of the plastics. As time progressed pores were seen on the samples. The surface of the samples in the soil became

Fig. 10.3 SEM pictures for bioplastic samples that were placed in soil, compost, and water for 5 weeks (from left to right) at room temperature.

more granular each week, this is because the soil particles were getting attached to the surface of the bioplastics. Although all the samples showed evidence of degradation, the samples in compost had the most activity. This could be due to the many micro-organisms already present in compost, thereby speeding up biodegradation.

Controlled conditions:

Figure 10.4 shows an SEM picture for samples in the 25° C controlled environment, the surface of the samples in water was getting rough. For the samples in compost, the compost started getting stuck on the surface and in the third week, there were fibres and some pores on the surface, which indicated that fungi were growing on the surface of the bioplastics. For samples in soil, soil particles were stuck on the surface and then fibres started appearing. As weeks went by the surface

Fig. 10.4 SEM pictures for bioplastic samples that were placed in soil, compost, and water for 5 weeks (from left to right) at a temperature of 25 ° C

was getting more granular and more fibres were appearing indicating the breakdown of the bioplastic.

4.6 Visual Analysis

Figure 10.5 shows pictures of samples that were placed in water, compost, and soil 5 weeks after biodegradation. The bioplastics showed the steps involved in the biodegradation process. The first picture (a) shows a sample that was placed in water and has purple/black spots on the surface. This represents catalytic agents that are released by microorganisms. The samples also showed evidence of fragmentation which was caused by the presence of microorganisms. Picture (b) shows a sample that was placed in compost, it has a black colour because of the compost that was stuck on the surface of the bioplastic. The plastic has deteriorated and is now in fragments which shows that biodegradation was taking place. Picture (c) is a sample that was placed in soil, soil particles got stuck on the surface of the bioplastic and the sample showed evidence of deterioration.

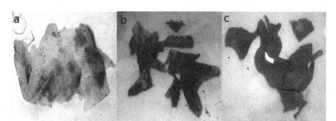

Fig. 10.5 Starch-based bioplastic samples after 5 weeks of biodegradation in a) water b) Compost c) Soil

5. Discussion

Different bioplastics were produced and allowed to biodegrade in mediums such as compost, water, and soil and two temperature conditions which are room temperature and 25° C. An FTIR analysis was performed on starch-only, starch-spirulina, hybrid (starch and gelatine) and gelatine-only bioplastics to compare the chemical compositions. The starch-only and starch-spirulina bioplastics had the same chemical compositions.

The addition of spirulina improved the physical properties of the starch-only film because it did not have bubbles and was smooth and rubbery, but it did not change the chemical composition. Spirulina is also known as Arthrospira and is a microalga which is multicellular and has a spiral shape (Ali & Saleh, 2012). Because spirulina is photosynthetic, it can be grown which is a benefit in the economic feasibility of producing starch-spirulina bioplastics. Further investigating the effect of spirulina-to-starch ratios on bioplastic films can improve the use of spirulina in the production of bioplastics. Spirulina is typically found in freshwater with high alkaline content (Zeller et al., 2013).

Corn starch and gelatine were mixed to investigate the differences that would arise compared to the starch-only and gelatine-only bioplastics. This hybrid bioplastic looked the same as the starch-only bioplastic. FTIR analysis also confirmed that the chemical composition of the hybrid and starch bioplastic only differ slightly. The addition of gelatine to the starch-based bioplastic improved the elongation from 13.25% to 21.85% and the increase in tensile strength was insignificant from 0.86 to 0.89 MPa. The gelatine-only bioplastic was hydrophilic. Gelatine-based bioplastic is clear, and it feels and looks more like conventional plastics compared to the ones made from starch. Sorbitol and microcrystalline cellulose can be added to starch-based bioplastics to improve their mechanical properties (Marichelvam et al., 2022).

The amount of gelatine added when producing the bioplastics decreases the tensile strength and the moisture content while it increases the density of the bioplastic (Marichelvam et al., 2022). This put a constraint on the amount of gelatine used, in this study 4 ml of glycerol was added to 1000 ml of distilled water to create a solution to which gelatine is later added. Decreasing the glycerol would have made the plastic stronger but less flexible. For the starch-based bioplastics, increasing the glycerol would have made the plastic weaker.

Because of the hydrophilic characteristic of gelatine-based bioplastic, it degrades faster as seen on the mass loss graphs. The gelatine placed in the water had disintegrated within the first week in both the 25°C and room temperature environments. The amount of moisture/water available affects the disintegration period of gelatine-based bioplastics. This limits the use of gelatine-based bioplastics because there is a need for plastics to be water-resistant. The produced bioplastic was not hydrophobic because the plasticizer used which was glycerol is a hydrophilic plasticizer like ethylene glycol, sorbitol, diethylene glycol and xylitol (Suderman et al., 2018). Using hydrophobic plasticizers would change the functional groups of the bioplastics and thus improve their resistance to water. Starch-based bioplastics can last longer in water.

When they degrade, they start by absorbing the moisture/water, and then they start degrading when they are saturated with water. The mass loss was higher in the room temperature environment because the average temperature was higher than 25 °C. Photodegradation has played a role in this instance because the samples were allowed to degrade where the sunlight reached. This shows that biodegradation is faster in higher temperatures (Folino et al., 2020).

The biodegradation process of bioplastics takes place in steps, SEM was used to monitor physical changes to the surface of the bioplastics. Fungi were seen on the surface of the bioplastics as fibres, the fibres accompanied by the fragmentation of the samples represent the first stage of biodegradation. Microorganisms secrete enzymes and other catalytic agents which help to reduce the molecular weight of the samples. This explains the purple/black colour seen on the surface of the bioplastics. There is a trade-off between the performance of the bioplastics and their biodegradability. Since it is important to produce bioplastics that can last longer in water, are flexible, and are strong, it is important to have blends of bioplastics and other materials that can improve performance. Because corn starch is an important food source, it is important to investigate the use of waste material from the production of corn starch as the main ingredient in the production of bioplastics.

The bioplastics underwent aerobic degradation because of the presence of oxygen. The products of this biodegradation process were carbon dioxide, water, biomass, and carbon residual (Shah & Alshehrei, 2017). These products can improve the quality of the soil when they degrade and return organic nutrients. The bioplastics had single films and thus biodegraded faster. Properties like water content, chemical composition and pH of the soil, water and compost affected the biodegradation of the bioplastics (Viera et al., 2021).

The application of gelatine-based bioplastics is limited because they are not resistant to water. Most plastic applications (grocery bags and containers) require bioplastic to be resistant to water to protect the products inside and to be able to support the product's weight. Although the gelatine-based bioplastic has a high tensile strength, its uses will be limited unless it is blended with other renewable materials to improve its water resistance and waterproofing. The starch-based and hybrid-based bioplastics sheets were used to produce bags to replace conventional plastic bags. The problem encountered here was the lowered strength of the bags, they were unable to carry a load of 1 kg without breaking (seen by the low tensile strength and strain). These bioplastics were resistant to water but not waterproof which limits their use. The starch-based bioplastics absorb and retain water because the glycerol molecules have a higher affinity for water, thus the addition of fructose which acts as a water-resistant agent can improve the bioplastics' waters resistance (Abotbina et al., 2021).

6. Conclusion

In this study, bioplastics were produced from corn starch, gelatine and a mixture of both using water and glycerol as the plasticizers. The gelatine-based bioplastic was weak in water compared to the starch-based bioplastics and completely disintegrated before the five-week period was complete, which indicated that the addition of a water-insoluble plasticizer could have reduced the time to complete disintegration. The benefit of the gelatine-based bioplastic was its higher tensile strength which indicated a better functional use in day-today applications. Mixing starch and gelatine to produce bioplastic only improved the elongation, but still completely disintegrated within the first few weeks. The mass of the starch-only and hybrid-based bioplastic had better resistance to degradation compared to the gelatine bioplastic. The mass initially increased during the first week because the samples were absorbing the moisture that was present in the soil and compost. After the absorption stage (once the bioplastics were saturated), the mass decreased of the samples decreased and started to degrade due to the activity of microorganisms. The samples in compost showed faster biodegradation compared to the samples in soil and water which could have been to the already present microorganisms. Microorganisms like fungi were seen on the surface of the bioplastics using SEM. Biodegradation is faster in high temperatures and moist conditions.

REFERENCES

1. Abotbina, W., Sapuan, S. M., Sultan, M. T. H., Alkbir, M. F. M., & Ilyas, R. A. (2021). Development and characterization of cornstarch-based bioplastics packaging film using a combination of different plasticizers. *Polymers*, *13*(20), 3487–3505. https://doi.org/doi.org/10.3390/polym13203487
2. Ali, S. K., & Saleh, A. M. (2012). Spirulina - An overview. In *International Journal of Pharmacy and Pharmaceutical Sciences* (Vol. 4, Issue SUPPL.3). https://doi.org/10.1201/9780203025901.ch14
3. Atiwesh, G., Mikhael, A., Parrish, C. C., Banoub, J., & Le, T. A. T. (2021). Environmental impact of bioplastic use: A review. *Heliyon*, *7*(9). https://doi.org/10.1016/j.heliyon.2021.e07918
4. Emadian, S. M., Onay, T. T., & Demirel, B. (2017). Biodegradation of bioplastics in natural environments. In *Waste Management* (Vol. 59, pp. 526–536). https://doi.org/10.1016/j.wasman.2016.10.006
5. Folino, A., Karageorgiou, A., Calabrò, P. S., & Komilis, D. (2020). Biodegradation of wasted bioplastics in natural and industrial environments: A review. *Sustainability (Switzerland)*, *12*(15). https://doi.org/10.3390/su12156030
6. Harding, K. G., Gounden, T., & Pretorius, S. (2017). "Biodegradable" Plastics: A Myth of Marketing? *Procedia Manufacturing*, *7*, 106–110. https://doi.org/10.1016/J.PROMFG.2016.12.027
7. Iñiguez, M. E., Conesa, J. A., & Fullana, A. (2018). Recyclability of four types of plastics exposed to UV irradiation in a marine environment. *Waste Management*, *79*, 339–345. https://doi.org/10.1016/j.wasman.2018.08.006
8. Marichelvam, M. K., Manimaran, P., Sanjay, M. R., Siengchin, S., Geetha, M., Kandakodeeswaran, K., Boonyasopon, P., & Gorbatyuk, S. (2022). Extraction and development of starch-based bioplastics from Prosopis Juliflora Plant: Eco-friendly and sustainability aspects. *Current Research in Green and Sustainable Chemistry*, *5*. https://doi.org/10.1016/j.crgsc.2022.100296
9. Mroczkowska, M., Culliton, D., Germaine, K., & Neves, A. (2021). Comparison of Mechanical and Physicochemical Characteristics of Potato Starch and Gelatine Blend Bioplastics Made with Gelatines from Different Sources. *Clean Technologies*, *3*(2), 424–436. https://doi.org/10.3390/cleantechnol3020024
10. Namazi, H., & Dadkhah, A. (2010). Convenient method for preparation of hydrophobically modified starch nanocrystals with using fatty acids. *Carbohydrate Polymers*, *79*(3), 731–737. https://doi.org/10.1016/j.carbpol.2009.09.033
11. Peña, C., de la Caba, K., Eceiza, A., Ruseckaite, R., & Mondragon, I. (2010). Enhancing water repellence and mechanical properties of gelatin films by tannin addition. *Bioresource Technology*, *101*(17), 6836–6842. https://doi.org/10.1016/j.biortech.2010.03.112
12. Rahman, M. H., & Bhoi, P. R. (2021). An overview of non-biodegradable bioplastics. In *Journal of Cleaner Production* (Vol. 294). https://doi.org/10.1016/j.jclepro.2021.126218
13. Ruggero, F., Onderwater, R. C. A., Carretti, E., Roosa, S., Benali, S., Raquez, J. M., Gori, R., Lubello, C., & Wattiez, R. (2021). Degradation of Film and Rigid Bioplastics During the Thermophilic Phase and the Maturation Phase of Simulated Composting. *Journal of Polymers and the Environment*, *29*(9), 3015–3028. https://doi.org/10.1007/s10924-021-02098-2
14. Shah, A., & Alshehrei, F. (2017). Biodegradation of Synthetic and Natural Plastic by Microorganisms. *Journal of Applied & Environmental Microbiology*, *5*(1), 8–19. https://doi.org/10.12691/jaem-5-1-2
15. Suderman, N., Isa, M. I. N., & Sarbon, N. M. (2018). The effect of plasticizers on the functional properties of biodegradable gelatin-based film: A review. In *Food Bioscience* (Vol. 24, pp. 111–119). https://doi.org/10.1016/j.fbio.2018.06.006
16. Tan, S. X., Ong, H. C., Andriyana, A., Lim, S., Pang, Y. L., Kusumo, F., & Ngoh, G. C. (2022). Characterization and Parametric Study on Mechanical Properties Enhancement in Biodegradable Chitosan-Reinforced Starch-Based Bioplastic Film. *Polymers*, *14*(2). https://doi.org/10.3390/polym14020278
17. Viera, J. S. C., Marques, M. R. C., Nazareth, M. C., Jimenez, P. C., Sanz-Lázaro, C., & Castro, Í. B. (2021). Are biodegradable plastics an environmental rip off? *Journal of Hazardous Materials*, *416*. https://doi.org/10.1016/j.jhazmat.2021.125957
18. Zeller, M. A., Hunt, R., Jones, A., & Sharma, S. (2013). Bioplastics and their thermoplastic blends from Spirulina and Chlorella microalgae. *Journal of Applied Polymer Science*, *130*(5), 3263–3275. https://doi.org/10.1002/app.39559

Note: All the figures in this chapter were compiled by the author.

Sustainable Materials Processing and Manufacturing – Lin Zhu et al. (eds)
© 2024 Taylor & Francis Group, London, ISBN 978-1-032-88599-5

Design of an Automatic Soya Beans Cake-Cutting Machine

Olayinka Olaogun[1], Samuel Faleti[2],
Abdulrasaq Lawal[3]
Department of Mechanical Engineering, Faculty of Engineering,
Kwara State University, Malete, Nigeria

ABSTRACT: Due to price rises, there is a growing shift from animal proteins towards plant-based, health-focused products like soya bean cake. COVID-19 pandemic has aided this trend. Despite its high protein content, which improves the product's quality, soya bean cake is not widely accepted as a meat substitute due to its texture, cut, and packaging. Manual cake cutting is taxing on the operators especially for extending cutting periods. Automating the process is crucial for overcoming these challenges. This work focuses on the design of an automated soya bean cake-cutting machine minimizing waste to improve cutting effectiveness and quality. The automation was based on a pneumatic double-acting cylinder actuator and an ultrasonic proximity sensor. Multi-criteria decision matrix was used to select an optimum concept. Design analysis and motion simulation of the selected model was simulated using ANSYS Workbench, a commercial simulation software. The accessories and fittings that constitute the control system for automation were selected based on simulation data. When the sensor detects the presence of soya bean cake, the pneumatic cylinder is actuated, which forces the connected pressing plate, coupled with the coagulation plate and cutting mesh to press and cut the cake uniformly. The pressing and cutting of the soya bean cake were analysed to be achieved within 80 seconds producing 16 pieces of cuts at a production rate of 720 cakes per hour. The machine design was concluded safe and will help reduce manual labour input and ensure adequate packaging with proper hygiene.

KEYWORDS: Pneumatic double acting cylinder, Ultrasonic proximity sensor, Coagulation plate, Cutting mesh, Multi-criteria decision matrix

1. Introduction

The development of cutting machines over the years has made remarkable strides; this is driven by the rising number of product launches and the steady growth of the manufacturing industry. The machine has a wide usage, primarily for cutting an item into layers. Obtaining an effective cutting depends on the item's thickness, properties as well as design of the cutting machine (ReportLinker, 2022). Cutting operation requires separating items into a predefined geometry; thus, measures need to be in place in terms of both worker and product safety (Demetrakekes, 2019). Manual cake cutting is taxing on the operators especially for extending cutting periods, which offers low productivity (Dinesh et al. 2017). A wide range of food products with various components, textures, and structures, pose enormous challenges to conventional cake cutting. Some processing parameters have a significant impact on how well the cutting performs, and choosing the right ones generally involves trial-and-error or empirical methods, which waste time and resources (Demetrakekes, 2019; Xu et al. 2022). For these reasons, new and more efficient cutting methods have been developed and introduced. The modern trend in the food industry is to automate machine operations. As demand increases in the food industry, so does the need

[1]yinka.olaoluwa@live.com, [2]samphalet2030@gmail.com, [3]aarskl.la@gmail.com

DOI: 10.1201/9781003538646-11

to use technology to find efficient ways to manufacture processing machines. Advancement in technology focuses on the creation of series of mechanisms, equipment and machines that meet a certain functionality, which facilitates and improves the creation of different products. Such equipment must comply with safety and hygiene standards. This ensures the quality of the final finished product (Edwin et al. 2018). It is well acknowledged nowadays that automation increases productivity, output uniformity, quality, and process robustness (Vilumsone-Nemes, 2018; Babu1 et al. 2015; Olukorede et al. 2014). Pneumatics as a channel of automation is economically cheap and easy to handle; hence, its utilization in production of protein rich soya-beans cake is a welcome development. However, recent economic issues and trends together with the COVID 19 pandemic have led to a rise in the prices of well-known sources of protein, such as animal proteins - pork, chicken, beef, and so on. As a result, there is a growing trend toward plant-based and health-focused products like soya bean cake rather than these animal-derived proteins. Factors, such as price, availability, suitability, and functional properties are also affecting this demand (Haque et al. 2016; Malav et al. 2015; Hoek et al. 2013). Soya beans are an inexpensive and excellent source of protein with high nutritional value. It produces so many edible commodities such as soya bean cake, soya milk and soya sauce. Soya bean cake is an easily prepared and tasty snack made from blended soya beans with a gel-like high absorbing structure. It can be spiced, dressed, and deep-fried. It serves as a substitute for meat and a food supplement, which provides dietary elements for optimal health; therefore, its consumption is encouraged (Akpomie et al. 2020; Aletor et al. 2007; Kyriakopoulou et al. 2019). However, soya bean cake is not yet widely accepted as a substitute due to its texture, cut, exposure to unhygienic

conditions and packaging, which all contribute to the product's quality (Hoek et al. 2011; Faluyi et al. 2019). Thus, the purpose of this design, to reveal an alternative method to manual cake cutting, ensuring the cake is now appealing and acceptable by people.

2. Structural Design of Soya Bean Cutting Machine

2.1 Design Requirement

To achieve the design aim, there is a need to satisfy the following requirements as shown in Table 11.1 below:

2.2 Concept Development and Configuration

Comprehensive literature research is conducted to determine the state of the art in soya beans cake production. The production process of soya bean cake is relatively not complex. The concerned aspect is the compression and cutting process basically achieved manually. Hence, the design of an automated soya bean cake-cutting machine will compress and simultaneously cut uniformly the soya bean cake, minimizing waste to improve cutting effectiveness, quality, and packaging. Various designs were proposed to offer the flexibility of pressing and cutting of the soya beans extract gel into uniform cakes. Two designs out of the proposed designs were focused on. For design 1, horizontal arrangement was considered. The mechanism for cutting the soya beans cake is a straight cutter blade positioned in a two-dimensional space (X-axis/Y-axis). The cutter movement is powered by 2 fixed motors. A conveyor aids the movement of the cakes. The cakes are collected below the machine chamber through the collecting channel. A slot design is used

Table 11.1 Design requirement

S/N	Requirement	Description
1	Cost	Moderate – the cost of the machine should be within the buying capacity of users.
2	Ergonomics	Moderate size, Aesthetic viability, easily accessibility, properly positioning of parts, Simplicity in user interaction with displays and controls, Height of the machine should match with the user for operation, Less noise.
3	Safety, quality, and hygiene	Versatile, Easy to use, Adequate protection of moving components, Sensor imposed, Detachable for easy cleaning and maintenance, Suitable food handling material.
4	Functionality	The equipment should cut the soya bean cake efficiently.
5	Availability	The machine should be made with readily available materials
6	Performance	It should reduce labor input in manual cake cutting
7	Capacity	The capacity should be higher compared to manual cake cutting
8	Design for manufacturing and Assembly	Simplified design and reduced number of components, all components or sub-assemblies should fit into each other to make the final assembly. Ease of assembling and disassembling for the sake of servicing and maintenance.

Source: Edwin, E.B., Armando, Q.A., Carlos, A.P., (2018). Design of an Automated Cheese Cutting Machine Prototype. Contemporary Engineering Sciences,11(101), 5005- 5015. https://doi.org/10.12988/ces.2018.810548z

Table 11.2 Decision matrix for the soya beans cake cutting machine

Criteria	Design 1		Design 2	
Design Scope [5]	Cutting only	[2 x 5]	Both Pressing and Cutting	[4 x 5]
Complexity [4]	Lots of parts and quite complex design.	[2 x 4]	Not very complex design	[3 x 4]
Manufacturability [5]	No very high accuracy and tolerances needed in fabrication. However, the shapes to be cut is limited though the cutters can be adjusted.	[3 x 5]	High level of precision and accuracy needed. Various shapes and sizes can be cut based on the geometry of the cutting mesh.	[3 x 5]
Processing time [4]	Not very fast as it requires both vertical and horizontal cutting to get the desired sizes.	[3 x 4]	Very fast as it cut the cakes at once.	[4 x 5]
Stability [4]	Low in height	[4 x 4]	The height is quite high.	[3 x 4]
Cost [5]	Costly – based on its complexity.	[2 x 5]	Moderate - Not so costly considering parts.	[3 x 5]
Feeding system [3]	Manual	[1 x 3]	Automatic – Push from pneumatic actuator through the pressing plate	[2 x 3]
Total	74		100	

Marks: 5 = excellent   4 = very good   3 = good   2 = intermediate   1 = poor
Source: Dr Rafiq Elmansy, (2022). How to Use the Decision Matrix to Make Decisions? https://www.designorate.com/decision-matrix-decision-making/

to feed in the soya beans gel manually. Design 2, consists of a pneumatic double-acting cylinder actuator, pressing plate, coagulation plate, and cutting mesh. As soon as the pneumatic cylinder actuates, the pressing plate is forced to contact both the coagulation plate and cutting mesh bringing about pressing and cutting. Multi-criteria decision matrix (MCDM) was used to evaluate a set of options against a set of criteria to select the optimum concept. Marks were given for each criterion in achieving a better design prototype. Table 11.4 shows the decision matrix. From the analysis, design 2 has the highest mark and was selected. To further enhances the design and control of the machine system, an ultrasonic proximity sensor is introduced.

When the sensor detects the presence of the soya beans gel, the pneumatic cylinder is actuated, forcing the connected pressing plate with the coagulation plate/cutting mesh to press, and cut uniformly.

2.3 Design Specifications

Identifying precisely what a product must satisfy is essential. (Richard G. Budynas, and J. Keith Nisbett, 2012). The following specifications provide an appropriate framework for this design task:

- Compressor is used for driving system and must be able to provide an ample power needed by the pneumatic cylinder actuator.
- Able to uniformly cut soya beans cake based on the geometry of the cutting mesh with minimal waste (Waste Rate: 2% - 5%)
- Integration of a main panel for all electrical and electronic elements for the control of the operation.

- Use of non-corrosive and non-toxic materials.
- Semi-automatic and automatic handling
- Machine height between 0.8 m – 1.2 m
- Moisture Content: 15% - 30% (Experimental - using Moisture Analyzer)
- Cut product Output: $44.5 \times 47.1 \times 20 = 41919$ mm^3
- Number of cakes per cut: 16 cakes
- Pressing time - 60 Secs, Dwelling time - 30 Secs, Cutting time - 30 Secs, Processing time - 120 seconds
- Capacity per hour: 720 pieces

2.4 Material Selection Criteria

Material selection is of utmost importance to ensure that the components designed meet design requirements. Since some component parts of the automated soya bean cake-cutting machine would be subjected to varying forms and degrees of loading, the material with the appropriate engineering property was chosen (Arunkumar et al. 2020). The materials selected were based on the design requirements and specifications. Due to economic considerations, food processing hygiene, and availability of raw materials, Stainless steel is chosen for product contacting parts and Perspex is used for the collector to appreciate the see-through characteristics. The pneumatic cylinder is procured based on specifications. - Stainless steel is used for product contacting parts and Perspex is used for the collector to appreciate the see-through characteristics.

2.5 Design of the Machine System

The design of the automatic soya beans cake cutting machine was modelled using SolidWorks. The simulation of the selected models was done using a commercial simulation software - ANSYS. The accessories and fittings that constitute the control system for automation were selected based on simulation.

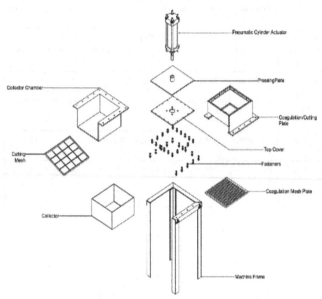

Fig. 11.1 Component parts of the machine system
Note: Figure is generated from solid works. Own work

3. Components of the Automatic Soya Beans Cake Cutting Machine

3.1 Pneumatic Cylinder Actuator

The pneumatic cylinder brings about the pressing and cutting of the soya bean cake. The movement of the piston is triggered by compressed air controlled by a directional valve (Festo, n.d.). The direction is defined by a chamber into which the compressed air is allowed to follow inside the cylinder. The force is transferred by the piston rod. The actuator consists of two ports. A control medium of the air flow pressure was introduced. This includes the pressure regulator, pressure sensor and an orifice introduced at each port as a reducer.

Selection and sizing of the pneumatic cylinder actuator

Parameters considered in the sizing of the pneumatic cylinder actuator include:

Cutting Force

$$Cutting\ force = VT_{max} \qquad (1)$$

where

$V = A \times S$

$V = Volume\ of\ the\ cake\ to\ be\ cut\ in\ mm^3$

$A = Area\ of\ the\ cake$

$S = Product\ thickness\ or\ depth\ in\ mm$

$T_{max} = shear\ strength\ of\ the\ cake\ in\ \dfrac{N}{mm^2}$

Note: Shear strength is 80% of tensile strength.

Striping force = 10% – 20% of cutting force

Press force = Cutting force + striping force

$$Working\ force\ (E) = \rho Vg \qquad (2)$$

where

$\rho = product\ density;$

$V = volume\ of\ the\ product\ and;$

$g = gravity = 9.81\dfrac{m}{s^2}$

The force generated by a cylinder depends on the operating pressure, diameter of the cylinder & piston rod, and friction of the inner parts.

Thus,

Diameter of piston rod (D) = 16 mm (Based on the pressing plate which is to be attached)

Diameter of cylinder (d) = 40 mm (Based on design chart)

$$Effective\ Area\ (A) = \frac{\pi D^2}{4} - \frac{\pi d^2}{4} = \frac{\pi(40)^2}{4} -$$

$$\frac{\pi(16)^2}{4} = 1055.7\,mm^2$$

Selected Operating pressure (P) = 6 bar = 0.6 N/mm^2

Force = P * A = 0.6 * 1055.7 = 633.42 N

Due to system friction between the piston and the cylinder, the theoretically available (or actual) force is usually a fraction of the total available force. These losses are usually accounted for using an efficiency fraction, η. The theoretically available force can be calculated using:

$$F = A * P * \eta$$

where

$\eta = efficiency\ factor$

However, as rule of thumb 5% can be deducted for friction. Therefore, the cylinder can exert a force of approximately 602N.

Hence,

$$F = M * g$$

$$M = \frac{602}{9.81} = 61.37\,kg$$

Therefore, the cylinder can hold a mass of about 62 kg.

Yield stress, $\sigma_y = 37\,kgf/mm^2 = 362.97\,N/mm^2$

Factor of Safety, n = 2   (Gujar et al. 2013)

$$Design\ stress = \frac{\sigma_y}{n} = \frac{362.97}{2} = 181.485\,N$$

Other factors considered are:

- *Air Consumption: This has two factors: the volume of air displaced by the piston during operation and the volume of contaminated air that passes through valves, ports, tubing, and cavities. A pneumatic cylinder capable of supplying air even in a worst-case scenario was considered to guarantee optimal performance.*
- *The mass of the item to be actuated.*
- *The distance the object must move (stroke length)*
- *The speed of actuation*

3.2 Ultrasonic Sensor

An ultrasonic sensor detects the presence of the soya beans cake without any physical contact causing the actuation of the pneumatic cylinder. The efficiency is highly tolerant of dirt. It calculates the distance to be moved by the piston. The output from the sensor is processed using a microcontroller. The results from the microcontroller are signaled to the users and fed to the LCD display.

3.3 Collection Chamber

It accommodates the collector.

Fig. 11.2   Collection chamber

Note: Figure is generated from solid works. Own work

3.4 Collector

The collector is a receptacle for the collection of both the moisture and the cakes. The top of the collector is opened for easy displacement of items.

3.5 Pressing Plate

This is the unit attached to the piston rod of the pneumatic cylinder, which brings about both the pressing and cutting. The sizing of the pressing plate is based on the geometry of the coagulation/cutting chamber and the load required to press and cut.

Fig. 11.3   Pressing plate

Note: Figure is generated from solid works. Own work

3.6 Coagulation Plate

The coagulation plate brings about effective pressing separating moisture from the soya beans extract through the mesh. The plate is located inside the coagulation/cutting chamber. After pressing, the plate is removed and replaced with the cutting mesh.

Fig. 11.4   Coagulation mesh plate

Note: Figure is generated from solid works. Own work

3.7 Cutting Mesh

The cutting mesh cuts into uniform cakes. The mesh sizes were determined based on the product dimension of observed cakes done manually. The edges of the cutting mesh were designed like a knife edge to ensure easy cutting, flexibility, and minimal waste.

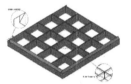

Fig. 11.5   Cutting mesh

Note: Figure is generated from solid works. Own work

3.8 Coagulation/Cutting Chamber

The chamber encloses both the coagulation plate and the cutting mesh. It offers flexibility to users without injuries.

Fig. 11.6   Coagulation/Cutting chamber

Note: Figure is generated from solid works. Own work

Other component parts include Top plate, Solenoid valve, Arduino (UNO) microcontroller, LCD display, FESTO Pneumatic fittings, Pressure Sensor, and Regulator etc.

4. Part Analysis (Finite Element Analysis – FEA)

It is imperative that a design should have a sufficient resistance against failure though it is not always possible to alter the operational loading to suit the design concept (Yuo-Tem Tsai et al. 2012). To assure a workable design, finite element analysis was done on some selected models. The behavior of these parts of the machine were simulated and analyzed under cyclic loading using ANSYS Workbench. A mesh convergence analysis was carried out for various mesh sizes to determine the optimum mesh size for the FEM solution. A mesh size of 5 mm is used.

Table 11.3 Convergence of the FEM result with respect to mesh size

Mesh Size	12	9	5	2.5
Cycles (10^7)	100.21	92.78	10	5.96

Figure 11.7 shows the S-N curve of the material which describes the relation between cyclic stress amplitude and number of cycles to fail given on a logarithmic scale. Cyclic stress with constant amplitude was applied on the material until failure which was stopped at $N = 10^6$ (Endurance limit).

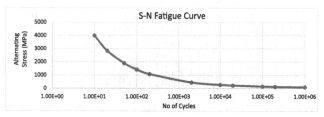

Fig. 11.7 S-N Fatigue Curve of the material used.

Note: Figure is generated for present work

4.1 Pressing Plate

The geometry of the pressing plate was fully defined. A static loading analysis was performed to prove that the stress due to load is far below the yield point of the material (Kurowski, 2015). A repeated point pressure load of 50 MPa was applied. The pressing plate has an average equivalent stress of 34.898 MPa. Fig.11.8(a) shows the minimum and maximum Von Mises stress values which was compared to the allowable stress of the material based on yield strength and ultimate strength. The pressing plate has a yield strength and ultimate strength of 250 MPa and 460 MPa respectively. From the analysis, the minimum equivalent (von-mises) stress of the pressing plate is 21.639 MPa and a maximum of 167.4 MPa. Comparing the maximum Von Mises stress with the yield strength shows a design that is acceptable considering the design criterion that says Von Mises stress of a design must be less than the yielding strength of the material (Khurmi et al. 2005; David et al 2018). The Fatigue Sensitivity was determined using Goodman as the mean stress theory. A zero-based constant amplitude was assumed. The fatigue life shows the available life for a given fatigue analysis representing the number of cycles until failure due to fatigue (Vidhya et al. 2020).

Figure 11.8(c) shows that the minimum fatigue life of the pressing plate is 49234 cycles i.e., the pressing plate will fail after 49234 cycles. Fig. 11.8(d) shows that maximum damage will occur at the upper tip of the pressing plate with a value of 20,311. Fig. 11.8(f) shows the equivalent alternating

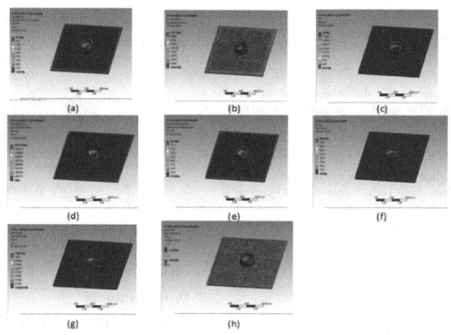

Fig. 11.8 (a) Equivalent (Von Mises) Stress; (b) Biaxiality Indication; (c) Life; (d) Damage; (e) Total Deformation; (f) Equivalent Alternating Stress; (g) Strain Energy (h) Safety Factor

Note: Figure is generated from ANSYS Workbench. Own Work.

stress with maximum value of 167.4 MPa which occurs at the upper tip of the pressing plate. The equivalent alternating stress expresses the stress used to query the fatigue S-N curve after accounting for fatigue loading type, mean stress effects, multiaxial effects, and other factors in the fatigue analysis (Sinan Köksal, 2013). Fig. 11.8(g) shows the fatigue factor of safety at $1x10^9$ cycles design life. The minimum value occurs at the lower tip of the pressing plate as 1.4934, which is approximately 2 i.e., the pressing plate can withstand twice the prescribed load before failure begins) which indicates a better design (Gujar, 2013). The sensitivity of the model's life was observed taking load changes from 50% (lower variation) of the current load up to 150% (upper variation) of the current load. It was deduced from the figure that when the load is increased up to 150%, the life decreases to 11566 cycles.

4.2 Coagulation Plate

The coagulation plate has a mass of 2.1 kg with an average surface area of 119,96 mm^2. A repeated uniformly distributed pressure load of 50 MPa was applied. A zero-based constant amplitude was assumed. Fig. 11.9(a) shows that the coagulation plate will fail after 1000000 cycles. Fig. 11.9(b) shows the minimum and maximum Von Mises stress values. The values were compared to the yield strength and ultimate strength of the material which is 250 MPa and 460 MPa respectively. The mesh plate has an average equivalent stress of 37.261 MPa with a minimum equivalent stress of 23.275 MPa and a maximum of 71.894 MPa, which shows a better design. Goodman mean stress correction theory was used to

determine fatigue sensitivity. Fig. 11.9(c) shows the fatigue factor of safety at $1x10^9$ cycles design life. The minimum value is 1.199, which indicates failure after the design life is reached (Vidhya et al. 2020). Fig. 11.9(f) shows fatigue damage, the maximum damage occurs all through the plate with a value of 1000.

The sensitivity of the model's life was observed taking load changes from 50% (lower variation) of the current load up to 150% (upper variation) of the current load. It was deduced from the figure that when the load is increased up to 150%, the life decreases to 275380 cycles. It was observed from the fatigue sensitivity graph that as the loading increases the average life of the component decreases.

4.3 Cutting Mesh

The geometry was fully defined. It has a mass of 0.84 kg with a volume of 1.07×10^5 mm^3. The cutting mesh will cut 16 pieces of cake at a time. A uniformly distributed pressure load of -5 MPa (ramped - z component) was applied for the simulation. A zero-based constant amplitude was assumed with a minimum biaxiality indication of -0.40388 and maximum of 0.27233. Fig. 11.10(a) shows that the cutting mesh will fail after 1000000 cycles. The mesh has an average equivalent stress of 17.313 MPa with a minimum and maximum Von Mises stresses of 3.958 MPa and 26.897 MPa respectively. Goodman mean stress correction theory was used to determine fatigue sensitivity. Fig. 11.10(c) shows the fatigue factor of safety at 1×10^9 cycles design life. The minimum value is 3.2048. Fig. 11.10(f) shows fatigue damage. The maximum damage occurs at a value of 1000.

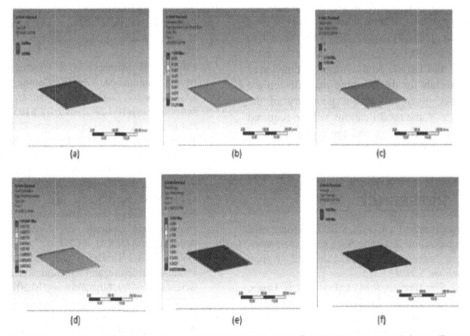

(a) (b) (c)

(d) (e) (f)

Fig. 11.9 (a) Life; (b) Equivalent (Von Mises) Stress; (c) Safety factor; (d) Total deformation; (e) Strain Energy (g) Damage
Note: Figure is generated from ANSYS Workbench. Own Work.

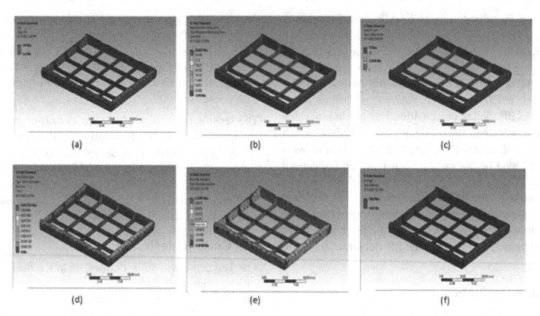

Fig. 11.10 (a) Life; (b) Equivalent Alternating Stress; (c) Safety factor; (d) Total Deformation; (e) Biaxiality indication (f) Damage

Note: Figure is generated from ANSYS Workbench. Own Work.

The sensitivity of the model's life was observed taking load changes from 50% of the current load up to 150% of the current load. It was deduced from the figure that when the load is increased up to 150%, the line graph remains at 1000000 cycles appearing as a straight line.

5. Conclusion

The machine was successfully designed starting with the conceptual development which was achieved through the multi criteria decision matrix. Finite element analysis was conducted on some selected parts using ANSYS Workbench to ensure that the machine works as desired. Based on the result from the static study and fatigue study, it can be concluded that the selected materials for the machine parts design are suitable. However, for other subsequent geometry of the cake with uniform size, some modifications will be required in the coagulation/cutting chamber and the replacement of coagulation plate with the cutting mesh in relationship with the product.

REFERENCE

1. Akpomie, T., Ogungbemiro, F., Anwani, S., (2020). Nutritional and elemental composition of awara (Soya bean cake) snack eaten in northern Nigeria. *International Journal of Food Science and Nutrition, 5(2), 113-115.*

2. Arunkumar, G.S., Siva Bharath, R.M., Lakshmi, S.S., James, M.I., (2020). Design and development of automatic sheet metal cutting machine. https://doi.org/10.1063/5.0034349

3. Aletor, O., Ojelabi, A., (2017). Comparative Evaluation of the Nutritive and Functional Attributes of Some Traditional Nigerian Snacks and Oil Seed Cakes. *Pakistan Journal of Nutrition, 6(1), 99-103.*

4. Babul, M.V.S., Rama Krishna, A., and K.N.S. Suman, K.N.S. (2015). Review of Journal Bearing Materials and Current Trends. *American Journal of Materials Science and Technology, 4(2),72-83.*

5. David, A., Barsanescu, P.D., Comanici, A.M., (2018). About the sensitivity to hydrostatic pressure of Mohr-Coulomb criterion with circular failure envelope, dedicated to ductile materials. *IOP Conference Series: Materials Science and Engineering PAPER* 400.

6. Dinesh, L., Akash, N., Rahul, C., Ajay, M., (2017). International Research Journal of Engineering and Technology, pp.1024-1032.

7. Edwin, E.B., Armando, Q.A., Carlos, A.P., (2018). Design of an Automated Cheese Cutting Machine Prototype. *Contemporary Engineering Sciences,11(101), 5005- 5015.* https://doi.org/10.12988/ces.2018.810548z

8. Faluyi, O., Opadoja, D., Adedoyin, R.A., (2019). Design and Fabrication of Soya Milk Extracting Machine. *International Journal of Engineering Research & Technology (IJERT). 8(9).*

9. FESTO – *Automation Technology, Pneumatics and electrical components.* www.festo.com/catalogue

10. Gujar, R.A., and Bhaskar, S.V., (2013). Shaft Design under Fatigue Loading by Using Modified Goodman Method. *International Journal of Engineering Research and Applications (IJERA). 3 1061–6.*

11. Haque M.A., Timilsena Y.P., Adhikari B., (2016). Food Proteins, Structure, and Function, Reference Module in Food Science. *Elsevier.* https://doi.org/10.1016/B978-0-08-100596-5.03057-2

12. Hoek, A.C., Elzerman, J.E., Hageman, R., Kok, F.J., Luning, P.A., de Graaf, C., (2013). Are meat substitutes liked better over time. A repeated in-home use test with meat substitutes

or meat in meals. *Food Quality and Preference 28, 253e263.* https://doi.org/10.1016/j.foodqual.2012.07.002

13. Hoek A.C., Luning P.A., Weijzen P., Engels W., Kok F.J., de Graaf C., (2011). *Replacement of meat-by-meat substitutes. A survey on person- and product-related factors in consumer acceptance appetite.* 56, 662e673. https://doi.org/10.1016/j.appet.2011.02.001

14. Khurmi, R.S., Gupta, J.K., (2005). A Textbook of Machine Design (S.I. Units), Vol 45. *Eurasia Publishing House (PVT.) LTD.*

15. Kurowski, P.M., (2015). Engineering Analysis with SOLIDWORKS' Simulation.

16. Kyriakopoulou, K., Dekkers, B.L., Van der Goot, A.J., (2019). Chapter 6 - Plant-Based Meat Analogues. *Sustainable Meat Production and Processing. 103-126.*

17. Malav, O.P., Talukder, S., Gokulakrishnan. P.,Chand S., (2015*).* Meat analog: A review. Critical Reviews in Food Science and Nutrition 55,1241e1245 https://doi.org/10.1080/10408398.2012.689381.

18. Olukorede, T.A., Khumbulani, M., (2014). Control system for electro-hydraulic synchronization on RBPT. *Procedia CIRP 17: 835 – 840.*

19. Pan Demetrakekes, (2019). Automation Makes Meat Cutting Faster Safer. *The Magazine of the Food Industry.* https://www.foodprocessing.com/.

20. ReportLinker, (2022). Global Industrial Food Cutting Machines Market 2023-2027 (Report ID. 5060888). *Infiniti Research Limited.* http://www.reportlinker.com/p05060888/Global-Industrial-Food-Cutting-Machines-Market.html.

21. Richard G. Budynas, and J. Keith Nisbett, (2012). Shigley's, Mechanical Engineering Design, Ninth Edition.

21. Sinan Köksal, N., Kayapunar, A., Çevik, M., (2013). Fatigue Analysis of a Notched Cantilever Beam Using Ansys Workbench, *pp.111-118.*

23. Vidhya, M.S., and K V Merlyn Christina, K.V., (2020). Fatigue Life, Fatigue Damage, Fatigue Factor of Safety, Fatigue Sensitivity, Bixaiality Indication and Equivalent stress of a Radial connecting rod. *IRJET. Vol: 07.*

24. Vilumsone-Nemes,. I. (2018). Industrial Cutting of Textile Materials. *Elsevier.* https://doi.org/10.1016/B978-0-08-102122-4.00009-3.

25. Xu, W., Wang, J., Deng, Y., Li, J., Yan, T., Zhao, S., Yang, X., Xu, E., Wang, W., Donghong Liu, D., (2022). Comprehensive Reviews in Food Science and Food Safety, Advanced cutting techniques for solid food: Mechanisms, applications, modeling approaches, and future perspectives. 21(2), 1568-1590. https://ift.onlinelibrary.wiley.com/doi/pdf/10.1111/1541-4337.12896.

26. Yuo-Tem Tsai, Y., Kuo-Shong, W., and Jeng-Chung, W., (2012). Fatigue life and reliability evaluation for dental implants based on computer simulation and limited test data. *Journal of Mechanical Engineering Science, 2013227.* DOI: 10.1177/0954406212463532

Sustainable Materials Processing and Manufacturing – Lin Zhu et al. (eds)
© 2024 Taylor & Francis Group, London, ISBN 978-1-032-88599-5

Investigating Settleability Properties of Different Sludges to Enhance Optimum Performance of an Upflow Anaerobic Sludge Bed Reactor

Mmontshi L. Sikosana[1]

PhD Candidate, Department of Mechanical Engineering Science,
University of Johannesburg Johannesburg, South Africa

Keneiloe Sikhwivhilu[2]

Chief Scientist, Advanced Materials Division, DSI/Mintek Nanotechnology Innovation Centre,
Johannesburg, South Africa

Richard Moutloali[3]

Associate Professor, Engineering and Technology, Institute for Nanotechnology and Water Sustainability,
University of South Africa, Johannesburg, South Africa

Daniel M. Madyira[4]

Associate Professor, Department of Mechanical Engineering Science, University of Johannesburg,
Johannesburg, South Africa

ABSTRACT: The performance of the upflow anaerobic sludge blanket (UASB) reactor depends largely on the settling properties and stability of the sludge bed. The investigation of the settling characteristics of three sludge samples collected from the municipal plant were tested. In this work, the temperature, pH, total dissolved solids and electrical conductivity were not controlled. These properties are known to influence the settleability of sludge and in this case, they were not taken into consideration. The settling of the various solid fractions in the sludge were measured in a 1 litre granulated flask to determine settleability properties. The 30 minutes sludge bed volume SV_{30} and 30 minutes sludge volume index (SVI_{30}) were employed as measures of performance. The secondary sludge indicated better settling characteristics compared to the other two primary samples based on SV_{30} (280 mL) and SVI (47.27 mL/g), The other two primary sludge samples had SV_{30s} and SVIs of 369, 880 mL/L and 22.43,37.22 mL/g, respectively. The secondary sludge has shown to be most suitable for the optimization of the UASB reactor system.

KEYWORDS: Batch settling curve, Zone settling velocity, Sludge volume index, Solid flux theory

1. Introduction

Technologies to produce clean water and clean energy have received global attention owing to water scarcity, resource depletion and global warming (Chung, et al. 2012). Recovered municipal wastewater treatment plants effluents have the potential to become net producers of renewable energy, converting the chemically bound energy content in the organic pollutants of raw municipal wastewater to useful energy carrier while producing other recyclable and reusable products (Shizas and Bagley 2004). The upflow anaerobic sludge blanket (UASB) reactor has been identified as one of the preferred high rate wastewater treatment technologies (GmbH 2001) (Lorenzen and Musee 2009) (Yu, et al. 2019). The most characteristic device the UASB reactor is the phase separator, which is placed in the top part of the reactor. The separator divides the reactor between a lower anaerobic digestion zone filled with biomass and an upper

[1]mmontshis@gmail.com, [2]keneiloes@mintek.co.za, [3]moutlrm@unisa.ac.za, [4]dmadyira@uj.ac.za

DOI: 10.1201/9781003538646-12

settling zone, having an intermediate transition zone. The influent is distributed evenly over the base of the reactor and flows upstream sequentially passing through the digestion, transition and settling zones to the top of the reactor where the effluent is collected and discharged. The digestion zone contains the biological sludge mass that transforms organic material present in the influent into biogas. The biogas desorbs from the liquid phase and is captured by the phase separator elements placed above the digestion zone. The liquid phase passes to the settling zone through the openings of the separator.

The performance of the UASB reactor depends largely on the settling properties and stability of the sludge bed (Wentzel, Poinapen and Ekama 2009). In the UASB reactor, equilibrium is established between the zone settling velocity (ZSV) of the solids and ascending velocity of the liquid phase (Van der Lubbe and Van Haandel 2019). The concentration of the stationary phase that forms depends on the settleability of the sludge and the upward velocity of the liquid phase. Sludge volume index (SVI) has been confirmed to be the most used index for routine operational and design tasks (Jin, Wilen and Lant 2003) in terms of sludge settleability. The SVI is defined as the volume in mL occupied by one gram of activated sludge which has settled for 30 min in a 1000 mL graduated cylinder. In a study where temperature was varied, the increases were identified as having a significant and positive effect on settleability of sludge (Rossle and Pretorious 2008). The SVI has shown to decrease by 14.8 mL/g per 1 °C increase in temperature (Rossle and Pretorious 2008). SVI varies between 30 to 400 mL/g and usually indicates good settleability when its less than 150 mL/g (Janczukowicz, et al. 2001) (Shahzad, Khan and Paul 2015). In this context, bulking sludge is classified as that sludge with SVI larger than 150 mL/g (Janczukowicz, et al. 2001). It is reported that if the SVI is equal to or less than 150 mL/g, the sludge has a very good settling characteristic whilst a SVI of above 150 mL/g usually indicates the presence of filamentous bacteria, which prohibit floc settling (Spellman 2003). Poor floc settling can lead to biomass washout with subsequent increased total suspended solids (TSS) levels in the effluent and reduced mixed liquor suspended solids (MLSS) levels in the bioreactor, leading to inefficient overall biological oxygen demand (BOD), chemical oxygen demad (COD), and TSS removals. Despite its widespread use, SVI has been criticised due to its strong dependence on initial sludge concentration (K. E. Renko 1996).

This paper serves to provide the results on the work that was undertaken to investigate the optimum performing sludge in terms of settleability among the three sludge samples that were collected from the Municipal Wastewater Treatment Plant. These sludge comprise of two primary (not treated at the plant) and secondary (treated with higher VSS which

favours biogas production) samples. The study will provide information that would save time when the designed in-house designed prototype is tested for the co-production of irrigation water and biogas.

2. Methods

$SV_{(t)}$ is determined by reading the volume of the settled sludge at time t (min) sedimentation period. SVI is measured by an expression shown in equation 1:

$$SVI(t) = \frac{SV(t)}{TSS} \qquad (1)$$

where,

$SVI_{(t)}$ = sludge volume index (mL/g) at time t

$SV_{(t)}$ = sludge volume (mL) at time t

TSS = total suspended solids (g/L)

t = sludge settling duration/period (minutes)

In practice, the SVI is usually taken at 30 minutes sludge settling duration in a settler.

3. Experimental Procedure

The aim of these experiments was to select the sludge sample based on its settleability performance. The selected sample was then to be used to test the performance of the in-house designed reactor. It is believed that since the design prototype is expected to exhibit the characteristics of the UASB reactor, a well settling sludge will be needed.

The sludge was collected from the wastewater plant from two points and the primary sludge was sieved to remove debris. This primary sludge was then divided into two parts, one smaller and large particles denoted as Sieve 1 and Sieve 2, respectively). The secondary sludge was found to be ready for testing as is. The collected samples were then analysed for their total suspended solids concentrations for application in equation 1.

3.1 Sludge Samples Solids Analysis

Sludge samples (50 mL) were placed in 60 mL crucibles and weighed, followed by heating at 103 °C for 5 hours in an oven to remove moisture. The final mass was converted to concentration by dividing with the initial sample volume in litres. The sludge samples were determined to have; TSS (g/L) of 16.45, 23.64 and 5.87 for sieve 1, sieve 2 and secondary, respectively.

3.2 Sludge Settleability Tests

The graduated cylinder and the associated apparatus were placed in a fumehood to capture the smell from the sewage sludge. The sludge samples were stirred with a glass rod to homogenise them before the settleability experiments were undertaken.

4. Results and Discussion

The SV_{30} and SVI_{30} are discussed in this section to find the sludge with superior settleability properties in comparison to the other two. It is intended to use the sludge in the optimization of a UASB reactor to produce methane as an energy source.

4.1 Sludge Samples Comparison Employing SV_{30} and SVI

The three sludge samples were placed in the graduated flask and allowed to settle by gravitational pull (illustrated in Fig. 12.1). The timer was set at zero minutes, followed by reading the volume of the settled sludge at 30 minutes. This procedure was performed in duplicate to ensure that the results were reliable under the given experimental conditions.

(a)   (b)   (c)

Fig. 12.1 Settled sludge at 30 minutes (a – sieve 1 sludge, b – sieve 2 sludge and secondary sludge as received)

Source: Author's compilation

The secondary sludge has a better settleability with respect to SV_{30} (280 mL/L) and SVI (47 mL/g) as compared to the other two sample, viz. sieve 1 (SV_{30} = 369 ml/L and SVI = 22.43 mL/g) and sieve 2 (SV_{30} = 880 mL/L and SVI = 37.22 mL/g), respectively. The criterion for good settleability in terms of SV_{30} is that it lies between 150 and 250 mL (van Loosdrecht, et al. 2016), at 280 mL for the secondary sludge, it is closest to this range. The SVI has good settleability when equal to or less than 150 mL/g as described above, and all these sludge samples are settling well. Based on the observation that SVI for the secondary sludge at 48 mL/g, which is closer to 150 mL/g in comparison to the other two, it is deemed better settling. These results, therefore, show that the secondary sludge has a superior settleability performance under the experimental conditions.

5. Conclusion

In conclusion, the secondary sludge has been shown experimentally to be more suitable for the optimisation of a UASB reactor to produce methane and water suitable for irrigation. All performance parameters have shown to be better with regards to the secondary sludge. The work has proven, the suitability of the secondary sludge for anaerobic commercial plants is generally employed instead of its primary counterpart. It is anticipated that high sludge settleability should reduce the amount of nutrients leaving the reactor with the effluent irrigation water.

Acknowledgement

This work is based on the research supported in part by the LIRA 2030. Africa Programme, which is implemented in partnership with the Network of African Science Academies (NASAC) and the International Science Council (ISC), with support from the Swedish International Development Cooperation Agency (Sida). The authors are thankful to the support received from the Department of Mechanical Engineering Science and Chemical Engineering Sciences, and the Department of Applied Chemistry of the University of Johannesburg. The authors are also grateful to the Department of Science and Innovation (DSI)/Mintek Nanotechnology Innovation Centre for the funding and permission to present the work.

REFERENCES

1. A model for batch settling curve. (1996). (Tiototie).
2. Bai , D., X. Zhang, G. Chen, and W. Wang. (2012). "Replacement mechanism of methane hydrate with carbon dioxide from microsecond molecular dynamics simulations." Energy and Environmental Science (5): 7033 - 7041.
3. Cacossa, K F, and D A Vaccari. (1994). "Calibration of a compresive gravity thickening model from a single batch settling curve." Water Science and Technology 30 (8): 107 - 116.
4. Chen, C., W. Guo, H. H. Ngo, S. W. Chang, D. D. Nguyen, P. D. Nguyen , X. T. Bui, and Y. Wu. (2017a). "Impact of reactor configurations on the performance of a granular." International Biodeterioration & Biodegradation (121): 131 - 138.
5. Chen, R, Y. Nie, H. Kato, J. Wu, T. Utashiro , J. Lu, S. Yue , H. Jiang, L. Zhang, and Y. Y. Li. (2017d). "Methanogenic degradation of toilet-paper cellulose upon sewage treatment in an anaerobic membrane bioreactor at room temperature." Bioresource Technology (228): 69–76.
6. Cho , S H, F Colin, M Sardin, and C Prost . (1993). "Settling velocity of activated sludge." Water Res (27): 1237 - 1242.
7. Chung, T S, X Li, R C Ong, Q Ge, and H Wang. (2012). ", Emerging Forward Osmosis (FO) Technologies and Challenges Ahead for Clean Water of Energy Application." Current Opinion in Chememical Engineering (1): 246 - 257.
8. Daigger , G T. (1995). "Development of refined clarifier operating diagrams using an updated settling characteristics database." Water Environmental Ressources (67): 95 - 100.

9. Deible, M. J., O. Tuguldur, and K. D. Jordan. (2014). "Theoretical Study of the Binding Energy of a Methane Molecule in a (H2O)20 Dodecahedral Cage." Journal of Physical Chemistry 1 - 7.

10. Dzyuba, A. V., and I. S. Zektser. (2013). "Variations in Submarine Groundwater Runoff as a Possible Cause of Decomposition of Marine MethaneHydrates in the Artcic." Water Resources 40 (1): 74 - 83.

11. Ekama, G A, J L Barnard, F W Gunthert, P Krebs, J A Mc-Corquodale , D S Parker , and E J Wahlberg . (1997). Secondary settling tanks: theory, modeling, design and operation. London: IAWQ Scientific and Technical Report (6).

12. Gambelli, A. M., B. Castellani, A. Nicolini, and F. Rossi. (2019). "Experimental study on natural gas hydrate exploitation: Optimization of methane recovery, carbon dioxide storage and deposit structure preservation." Journal of Petroleum Science and Engineering (177): 594 - 601.

13. Garmsiri, M R, H Haji , and A Shirazi. (2012). "A new approach to define batch settling curves for analyzing the sedimentation characte." Journal of Mining & Environment 3 (2): 103 - 111.

14. GmbH, T. (2001). Anaerobic treatment of municipal wastewater in UASB-reactors," Technical Information". Frankfurt,: W6e gtz.

15. Gouveia, J., G. Plaza, G. Garralon, F. Fdz-Polanco, and M. Pena. (2015). "Long-term operation of a pilot scale anaerobic membrane bioreactor." Bioresource Technology (185): 225–233.

16. Hayet, C, S Hédi, A Sami, J Ghada, and M Mariem. (2010). "Temperature effect on settling velocity of activated sludge." Biological and Environmental Engineering 290 - 292.

17. Hopfstock, H. (1997). "Paint removal composition and system." Paint Ink International 10 (3): 1 -23.

18. Janczukowicz, W, M Szewczyk, M Krzemieniewski, and J Pesta. (2001). "Settling Properties of Activated Sludge from a Sequencing Batch Reactor (SBR)." Polish Journal of Environmental Studies 10 (1): 15 - 20.

19. Jin, B, B M Wilen, and P Lant. (2003). "A comprehensive insight imto floc characteristics and their impact on compressibility and settleability of activated sludge." Chemical Engineering Journal 95 (1-3): 221 - 234.

20. Kirov , M. V., G. S. Fanourgakis, and S. S. Xantheas. (2008). "Identifying the most stable networks in polyhedral water clusters." Chemical Physics Letters (461): 180–188.

21. Komatsu, H., T. Sasagawa, S. Yamamoto, Y. Hiraga, M. Ota, T. Tsukada, and R. L. Smith Jr. (2019). "Methane clathrate hydrate dissociation analyzed with Raman spectroscopy and a thermodynamic mass transfer model considering cage occupancy." Fluid Phase Equilibria (489): 41 - 47.

22. Lin, h., J. Chen, F. Wang, L. Ding , and H. Hong. (2011). "Feasibility evaluation of submerged anaerobic membrane bioreactor for municipal secondary wastewater treatment." Desalination (280): 120–126.

23. Liu , Z., H. Yin, Z. Dang, and L. Yu . (2014). "Dissolved Methane: A Hurdle for Anaerobic Treatment of Municipal Wastewater." Environmental Science & Technology (48): 889–890.

24. Lorenzen , L, and N Musee. (2009). Market Analysis for UASB. Pretoria: WRC Project No. KV 224/09.

25. McDonald, S., L. Ojama, and S. J. Singer. (1998). "Graph Theoretical Generation and Analysis of Hydrogen-Bonded Structures with Applications to the Neutral and Protonated Water Cube and Dodecahedral Clusters." Journal of Physical Chemistry 102 (17): 2824-2832.

26. Ohgaki, K., K. Takano, H. Sangawa, T. Matsubara, and S. Nakano. (1996). "Methane Exploitation by Carbon Dioxide from gas Hydrates - Phase Equilibria for CO2-CH4 Mixed Hydrate System." Journal of Chemical Engineering of Japan 29 (3): 478 - 483.

27. Ong, S L. (1992). "Effect of measurement error of settling velocity on secondary tank design." Journal Water Polish Conference Federation (64): 104 - 110.

28. Otterpohl , R, and M Freund. (1992). " Dynamic models for clari®ers of activated sludge plants with dry and wet weather ˉows." Water Sci. Technol 26 (5 - 6): 1391 - 1400.

29. Renko, E K. (1996). "A model for batch settling curve." Water SA Vol. 22 No.4 October 1996 22 (4): 339 - 344.

30. Renko, K E. (1996). "A model for batch settling curve." Water SA 22 (4): 339 - 344.

31. Rössle, W H. (2008). "The effect of short-term temperature variations on activated sludge settling." Pretoria: University of Pretoria.

32. Rossle, W H, and W A Pretorious. (2008). "Batch and automated SVI measurements based on short-term temperature variations." Water SA 34 (2): 237 - 243.

33. Shahzad, M, S J Khan , and P Paul. (2015). "Influence of Temperature on the Performance of a Full-Scale Activated Sludge Process Operated at Varying Solids Retention Times Whilst Treating Municipal Sewage." Water (7): 855-867.

34. Shizas, I, and D M Bagley. (2004). "Experimental determination of energy content of unknown organics in municipal wastewater streams." Journal of Energy Engineering (130): 45 - 53.

35. Songa, S., B. Shi, W. Yu, L. Ding, Y. Chen, Y. Yu, C. Ruan, Y. Liu, W. Wang, and J. Gong. (2019). "A new methane hydrate decomposition model considering intrinsic kinetics and mass transfer." Chemical Engineering Journal (361): 1264 - 1284.

36. Souza, C. L., C. A> Chernicharo, and S. F. Aquino. (2011). "Quantification of dissolved methane in UASB reactors treating domestic wastewater under different operating conditions." Water Science & Technology 64 (11): 2259 - 2264.

37. Spellman, F P. (2003). Handbook of Water and Wastewater Treatment Plant Operation. Florida: CRC Press.

38. Svoronos, S A, B Koopman, and R W Watts R. W. . (1996). "One-dimensional modeling of secondary clari®ers using a concentration and feed velocity-dependent dispersion." Water Resources 33: 2112±2124.

39. Takacs , I, G Patry , and D Nolasco. (1991). "A dynamic model of the clari®cation-thickening process." Water Resources (25): 1263 - 1271.

40. Umaiyakunjaram, R., and P. Shanmugam. (2016). "Study on submerged anaerobic membrane bioreactor (SAMBR)

treating high suspended solids raw tannery wastewater for biogas production." Bioresource Technology (216): 785–792.

41. Van Der Hasselt , A, A Peter, and E A Van Rolleghem. (2000). "Estimation of Sludge Sedimentation Parameters from Single Batch Setling Curves." Water Resources 34 (2): 395 - 406.

42. Van der Lubbe, J, and A Van Haandel. (2019). "Sludge settleability." In Anaerobic Sewage Treatment, 415 - 421. London: IWA Publishers.

43. van Loosdrecht, M C, P H Nielsen, C M Lopez-Vazquez, and D Brdjanovic. (2016). Experimental Methods In Wastewater Treatment. London: IWA Publishing.

44. Vesilind , P A. (1968). "Design of prototype thickene batch settling tests." Water Sewage Works 115 (7): 302 - 307.

45. Vesilind , P A, and G N Johes. (1990). "re-examination of the batchthickening." Resource Journal 62 (7): 887-893.

46. Wei , N., W. T. Sun, Y. F. Meng, A. Q. Liu, S. W. Zhou, P. Guo, Q. Fu, and X. Lv. (2018). "Analysis of Decomposition for Structure I Methane Hydrate by Molecular Dynamics Simulation." Russian Journal of Physical Chemistry A 92 (5): 840–846.

47. Wentzel, M C, J Poinapen, and G A Ekama. (2009). "Biological sulphate reduction with primary sewage sludge in an upflow anaerobic sludge bed (UASB) reactor – Part 4: Bed settling characteristics." Water 35 (5): 553 - 560.

48. Yu, Y, S Tabr, A Yakubu, T P Curtisa , and J Dolf. (2019). "High rate domestic wastewater treatment at 15 °C." Water Research & Technology 5 (70): 70 - 82.

49. Zheng, Y, and D M Bagley. (1999). "Numerical Simulation of Batch Settling Process." Journal of Environmental Engineering 1007 - 1013.

Sustainable Materials Processing and Manufacturing – Lin Zhu et al. (eds)
© 2024 Taylor & Francis Group, London, ISBN 978-1-032-88599-5

Wireless Charging System for Unmanned Aerial Vehicle Using Lightweight and Compact Receiver Module

Hua Yin[1]

College of Mechanical and Electrical Engineering, Jiangsu Vocational College of Agriculture and Forestry, No. 19 Wenchang East Road, Jurong 212400, China

Junhua Wu*

College of Automotive and transportation engineering Nanjing Forestry University, No. 159 lung Poon Road, Xuanwu District, Nanjing, 210037, China

ABSTRACT: This paper presents a novel wireless charging system (WCS) designed specifically for unmanned aerial vehicles (UAVs). Employing the constant current (CC) and constant voltage (CV) charging method, the system integrates a receiver module that is both lightweight and compact. Through the optimization of the LCC-None compensation topology, the size and weight of the receiver module are significantly reduced. This optimization is achieved by eliminating the need for secondary-side resonance capacitance while ensuring that the system maintains high performance levels comparable to those achieved with the LCC-S topology. The magnetic coupler utilized in the system is customized to suit the unique structure of UAVs and features dual power transmission channels. By optimizing the parameters of the magnetic coupler, the optimal charging zone can be determined. Furthermore, a primary-side PI-controlled buck converter is implemented to facilitate efficient CC/CV charging while simplifying control of the secondary circuit, particularly within an acceptable misalignment range. Software simulation studies and experimental trials validate the feasibility of the WCS. Remarkably, the weight of the coil in the signal receiver is reduced to a mere 54 g. The system achieves a maximum output power of 91 W, with an efficiency rating of 87.3% for 5 A CC charging.

KEYWORDS: Wireless power transfer, Unmanned aerial vehicle(UAV) , LCC-None, Compact receiving module

1. Introduction

Presently, unmanned aerial vehicles (UAVs) find utility in various tasks such as real-time power line inspections and aerial photography [1, 2]. However, their limited battery capacity results in short flight times (typically 20-30 minutes), constrained by takeoff weight. Augmenting battery capacity enhances endurance but invariably escalates weight and cost. Moreover, recurrent battery charges with conductive chargers constrain UAV flexibility. Thankfully, the wireless charging system (WCS) offers a viable remedy, facilitatin, safety, and automated charging [3, 4]. Notably, the design of coil structures, system circuits, and control

methods holds paramount importance for WCS efficacy. This paper endeavors to design and refine a lightweight, compact receiver for WCS, featuring constant current/constant voltage (CC/CV) charging capabilities for UAS [5, 6]. Subsequently, it delves into the optimization and analysis of three pivotal WCS components.

1.1 From the View of Different Compensation Topologies

Examining various compensation topologies in magnetic resonant wireless charging systems reveals the role of resonant capacitors in offsetting the magnetic coupler's reactive power. The substantial weight and volume of the secondary resonant

*Corresponding author: wj_h@163.com
[1]81996931@qq.com

DOI: 10.1201/9781003538646-13

capacitor within the receiving module prompt researchers to explore methods for its elimination while maintaining system performance. In [7] , the researchers introduced compact and lightweight receiver modules that utilize cl-none and series-uncompensated topologies. However, strong coupling between magnetic couplers is usually required to achieve high system performance. Unfortunately, the structure of UAVs often leads to a weak coupling between these couplers, resulting in a relatively low coupling coefficient. As a result, ensuring the necessary mutual inductance requires either the primary and secondary coil self-inductance to be sufficiently large. For UAV applications, designing the receiver with minimal weight is imperative, necessitating primary coils with substantial self-inductance. Employing LCL-None topology technology presupposes identical primary side inductors. Yet, employing two inductors with considerable inductance, weight, volume, and cost proves impractical. Hence, a novel LCC-None topology design emerges as a pragmatic solution for applications like UAVs characterized by weak coupling.

1.2 From the View of Various Magnetic Couplers

When exploring different designs for magnetic couplers, the primary focus is on steering clear of bulky and fragile ferrite cores to Reducing weight reduces economic costs, all while improving the structural integrity of receiver modules intended for UAVs. Customizing coil structures and the positioning of magnetic couplers to suit the unique structures and dimensions of various UAV models is imperative. As depicted in Fig. 13.1, this paper utilizes a UAV model as an example for analysis, outlining three distinct installation methods for UAV receiving coils.

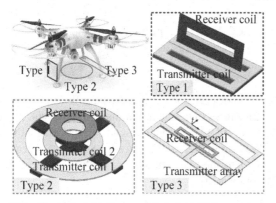

Fig. 13.1 Three installation methods for UAV receiving coils

In [8], the Type 1 receiver coil is positioned centrally to the transmitting coil, orthogonal in design. However, stringent misalignment tolerances necessitate precise UAV landing for optimal system performance. Additionally, metal landing legs may impact magnetic coupler performance. In [9], while transmitters with two coils in series enhance anti-misalignment, Type 2 receiver coils are larger and

bulkier. Both Type 1 and Type 2 share drawbacks: potential obstruction of the camera by the receiving coil during rotation and interference with the wireless communication module within the ground leg due to the surrounding magnetic field.

In light of these challenges, [10] introduces the Type 3 receiver coil. Nonetheless, the approach and circuitry for managing the transmitter array are considerably more intricate. This study opts to enhance the Type 3 receiving coil, tackling the aforementioned concerns through a refinement process guided by the examination of dual power transmission channel magnetic couplers elaborated in Section 3.

1.3 From the View of Different Control Methods

CC/CV Charging is attained via closed-loop control mechanisms, utilizing DC-DC converters, active rectifiers, and controlled switches for secondary side regulation [11, 12]. However, this methodology increases the weight and size of the receiver module, making it unsuitable for drone applications. Primary side control, employing DC-DC converters and H-bridge inverters, offers distinct advantages [13, 14]. While maintaining a zero voltage switch (ZVS) during charging presents challenges for phase-shifted H-bridge inverters, H-bridge variable frequency inverters typically adjust the the frequency range is adjusted according to the standard [15,16] . Therefore, a main step-down converter with duty cycle adjustment is used to achieve CC and CV charging,, enabling the development of a lightweight and compact receiving module suitable for UAV applications.

The paper's organization is as follows: Section 2 delves into the topology optimization of LCC is deeply studied, while Section 3 devises a magnetic coupler with double power transmission channels. Section 4 investigates the primary controller, and Section 5 verifies the feasibility of WCS design through experimental findings. Finally, a conclusion is drawn in section 6.

2. System Structure of WCS

Figure 13.2 depicts the primary side circuit, which consists of H-bridge inverter, LCC compensator, DC voltage source, step-down converter and controller. Employing LCC compensation offers several benefits, including the maintenance of a constant resonant current in the transmitter coil, ensuring a stable induced voltage on the secondary side, and enabling no-load operation, thereby improving system reliability. The receiving coil is directly connected to the secondary side of the full bridge rectifier and capacitor filter. The charging current Io and charging voltage Uo are transmitted to the main controller through the wireless communication module, and then the main controller adjusts the Buck converter, which is controlled by pi, and finally

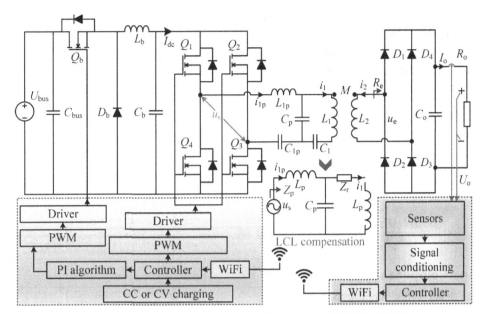

Fig. 13.2 Circuit block diagram of the designed WCS for UAVs

realizes CC/CV charging. The variable us in the figure represents the output voltage of the H-bridge inverter.

The LCC compensation system consists of components including a series coil L_{1p}, a transmitter coil L_1, and compensating capacitors C_{1p}, C_p, and C_1. Within this system, i_{1p} and i_1 respectively represent the currents flowing through L_{1p} and L_1, with M symbolizing mutual inductance. The current flowing through the receiving coil L_2 is denoted as i_2, R_e represents the equivalent input resistance of the rectifier circuit and U_e represents the equivalent input voltage.

In LCC-None circuits, Z_r denotes the reflected impedance, considered resistive in the resonant state of LCC-None compensation topology, yielding equation (1) below. This assumption's validity is further affirmed through subsequent analysis, where ω signifies the system's angular frequency.

$$\omega = \frac{1}{\sqrt{\left(L_1 - L_p\right)C_1}} = \frac{1}{\sqrt{\left(L_{1p} - L_p\right)C_{1p}}} = \frac{1}{\sqrt{L_p C_p}}$$

* MERGEFORMAT (1)

L_p, representing inductance in the LCC partially equivalent to the LCL circuit depicted in Fig. 13.2, enhances parameter flexibility. The fundamental principles of LCC and LCL being akin, equation (1) establishes equivalence between the two topologies.

Based on equation (1), C_1 and C_{1p} offer enhanced circuit design flexibility. Consequently, inductors in LCC topology prove more adaptable compared to those in LCL topology. Firstly, for a lightweight and compact receiving coil, minimizing L_2 is preferable. Nonetheless, achieving desired

mutual inductance necessitates a larger L_1 due to decreased coupling coefficient from reduced L_2. In such cases, L_1 in LCL compensation significantly exceeds expected L_p, a challenge effectively addressed by compensating L_1 with C_1 in LCC topology. Secondly, opting for a larger L_{1p} diminishes total harmonic distortion of i_{1p}. To compensate for ($L_{1p}-L_p$), C_{1p} serves its purpose. In practical scenarios, judicious selection of L_{1p} avoids unnecessary cost, power loss, and volume.

Secondary side series compensation, typically employed to attain lightweight and compact receivers, contrasts with composite compensation topology utilizing additional passive components. Leveraging the LCC-None compensation topology bolsters this characteristic, compared to LCC-S topology, elucidating its advantages.

By disregarding the resistances of coils and capacitors during the deduction of equations, Z_{r_N} and Z_{r_S} denote the reflected impedance of LCC-None and LCC-S topologies, respectively, as specified in equation (2). The subscript N associated with I_o and η represents LCC-none, and S represents LCC-S compensation topology. When the value of ωL_2 significantly exceeds that of R_e, Z_{r_N} and Z_{r_S} converge, emphasizing the critical importance of selecting ωL_2 in the design of LCC-None compensation topology.

$$\text{LCC-None: } Z_{r\_N} \approx \left.\frac{(\omega M)^2}{R_e}\right|_{R_e \gg j\omega L_2}$$

$$\text{LCC-S: } Z_{r\_S} \approx \left.\frac{(\omega M)^2}{R_e}\right|_{j\omega L_2 + \frac{1}{j\omega C_2} = 0}$$

(2)

Derived from the equation above and the equivalent input impedance Z_p, we obtain the RMS (root mean square) value of i1 as (4), D representing the Buck converter's duty cycle.

The induced voltage on the secondary side is determined by the ratio α, denoting the distortion factor in equation (5).

$$I_1 = \frac{2\sqrt{2}DU_{bus}}{\pi\omega L_p} \quad \backslash\text{* MERGEFORMAT} \qquad (3)$$

$$\text{LCC-None:} \quad j\omega M\dot{I}_1 \approx \dot{U}_e\Big|_{R_e \gg \omega L_2}$$
$$\text{LCC-S:} \quad j\omega M\dot{I}_1 \approx \dot{U}_e\Big|_{j\omega L_2 + \frac{1}{j\omega L_2}=0} \qquad (4)$$

$$\alpha = \frac{I_o}{I_2}, \ I_o = \alpha I_2 = \frac{\alpha DMU_{bus}}{L_p R_o} \qquad (5)$$

2.1 The LCC-None Compensation Design

In Figure 13.2, R_e denotes the input impedance of the rectifier, while R_o represents the equivalent load resistance. The correlation between R_e and R_o can be derived as follows.

$$R_e = \frac{8}{\pi^2}R_o \quad \backslash\text{* MERGEFORMAT} \qquad (6)$$

Selecting an appropriate value for ωL_2 necessitates taking into account the range of R_o that is equivalent to R_e. Gamma is defined as Z_{r_N} and Z_{r_S} by.

$$\gamma = \frac{Z_{r\_N}}{Z_{r\_S}} \quad \backslash\text{* MERGEFORMAT} \qquad (7)$$

When ωL_2 falls significantly below the minimum value of R_o, γ tends to approach 1. For instance, if R_o is maintained at 3 Ω and ω_{L2} remains below 0.7 Ω, γ surpasses 0.95. Consequently, the operational efficiency of both LCC-None and LCC-S compensation topologies becomes nearly indistinguishable. The design of systems with exceedingly small ω_{L2}, achieved by reducing both f and L_2, may present challenges in practical applications. While f is configured at 85 kHz to accentuate the parameterization of the magnetic coupler and the design of LCC-none compensation topology, it is subject to variation based on the specific application. Therefore, further optimization of L_2 was pursued. Table 13.1 consolidates software simulation outcomes of L in correlation with I_o and system efficiency η, as depicted in Fig. 13.3, where D is fixed at 0.64, and ΔI and $\Delta\eta$ respectively indicate disparities between LCC-S and LCC-None compensation topologies.

In Fig. 13.3(a), when L_2 equals 2 μH, $\Delta\eta$ stands at 1%, and ΔI is 0.15 A. Eliminating bulky and unnecessary secondary-side resonant capacitors leads to a reduction in both the weight and cost of the UAV. As observed in Fig. 13.3(b), when R_o significantly surpasses ωL_2, I_{o_N} closely matches I_{o_S}. Moreover, in both Fig. 13.3(a) and Fig. 13.3(b), as L_2 increases, $\Delta\eta$ also rises.

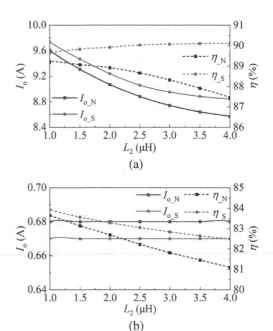

Fig. 13.3 Software simulation results (a) R_o=2 Ω. (b) R_o=30 Ω.

When ω_{L2} is significantly below the minimum R_o, ω approaches nearly 1. For instance, if R_o equals 3 Ω and L_2 is less than 0.7 Ω, γ exceeds 0.95. Consequently, the operational performance of both LCC-None and LCC-S is nearly identical. Implementing very small ω_{L2} based on f and L_2 in system design poses challenges in practical applications. The frequency f is set at 85 kHz to highlight magnetic coupler parametric design and LCC-none compensation topology, though it may vary for different applications. Therefore, further optimization of smaller L_2 is necessary. Fig. 13.4 presents the software simulation outcomes of L_2 concerning I_o and system efficiency η, complementing the data in Table 13.1. Here, D is held constant at 0.64, while ΔI and $\Delta\eta$ indicate variations in I_o and η between the LCC-S compensation topology and LCC-none compensation topology.

The parameters of the wireless charging system used in this paper are shown in Table 13.1.

Table 13.1 The Parameters of the WCS for UAVs

Symbol	Note	Value
U_{bus}	Input voltage	96 V
f	Frequency	85 kHz
d	Air gap	3 mm
L_{1p}	The series coil inductance	85 μH
L_1	The transmitter coil inductance	1.14 mH
L_2	Receiver coil inductance	1.8 μH
L_p	LCL inductance of compensation	45 μH
M	Mutual inductance	14 μH
U_o	Battery voltage	12 V~18 V
I_o	Charging current	5 A

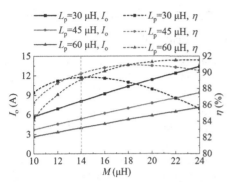

Fig. 13.4 Software simulation results of M versus I_o and η.

3. Design of the Proposed Magnetic Coupler

3.1 Modeling Analysis

The receiver coil is constructed with two coils connected in series, strategically positioned at the base of both landing legs of the drone to optimize the utilization of its distinctive shape. Illustrated in Fig. 13.5, a magnetic coupler, denoted as CHi (i=1,2), features dual power transmission channels within the same structure, enhancing power transmission capability. L_{1i} and L_{2i} denote the self-inductance of transmitting coil T_i and receiving coil R_i. Mutual inductance between CH1 and CH2 is represented by M_1 and M_2, respectively. Cross-coupled mutual inductance between T_1 and T_2 is denoted as M_{11}, while that between T_1 and R_2 is M_{12}. Similarly, M_{22} and M_{21} have analogous definitions.

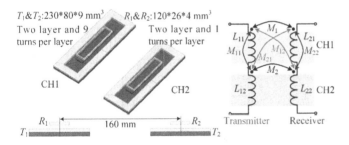

Fig. 13.5 The magnetic coupler model

Figure 13.5 provides a comprehensive overview of the magnetic coupler parameters. Assuming that the UAV docks onto the charging pad with a minimal air gap and taking into account the dimensions of the landing legs, with L_2 established at 1.8 μH, the receiver coil's optimal length and width are determined to be 145 mm and 30 mm, respectively. Within CH1, the receiver coil consists of 2 turns, with one turn per layer. Furthermore, the transmitter coil's dimensions in CH1 are optimized at 160 mm in length and 110 mm in width, incorporating a total of 48 turns, with 12 turns per layer.

Due to the serial connection of T_1, T_2, R_1, and R_2 at their dotted terminals, the total inductances of the transmitter coil and receiver coil, L_1 and L_2, can be determined using equation (8). Effective design of the magnetic coupler enables M_{12} and M_{21} to be significantly smaller than M_1 and M_2, rendering them negligible. Consequently, their impact on system performance is minimized, eliminating the need for extra compensation methods. Total inductance for power transmission equals (M_1+M_2).

$$L_1 = L_{11} + L_{12} + 2M_{11}, \ L_2 = L_{21} + L_{22} + 2M_{22}$$

$\backslash$* MERGEFORMAT (8)

3.2 Charging Zone Analysis

Considering the inevitable misalignment between the UAV and the charging pad, the determination of a reasonable charging zone relies on the variation range of mutual inductance (M), taking into account the maximum values of power output (P_o) and efficiency (η). Analyzing the software simulation results of M on η and duty cycle (D), as illustrated in Fig. 13.6, considering the adjustable range of D from 0.1 to 0.9, and with the minimum value of M set at 9 μH.

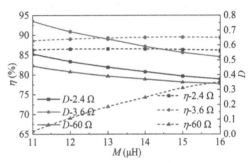

Fig. 13.6 Software simulation results of η and D

When the load resistance R_o equals 2.4 Ω, corresponding to the minimum value of P_o during constant current (CC) charging, the minimum value of η is 85.3%. Similarly, when R_o equals 60 Ω, corresponding to the minimum value of P_o during constant voltage (CV) charging, η is at least 57.2%. In summary, the designed magnetic coupler M ranges from 9 μH to 14 μH.

Figure 13.7 illustrates the software simulation outcomes of the x-axis (dx) and y-axis (dy) for misalignment distances of M_i and M_{ij} (j ≠ i). The acceptable ranges of dx and dy are -30 mm to 30 mm and -40 mm to 40 mm, respectively, when M varies within the range of 9 μH to 14 μH. M_{ij} (j ≠ i) exhibits significantly smaller values than M_i within the designed dx and dy ranges, thus exerting minimal impact on the system's performance.

Figure 13.8 illustrates the software simulation outcomes of the magnetic field distribution. The magnetic field diminishes

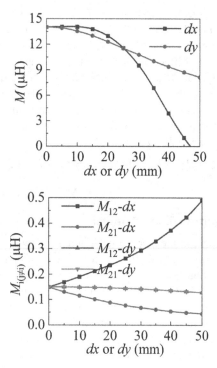

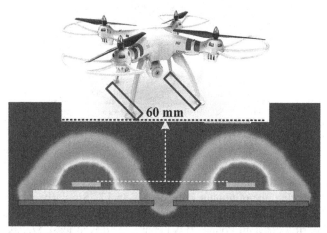

Fig. 13.7 *dx* and *dy* versus M_i and $M_{ij(i \neq j)}$

Fig. 13.8 The software simulation results of magnetic field distribution

significantly when the vertical distance from the top of the receiver coil surpasses 60 mm. This indicates minimal impact on the UAV, given that the length of the landing leg exceeds 100 mm. Additionally, no aluminum plate or ferrite core was employed to shield the magnetic field, thereby reducing both the weight and economic cost of the receiver module. Ultimately, the receiver coil, weighing only 27 grams, takes full advantage of the UAV's structure.

4. Primary-side Controller Analysis

4.1 Working Principle

Based on the insights derived from Fig. 13.9, the intricate operational mechanism of the main control methods is elucidated as follows:

(1) Voltage and current sensors installed on the secondary side measure U_o and I_o, respectively. These measurements undergo processing through a signal conditioning circuit and are subsequently converted into digital signals via an analog-to-digital converter. Following this, the digital signals are wirelessly transmitted to the primary side controller through a communication module.

(2) The measured U_o is compared with the predetermined charging voltage, U_{o_set}, to determine the charging mode. In the event that U_o falls below U_{o_set}, the constant current charging proportional-integral (PI) control mechanism is engaged to achieve the preset charging current. I_{o_set}, resulting in an increase in U_o Once U_{o_set} is attained, continual voltage PI control (CV) initiates to stabilize Uo at U_{o_set}, thereby decreasing I_o.

(3) The battery charging process concludes when Io reaches the stop charging current (I_{o_stop}). Users have the flexibility to set I_{o_set} to different values within the limitation of maximum power output (P_o).

By adhering to this control strategy, the primary-side control method effectively regulates U_o and I_o, ensuring safe and efficient charging of the battery.

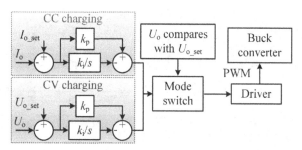

Fig. 13.9 The working principle of primary side control

4.2 Simulation Analysis

When R_o ranges from 2.4 Ω to 3.5 Ω for constant current charging and from 10 Ω to 60 Ω for constant voltage charging, the closed-loop software simulation waveforms depicted in Fig. 13.10 illustrate the following behavior: Increasing D leads to a rise in U_o while maintaining the charging current I_o at 5 A. Conversely, reducing D results in a decrease in I_o, while U_o is maintained at 18 V.

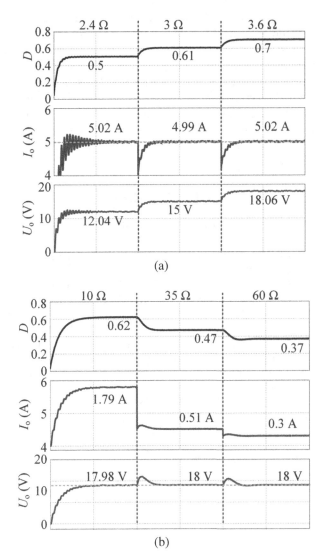

(a)

(b)

Fig. 13.10 The closed-loop waveforms. (a) CC charging. (b) CV charging

Fig. 13.11 The experimental setup

5. Experimental Verification

5.1 Experimental Setup

To validate the proposed method's feasibility, an experimental system, as depicted in Fig. 13.11, was constructed. For practical implementation, further optimization of the circuit and control method is feasible. On the first side, the MOSFETs and their driver chips for the Buck converter and full-bridge inverter are STW48N60DM2 and 1EDI20H12AH, respectively. The rectifier comprises four Schottky diodes on the secondary side, specifically the low forward voltage VS-52CPQ030-N3 from Vishay Semiconductor. Non-polarized capacitors constitute the filter.

For each power transfer channel, 2.5 mm diameter, 320 stranded Litz wire was utilized to construct the transmitting and receiving coils. Litz wire was chosen due to its lower resistance and lower proximity effect. The primary-side coil features a PC95 ferrite core and metalized polypropylene film capacitors. HCS-ES3.3 and HVS-AS3.3 are employed as current and voltage sensors, respectively, for measuring the charging current and voltage. The wireless communication module used is USR-WIFI232-A2. Additionally, ITECH's IT6524D and charging IT8816B serve as the DC power supply and electronic load, respectively.

5.2 Experimental Results

Experimental results comparing the efficiency (η) between the LCC-None and LCC-S compensated topologies were obtained using a power analyzer at 5 A for CC charging and 18 V for CV charging, as depicted in Fig. 13.12. The findings reveal that the efficiency difference ($\Delta\eta$) between the two topologies is less than 1.1%.

Despite the slightly lower efficiency η_N compared to η_S, the utilization of the LCC-none compensated topology and the dual power transfer channel magnetic coupler significantly diminishes the weight, size, and cost of the receiver module.

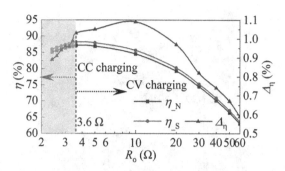

Fig. 13.12 Closed-loop experimental results of R_o versus η

Furthermore, the maximum power output and efficiency attain values of 91 W and 87.3%, respectively, positioned close to the transition point between constant current charging and constant voltage charging. These experimental findings serve to reinforce the feasibility of the future areas of wireless charging system.

For a more comprehensive understanding of the CC/CV dynamic charging process, Fig. 13.13 illustrates the system's ability to maintain CC and CV under variations in R_o.

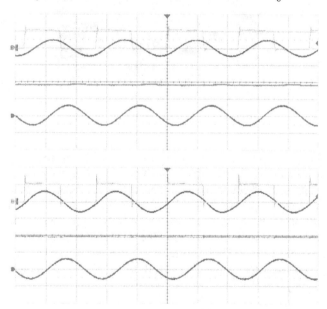

Fig. 13.13 Experimental results. CC/CV dynamic waveforms

6. Conclusion

Optimized for lightweight and compact UAV receivers in WCS, three primary components are refined. The developed compensation topology eliminates secondary side resonant capacitance, ensuring optimal performance for weakly coupled WCS setups. Introducing a magnetic coupler with dual power transmission channel function enhances misalignment resistance and leverages drone structure for a

lighter receiver module. Implementing a primary-side control methodology simplifies the secondary loop and reduces control complexity, thereby enabling efficient constant current and constant voltage charging. Validation through software simulations and experimental trials demonstrates that the receiver coil, weighing 54 g, attains a maximum output power of 91 W with an efficiency of 87.3%. This WCS design holds promise for applications in mobile phones and implantable devices, with future development geared towards these sectors.

REFERENCES

1. P. Chittoor, B. Chokkalingam, and L. M. Popa: A Review on UAV Wireless Charging: Fundamentals, Applications, Charging Techniques and Standards, IEEE Access. 9, 2169-3536. (2021)
2. P. Cao, Y. Lu, H. Zhang, J. Li, W. Chai, C. Cai, and S. Wu: Embedded Lightweight Squirrel-Cage Receiver Coil for Drone Misalignment-Tolerant Wireless Charging. IEEE Trans. Power Electron. 38(3), 2884-2888 (2023)
3. Yuvaraja Shanmugam, Narayanamoorthi R, Pradeep Vishnuram, Mohit Bajaj, Kareem M. AboRas, Padmanabh Thakur, and Kitmo: A Systematic Review of Dynamic Wireless Charging System for Electric Transportation, IEEE Access. 10, 133617-133642. (2022)
4. M. Huang, Y. Lu, and R. P. Martins: A Reconfigurable Bidirectional Wireless Power Transceiver for Battery-to-Battery Wireless Charging. IEEE Trans. Power Electron. 34(8), 7745-7753 (2019)
5. Y. Zhang, W. Pan, H. Wang, Z. Shen, Y. Wu, J. Dong, and X. Mao: Misalignment-Tolerant Dual-Transmitter Electric Vehicle Wireless Charging System With Reconfigurable Topologies. IEEE Trans. Power Electron. 37(8), 8816-8819 (2022)
6. X. Mou, D. T. Gladwin, R. Zhao, H. Sun, and Z. Yang: Coil Design for Wireless Vehicle-to-Vehicle Charging Systems, IEEE Access. 8, 172723-172733. (2020)
7. Y. Zhang, C. Liu, M. Zhou, and X. Mao: A Novel Asymmetrical Quadrupolar Coil for Interoperability of Unipolar, Bipolar, and Quadrupolar Coils in Electric Vehicle Wireless Charging Systems. IEEE Trans. Ind Electron. 71(4), 4300-4303 (2024)
8. Z. Li, H. Liu, Y. Tian and Y. Liu: Constant Current/Voltage Charging for Primary-Side Controlled Wireless Charging System Without Using Dual-Side Communication, *IEEE Trans. Power Electron.*, 36(12), 13562-13577. (2021)
9. Y. Zhang, Z. Yan, Z. Liang, S. Li, and C. T. Rim: A High-Power Wireless Charging System Using LCL-N Topology to Achieve a Compact and Low-Cost Receiver. *IEEE Trans. Power Electron.* 35(1), 131–137 (2020)
10. K. Song, B. Ma, G. Yang, J. Jiang, R. Wei, H. Zhang, and C. Zhu: A Rotation-Lightweight Wireless Power Transfer System for Solar Wing Driving. *IEEE Trans. Power Electron.* 34(9), 8816–8830 (2019)
11. C. Cai, S. Wu, L. Jiang, Z. Zhang, and S. Yang: A 500-W Wireless Charging System with Lightweight Pick-Up for

Unmanned Aerial Vehicles. *IEEE Trans. Power Electron.* 35(8), 7721–7724 (2020)

12. Y. Song, X. Sun, H. Wang, W. Dong, and Y. Ji: Design of Charging Coil for Unmanned Aerial Vehicle-Enabled Wireless Power Transfer. *2018 8th International Conference on Power and Energy Systems (ICPES).* (2019)

13. T. Campi, S. Cruciani, G. Rodriguez, and M. Feliziani: "Coil Design of a Wireless Power Transfer Charging System for a Drone," *2016 IEEE Conference on Electromagnetic Field Computation (CEFC).* (2017)

14. E. Gati, G. Kampitsis, and S. Manias, "Variable Frequency Controller for Inductive Power Transfer in Dynamic Conditions," *IEEE Trans. Power Electron.*, 32(2), 1684–1696. (2017)

15. B.-V. Vu, V.-T. Phan, M. Dahidah, and V. Pickert: "Multiple output inductive charger for electric vehicles," *IEEE Trans. Power Electron.*, 34(8), 7350–7368. (2019)

16. R. Mai, Y. Liu, Y. Li, P. Yue, G. Cao, and Z. He: "An active rectifierbased maximum efficiency tracking method using an additional measurement coil for wireless power transfer," *IEEE Trans. Power Electron*, 33(1), 716–728. (2018)

Note: All the figures and table in this chapter were compiled by the author.

Sustainable Materials Processing and Manufacturing – Lin Zhu et al. (eds)
© 2024 Taylor & Francis Group, London, ISBN 978-1-032-88599-5

Research and Design of Adaptive Control System for Driver's Seat

Wenxin Jin
Jiangsu Vocational and Technical College of Agriculture and Forestry,
Jurong, Jiangsu, 212400

Feng Jin*
Hohai University, Nanjing, Jiangsu, 213022
Jiangsu College of Transportation Technicians, Zhenjiang, Jiangsu, 212028

Jiabo Wang
Jiangsu Vocational and Technical College of Agriculture and Forestry,
Jurong, Jiangsu, 212400

ABSRTACT: The driver's seat is the device that the driver contacts most closely when driving. Whether the driver's seat is adjusted properly or not directly affects the driver's driving comfort, but there is little research on intelligent and adaptive seats at present.Aiming at the problem that the intelligent degree of the driver's seat adjustment control is not high at present, this paper proposes the height adjustment control method of the vehicle driver's seat based on human eye positioning and ranging and the horizontal adjustment method of the vehicle driver's seat based on fuzzy double loop control to realize the intelligent adjustment of the seat.The seat prototype is completed and installed on the vehicle.60 drivers were selected for the real vehicle test. After the intelligent adjustment of the driver's seat, the distance between the driver's eyes and point B of the roof was measured to be within 19.5 ~ 20.5cm. After the angle adjustment, the angle between the driver's right leg and thigh was within 118.5° ~ 121.5°. The total adjustment time was less than 8 seconds. The test results show that the adaptive adjustment system of the driver's seat designed in this paper achieves the intelligent control effect of precise adjustment and less time consumption.

KEY WORDS: Driver's seat; Adaptive; Eye location; Fuzzy control; Intelligent adjustment

With the rapid development of social economy, cars have entered thousands of households as a means of transportation. In order to meet people's demand for quality life, the design of cars is becoming more and more intelligent and humanistic. In view of the problem that the intelligent level of the driver's seat adjustment control is not high at present[1-7], this paper determines the relevant angle parameters and eye height positions of the best sitting posture of the human body when driving through literature review to ensure the comfort and safety of driving;Before adjusting the seat, the driver shall take corresponding simple actions to detect, analyze and control the work of the seat motor by using the human eye

positioning and ranging algorithm, fuzzy control algorithm, sensor technology, image acquisition technology, and single-chip technology, until the seat is adjusted to the best sitting position, so as to achieve intelligent adaptive control.

1. Driver Position Information Collection

This design is based on Kia KX7 model, and based on the research of Jingjie[8], the optimal vertical height between the human eye and the top of the vehicle is determined to be 20cm.From the perspective of ergonomics and safety,

*Corresponding author: 996271660@qq.com

DOI: 10.1201/9781003538646-14

Fig. 14.1 is a diagram of the best sitting posture angle of drivers[9] . The best angle of the right leg thigh calf angle A5 = 120° is taken.

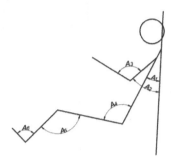

Fig. 14.1 Schematic diagram of human body angle in the best sitting position

*Source:*Adapted from the research of Jingjie[8]

1.1 Eye Height Information Collection

The height adjustment of the driver's seat is based on the height position of the human eye. This system uses the

human eye positioning and ranging to obtain this parameter. As shown in Fig. 14.2, position A is the installation position of the monocular camera (above the front windshield and directly above the human eye), position B is the roof position directly above the human eye, and position C is the human eye position|AC | is determined by the method of human eye positioning and ranging (single hole imaging principle), and | BC | can be calculated according to the sine cosine theorem of the triangle.The specific solution is as follows:

$$\sqrt{|AB|^2 + |AC|^2 - 2|AB||AC|\cos\left(\pi - \arcsin\frac{|AB|\sin B}{|AC|} - \angle B\right)}$$

(1)

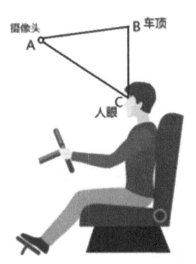

Fig. 14.2 Method of obtaining eye height information

Source: Anthor

1.2 Collection of Thigh and Calf Angle Information

Two rows of micro ranging sensors are arranged above the right calf, three in each row (Fig. 14.3). The minimum values D2 and D3 of ranging in each row are taken and sent to the single chip processor for processing. According to mathematical knowledge, it can be concluded that:

$$A_7 = A_9 = \tan^{-1}\frac{D_1}{D_2 - D_3}$$

(2)

$$A_5 = A_7 + A_8$$

(3)

A_8 is a fixed constant value, and A_7 is obtained by measuring D_2 and D_3 with the sensor, so the information acquisition of the thigh and leg angle (A_5) can be obtained through distance measurement.

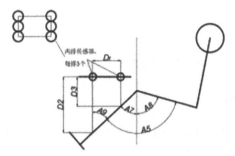

Fig. 14.3 Design drawing of thigh and calf angle signal acquisition

Source: Anthor

2. System Design

The auto driver seat adaptive adjustment control system is mainly divided into two modules: height adjustment system and level adjustment system. As shown in Fig. 14.4, the structure block diagram of the driver's seat adaptive adjustment control system is designed.

When the auto driving seat adaptive adjustment control system works, the master chip successively collects the digital image of the face and the signals of six laser range sensors, analyzes and processes the signals, obtains the motor adjustment signal through the corresponding algorithm, and then drives the two motors to run successively (first height adjustment, then angle adjustment). The main control chip selected in this design is ARM9 S3C2440;NandFlash type read-only memory chip is adopted;The processing chip model of the camera module is OV2640;The range finder adopts laser range finder (module) GY-530-VL53L0X;Closed loop stepper motor is selected as the seat height motor, and the model is 57CME13;The seat horizontal motor is a brushless DC motor, and the model is XD-WS60SRZ- 1.

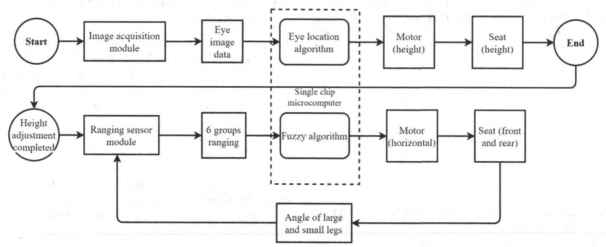

Fig. 14.4   Structure block diagram of driver's seat adaptive adjustment system

Source: Anthor

2.1 Mechanical Structure Design

According to the overall size of the original seat, the structural size of the newly selected components and the requirements of the control system, solidwords is used to design the height adjustment and horizontal adjustment mechanism of the new seat. The structural schematic diagram is shown in Fig. 14.5.

The auto driver's seat adopts adaptive height adjustment. Two stepper motors are used for synchronous control to ensure that the seat can rise and fall vertically. In the height adjustment mechanism, the number of worm heads q=2, the number of worm gear teeth z = 18, the lead of the screw is 5mm, the effective travel of the sliding table is 100mm, and its transmission accuracy can reach 0.01mm. The front and rear horizontal adjustment transmission system of automobile seat is mainly composed of fixed lower track, sliding upper track, DC motor, worm, worm gear box, worm gear, lead screw, etc. In the height adjustment mechanism, the number of worm heads q=2, the number of worm gear teeth z = 18, the lead of the screw is 5mm, the effective travel of the sliding table is 240mm, and its transmission accuracy can reach 0.01mm. Seat prototype and test platform are shown in Fig. 14.6.

2.2 Control System Design

Adaptive height adjustment of vehicle driver's seat based on human eye positioning and ranging

The control strategy of the height adjustment of the stepping motor is as follows: after the initialization of each module is completed and the face image taken by the camera is obtained,

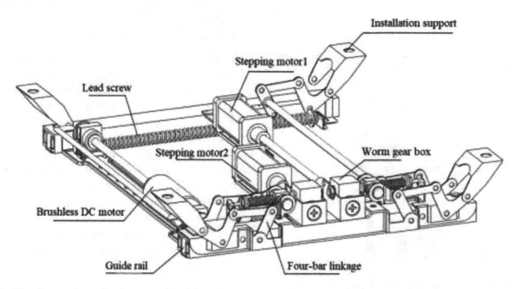

Fig. 14.5   Structure schematic diagram of height adjustment and horizontal adjustment mechanism of new driver's seat

Source: Anthor

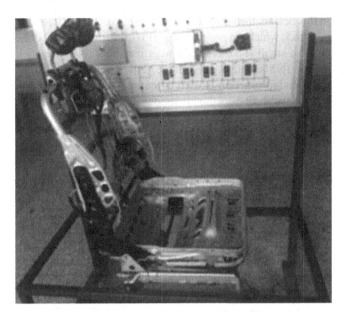

Fig. 14.6 Driver Seat Prototype Test Platform

Source: Anthor

the gray projection function algorithm is used to coarse locate the human eye, that is, to obtain the area of the human eye; Then the edge detection algorithm is used to precisely locate the human pupil and obtain the coordinates of the human pupil; Finally, the difference between the actual eye height and the optimal height of the initial position is calculated according to the eye positioning coordinates combined with the function algorithm, and the pulse number of the control stepping motor is calculated, and then the motor is driven to complete the height adjustment.

(1) Distance algorithm from the center of two eyes to the roof

In this paper, we choose the method based on gray projection function to carry out coarse eye location and accurate pupil location based on image edge extraction, and obtain the coordinates a (u1, v1), b (u2, v2)[11-14] of the center of human eye pupil.

Figure 14.8 shows a simplified camera pinhole imaging model. The distance from the center of two eyes to the camera can be calculated according to the triangle similarity principle. Point O is the camera lens (pinhole), f is the camera focal length, d is the distance between the two eyes from the camera, the actual coordinates of the two eyes are A (x1, y1), B (x2, y2), the imaging coordinates of the human eye are a (u1, v1), b (u2, v2), R is the actual pupillary distance of the two eyes, and r is the pixel distance of the two pupils in the image. According to the triangle similarity principle, it can be obtained that:

$$d = f \frac{R}{r} \tag{4}$$

Fig. 14.7 Center coordinate of human pupil

Source: Anthor

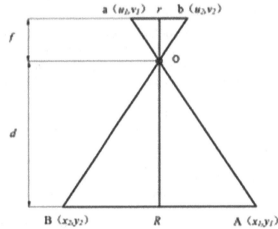

Fig. 14.8 Simplified camera pinhole imaging model

Source: Anthor

According to the literature, the pupillary distance of adults is basically the same[11], so R can be determined; From the above known physical size of each pixel on the x axis is dx, we can get: Let R=| x2- x1|, r=| u2 - u1|

$$r = dx \left| u_2 - u_1 \right| = \frac{f}{a_x} \Delta u \tag{5}$$

According to formula (4) and (5), we can get:

$$d = a_x \frac{R}{\Delta u} \tag{6}$$

Where: d -- distance between two eye centers and camera

R -- Actual pupillary distance

a_x ——Camera internal parameters

Δu ——Pixel distance of human pupil in image

After calculating d, the distance from the center of two eyes to the roof can be calculated according to the geometric relationship (see the previous article).

Adaptive horizontal adjustment of vehicle driver's seat based on double loop fuzzy control

During horizontal fore and aft adjustment, due to the inconsistent proportion of human body shape and leg length, there is no definite relationship between seat displacement and angle change (even if the same error angle, the adjustment amount of different driver's seat is different), so the sensor should always monitor during adjustment and constantly feedback the angle signal to the controller;In order to improve the adjustment efficiency and control accuracy, the speed of the horizontal adjustment motor should be able to change with the change of leg angle. This paper proposes a horizontal adjustment method based on double loop fuzzy control. The schematic diagram of double loop fuzzy control for seat horizontal adaptive adjustment is shown in Fig. 14.9 below.

(1) Design of fuzzy controller 1

In this system, the input of fuzzy controller 1 is the deviation e1 and deviation change rate ec1 between the angle of the thigh and the leg and the optimal value, and the output is the target speed of the DC motor $v°$ On the premise of ensuring safety, this design is based on comfort. The optimal value of the leg angle is 120°, and the maximum value of the leg angle is 180°. When the seat is adjusted to the optimal value of the angle, it will stop working. The physical universe of e1is [- 1.22, 1.22] rad. If the fuzzy universe E1 of e1 is [- 1.22, 1.22], the quantification factor is 1. The physical universe of ec1 is [-0.35,0.35]. If the fuzzy universe of ec1 is [- 3.5,3.5], the quantization factor is 10. The rated speed of the selected DC motor is 1200 rpm$v$. The physical universe of is [- 1200, 1200], let v If the fuzzy universe V of is [- 3,3], then the scale factor is 400.

In this design, the number of fuzzy subsets of E1, EC1, and V is set to 7, which are positive large (PB), positive middle (PM), positive small (PS), zero (Z), negative small (NS), negative middle (NM), and negative large (NB).The triangular trimf membership function is used as input and output variables, and the barycenter method is used to solve the ambiguity.

The control rules of fuzzy controller 1 are as follows (Table 14.1).

(2) Design of fuzzy controller 2

The error (e2, ec2) between the target speed output by fuzzy controller 1 and the actual speed detected by the sensor is taken as the input of fuzzy controller 2. The rated speed of the seat motor is 1200 rpm, so the physical universe of e2 can be selected as [- 1200, 1200], and the fuzzy universe E2 of e2can be set as [-3,3], so the quantization factor is 400; The physical universe of the rotational speed ec2is [-50,50]. If the fuzzy universe EC2 of ec2 is set to [-5,5], the quantization factor is 10;The electrical signal u output by the fuzzy controller 2 should be compared with the triangular wave with amplitude of 1 to generate PWM signal, so the physical universe of the control quantity u of the fuzzy controller 2 is [- 1, 1]. If the fuzzy universe U of the fuzzy controller 2 is set to [- 1, 1], then the scale factor is 1.

The number of fuzzy subsets of E2, EC2, and U is set to 7, which are positive large (PB), positive middle (PM), positive small (PS), zero (Z), negative small (NS), negative middle

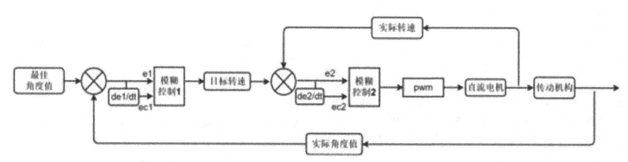

Fig. 14.9 Schematic diagram of double loop fuzzy control for seat horizontal adaptive adjustment

Source: Anthor

Table 14.1 Rules of fuzzy controller 1

EC₁ \ E₁	NB	NM	NS	ZERO	PS	PM	PB
NB	NB	NB	NB	NB	NM	NS	ZERO
NM	NB	NB	NM	NM	NS	ZERO	PS
NS	NB	NM	NM	NS	ZERO	PS	PM
ZERO	NB	NM	NS	ZERO	PS	PM	PB
PS	NM	NS	ZERO	PS	PM	PM	PB
PM	NS	ZERO	PS	PM	PM	PB	PB
PB	ZERO	PS	PM	PB	PB	PB	PB

Source: Anthor

(NM), and negative large (NB).Gbellmf membership function is used as input and output variables. The center of gravity method is used to solve the ambiguity.

The control rules of fuzzy controller 2 are as follows (Table 14.2).

(3) Simulation analysis of adaptive level adjustment of double loop fuzzy control for driver's seat

Use Matlab/Simulink to build the simulation diagram of the dual loop fuzzy control adaptive level adjustment system of the car driver's seat, as shown in Fig. 14.10:

During simulation, select two angle values of leg angle at the initial position, angle 1:180° (3. 14 rad), angle 2:90° (1.57rad).The simulation output curve is shown in Figure 14.11.

It can be seen from the output curve that when the initial position angle value is 180° (3. 14 rad), the adjustment time is 3.5 seconds, the curve is stable, and there is almost no overshoot. When the initial position is 90° (1.57 rad), the adjustment time is 2.5 seconds, the curve is stable, and there is almost no overshoot. Therefore, the adaptive horizontal

adjustment system based on fuzzy double ring driver's seat has good stability, responsiveness and accuracy, and the algorithm is applicable and reliable.

3. Test

3.1 Real Vehicle Test

In order to truly simulate the driving environment and ensure the reliability of test data, this test is directly conducted on the original vehicle (Kia KX7). Remove the original driver's seat and install the newly developed seat prototype on the vehicle. Select 60 drivers to participate in the seat adjustment test. Obtain the vertical distance (height data), thigh and calf angle (angle data) and adjustment time data between the point B of the roof and the centerline of the human eye after adjustment.

3.2 Test Analysis

Height adjustment analysis

The height adjustment data scatter plot is drawn according to the experimental data (Fig. 14.12).The abscissa in the figure is the height of 60 drivers, and the ordinate is the height from

Table 14.2 Rules of fuzzy controller 2

E_2 / EC_2	NB	NM	NS	ZERO	PS	PM	PB
NB	NB	NB	NB	NB	NM	NS	ZERO
NM	NB	NB	NM	NM	NS	ZERO	PS
NS	NM	NM	NM	NS	ZERO	PS	PM
ZERO	NM	NM	NS	ZERO	PS	PM	PM
PS	NS	NS	ZERO	PS	PM	PM	PM
PM	NS	ZERO	PS	PM	PM	PB	PB
PB	ZERO	PS	PM	PB	PB	PB	PB

Source: Anthor

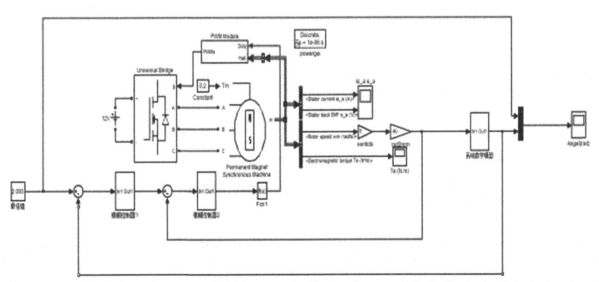

Fig. 14.10 Matlab/Simulink simulation model of driver seat double loop fuzzy control adaptive horizontal adjustment system
Source: Anthor

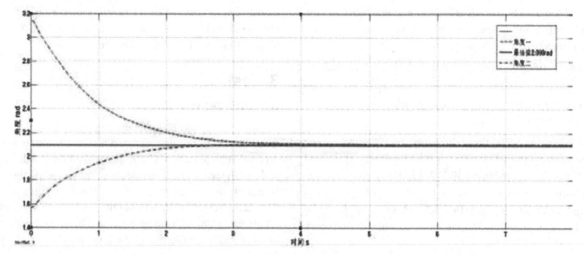

Fig. 14.11 Simulation output curve of double loop fuzzy control

Source: Anthor

point B to eyes after adjustment.It can be seen from the figure that the distance between the driver's eyes and point B on the roof after height adjustment is within 19.5~20.5cm, which meets the design requirements.

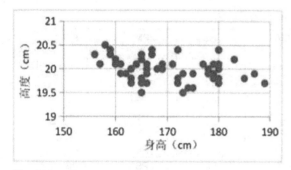

Fig. 14.12 Scatter diagram of height adjustment data

Source: Anthor

Horizontal regulation analysis

The horizontal adjustment data scatter plot is drawn according to the experimental data (Fig. 14.13).The abscissa in the figure is the height of 60 drivers, and the ordinate is the adjusted angle value of the right leg calf and thigh.It can be seen from the figure that the angle between the driver's right leg and thigh is 118.5° ~ 121.5° after the angle adjustment, which meets the design requirements.

Analysis of total regulating time

The scatter plot of the total adjustment time data is drawn according to the experimental data (Fig. 14.14). In the figure, the X axis is the height of 60 drivers, and the Y axis is the total adjustment time. It can be seen from the figure that the total adjustment time of 60 drivers is within 8 seconds, and the higher the height is, the less adjustment time is required.

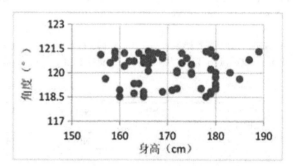

Fig. 14.13 Scatter diagram of horizontal adjustment data

Source: Anthor

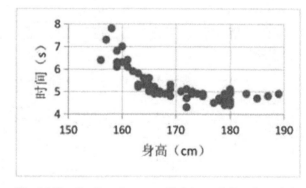

Fig. 14.14 Scatter diagram of total regulation time data

Source: Anthor

4. Conclusion

(1) This paper studies the problem that the intelligent degree of the driver's seat adjustment control is not high at present, proposes a method of collecting the driver's sitting posture information, designs a controller with high accuracy based

on human eye positioning and fuzzy algorithm, redesigns the seat adjustment mechanism and makes a prototype.

(2) After the design is completed, the real vehicle test is carried out. After the height adjustment, the distance between the driver's eyes and point B of the roof is within 19.5 ~ 20.5cm. After the angle adjustment, the angle between the driver's right leg and thigh is within $118.5° ~ 121.5°$. The total adjustment time of 60 drivers is within 8 seconds. The system achieves the intelligent control effect of precise adjustment and less time consumption.

REFERENCE

1. Zhu Hui, Meng Ni. Design and Implementation of Auto Electric Seat Control System [J]. Science and Technology Outlook, 2016,26 (02): 154

2. Dai Chao. Design of PEPS and driver seat intelligent adjustment system based on ARM [D]. Jiangsu University, 2017

3. Chen Wenda, Huang Wenkai, Zhu Jing, He Junfeng. Research on auto seats based on face recognition and autonomous memory [J]. Journal of Dongguan Institute of Technology, 2017,24 (01): 92-96

4. LIU H Y,GRINDLE G,CHUANG F C,et al.A survey of feedback modalities for wheelchair power seat functions[J]. Pervasive Computing, IEEE, 2012, 11(3):54-62.

5. CHEN H N,CHEN H,WANG L J.Analysis of vehicle seat and research on structure optimization in front and rear impact[J]. World Journal of Engineering and Technology, 2014(2):92-99.

6. Nicole Wakelin.GM Technology Could Automatically Adjust Driver Settings in Any Car[P].2015.7

7. Gong Zhipeng, Gao Qiurong, Pan Mi, Yu Weihao, Zhang Xinming. Design of intelligent car seats based on CAN bus [J]. Electronic Production, 2018 (07): 33-34+36

8. Jing Jie. Discussion on driver's vision design and verification in automobile design and development [J]. Small and medium-sized enterprise management and technology (first ten day issue), 2016 (05): 180- 181

9. Li Yanjing, Zhang Yaping, Yin Xinquan. Research on comfort design of automobile driving seat based on ergonomics [J]. Mechanical Research and Application, 2014, 27 (05): 28-30

10. Hou Xiangdan, Zhao Dan, Liu Hongpu, Gu Junhua. Human eye localization based on integral projection and differential projection [J]. Computer Engineering and Science, 2017,39 (03): 534-539

11. Li XianhuiMonocular ranging method based on human eye positioning and implementation of ARM platform [D]. Shenzhen University, 2017

12. Aimran M, M S U M, Rahman H, et al. Face Recognition using Ei genfaces[J]. International Journal of Computer Applications, 2015, 118(5):12- 16.

13. Ban Y, KimS K, Kim S, et al. Face detection based on skin color likelihood [J]. Pattern Recognition,2014, 47(4): 1573-1585.

14. Samir, Bandyopadhyay K. A Method for Face Segmentation, Facial Feature Extraction and Tracking[J]. 2014.

15. Zhao YuDesign of DC speed regulation system based on fuzzy control [D]. Harbin University of Science and Technology, 2019

16. Xia CL,Fang H w,Chen W,et al .Ant colony algorithm based fuzzy control for a brushless DC motor[C]. IEEE Proceedings of the World Congress on Intelligent Contorl and Automaton,China, 2016: 6498-6502.

17. Srinivase Y,Babu K,Tulasi R D G.Improvement in Direct Torque control of induction motor using fuzzy logic duty ratio controller[J]. ARPN Joumal of Engineering and Applied Sciences,2018, 5(4): 68-74.

Sustainable Materials Processing and Manufacturing – Lin Zhu et al. (eds)
© 2024 Taylor & Francis Group, London, ISBN 978-1-032-88599-5

Comparison of Three Sludge Cuts for Biomethanepotential from Selected Municipal Wastewater Treatment Plant

Mmontshi L. Sikosana[1]

PhD Candidate, Department of Mechanical Engineering Science, University of Johannesburg Johannesburg, South Africa

Keneiloe Sikhwivhilu[2]

Chief Scientist, Advanced Materials Division, DSI/Mintek Nanotechnology Innovation Centre, Johannesburg, South Africa

Richard Moutloali[3]

Associate Professor, Engineering and Technology, Institute for Nanotechnology and Water Sustainability, University of South Africa, Johannesburg, South Africa

Daniel M. Madyira[4]

Associate Professor, Department of Mechanical Engineering Science, University of Johannesburg, Johannesburg, South Africa

ABSTRACT: Anaerobic treatment of municipal wastewater has shown sufficient methane production potential for use as an energy source. Three sludge samples (two primary and one secondary) that were collected from a municipal wastewater treatment plant were tested for their production potential of biogas or methane. Yield expressed as a ratio of biogas or methane (normal litres (L_N)) and volatile suspended solids in the sample was used as a measure of performance. Two experiments were carried-out in which, the three sludges were digested with and without an inoculum. The secondary sludge was superior to the other two with an accumulated average methane yield of 420.43 to 528.85 $L_N CH_4/kg_{ODM}$ for original and inoculated samples, respectively. The non- inoculated biomethane production potential for sieve 1 and sieve 2 sludge samples were determined to be 146.96 and 234.71 $L_N CH_4/kg_{ODM}$l, whereas, for inoculated sieve1 and 2, values of 157.55 and 326.04 $L_N CH_4/kg_{ODM}$ were measured. The secondary sludge is to be used in future research in optimizing the designed bioreactor due to its superior performance.

KEYWORDS: Biomethane potential; Biomethane yield; Organic dry matter, Volatile suspended solids

1. Introduction

In particular, before using input substrates in an anaerobic digester, it is advised to obtain information regarding their biomethane potential (BMP) (Owen, et al. 1979). A lab-scale anaerobic digester with a sufficient bacterial inoculum is used to incubate the substrate. The most popular method for obtaining BMP is to track the substrate's degradation over time by measuring the amount of biogas produced and analyzing its composition, which primarily consists of carbon dioxide and methane (Angelidaki, et al. 2009). The batch test is undertaken at a defined temperature between 35 to 38°C for 30 to 35 days until no relevant gas production is takes place (Meyer , et al. 2011) (Wulf , Dohler and Roth 2011) (Muller, Frommert and Jorg 2004) (Gartiser, et al. 2007) . More than 50% of the solids content should be made up of organic dry matter (ODM) in the seeding sludge (Enwuff 2006). Methanogenic bacteria produce biogas as a byproduct of their metabolism when they break down large amounts of organic matter (Vindis, et al. 2008). When building a biogas plant (sizing, management, etc.) and determining its economic viability, the gas yield of various feedstocks—

[1]mmontshis@gmail.com, [2]keneiloes@mintek.co.za, [3]moutlrm@unisa.ac.za, [4]dmadyira@uj.ac.za

DOI: 10.1201/9781003538646-15

particularly the methane yield—is a critical consideration (Wulf, Dohler and Roth 2011). (Ramaraj and others, 2015). The three primary phases of the biological degradation process involved in the generation of anaerobic biogas are disintegration (hydrolysis), acidity, and methane production. Acidification is an important step prior to biogas production, methanogenesis reactions are represented by reactions 1 and 2 as shown below:

$$CH_3COOH \longrightarrow CH_4 + CO_2 \qquad (1)$$

$$2H_2 + CO_2 \longrightarrow CH_4 + CO_2 \qquad (2)$$

Sludge samples were tested with and without an inoculum using the gas yield as performance measure. The aim was to find the sample with the highest biomethane production potential with and without an inoculum.

2. Materials, Methods and Experimental

2.1 Materials

The primary and secondary sludge samples were collected from the Daspoort Wastewater Works in Pretoria.

The primary sludge was screened to remove debris. This sludge was divided into samples of different particle sizes of 0.5 and 1 mL (sieve 1 and sieve 2, respectively). The initial runs were performed to prepare the inoculum from each sample.

2.2 Sludge Solids Determination Procedure

After thoroughly mixing the sample, it was evaporated in a weighted plate and dried for five hours at 103°C to a consistent weight. Total solids were represented by the weight increase over the empty dish. The residue was then burned for 15 minutes at 550°C until it reached a consistent weight. The volatile solids were the ones that lost weight upon fire, whereas the remaining particles stood in for the fixed solids (ash).

2.3 Experimental Procedure

The experiments were performed in order to complement the intended research that is to be undertaken to investigate the water for irrigation methane employing in-house designed AnMBR system. In this exercise, the as received secondary and screened primary sludge samples were subjected to digestion. In Fig. 15.1, the experimental setup is displayed.

The set-up consists of 1 litre Erlenmeyer flasks, 0.5 litre burettes, collection bottles and tubing as shown in Fig. 15.1. The sludge samples were placed in the digesters (Elernmeyer flasks). Each sludge sample was performed in duplicate. The flasks were shaken for 120 min once a day throughout the respective experiments. The Elernmeyer flasks were maintained at 37°C for 35 days using a waterbath. The elevation of the collection bottles served to facilitate the pressure difference in response to the production of biogas. Prior to starting the experiments, the pH of the respective sludge samples was adjusted to be between 6,5 and 7.2 using sodium carbonate powder (Na2CO3) which is known to be ideal for a digestion pH adjustment process (Owen, et al. 1979) (Anderson and Yang 1992). These systems were purged with nitrogen to remove oxygen and create an anaerobic environment (Hansena, et al. 2004).

The pressure increases due to biogas formation dropped the volume of water in the burette from the original setting and the final reading atthe end of the experiment represents the

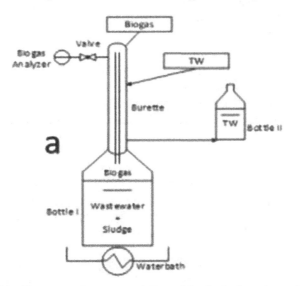
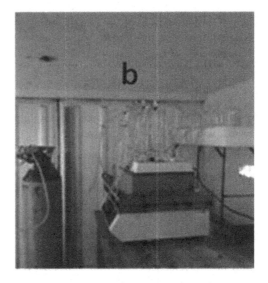

Fig. 15.1 Diagrammatic representation of the typical equipment test setup used to assess the organic content in wastewater's anaerobic biodegradability. (a) a picture of a real test setup in a lab, (b) a schematic drawing (TW = Tap Water)

Source: Adapted from Enwuff 2006 (a) and Authors compilation (b)

generated gas. The volume of the biogas formed from the biodegestion process was read on the burettes and recorded. The produced biogas was collected at the top of the burettes and the composition was determined using a Geotech G5000 equipment.

2.4 Methods

The input of volatile suspended particles and conversion to normalized conditions (0 °C and atmospheric pressure) are typically related to the biogas or methane yield (Enwuff 2006). The resultant gas yields are frequently displayed as a cumulative curve that shows the evolution of gas generation over time. The normalized volume of the fermentation gas, which developed during the intervals between observations, must be determined first. After calculating the biogas's water vapour concentration, the dry gas volume is determined using equation 1 (Deutsches Institut Fur Normung 2001) (Enwuff 2006):

$$VO = V \times \frac{(Pl - Pw) \times T_0}{P_0 \times T} \quad (1)$$

where,

Vo = volume of the dry gas in the normal state (mL_N)

V = volume of the gas as read off (mL)

Pl = pressure of the gas phase at the time of reading (mbar)

Pw = vapour pressure of the water as a function of the temperature of the ambient space (mbar)

To = normal temperature (273 K)

Po = normal pressure (1013 mbar)

T = temperature of the fermentation gas or of the ambient space (K)

Using equation 2 (Deutsches Institut Fur Normung 2001), the specific gas formation (VS) of the sample during the test duration is determined step- by-step, from readout to readout:

$$Vs = \frac{\Sigma Vn \times 10^2}{m \times wT} \quad (2)$$

where,

Vs = specific volume of gas generated during the test period, with respect to the dry weight (L_N/kg)

ΣVn = net volume of gas generated during the test duration under consideration (mL)

m = weight of the weighed sample (g)

wT = dry weight of the sample (%)

Changes of the dead volume, due to variation in temperature and pressure conditions between the readouts are insignificant and thus may be neglected (Deutsches Institut Fur Normung 2001).

The VSS removal of the substrates were calculated using equation 3 (Elsayed, et al. 2019).

$$VSS\ (removed) = \frac{VSS(in) \times VSS(out)}{VSS(in)} \times 100 \quad (3)$$

where,

VSS (removed) = the volatile suspended solids removed from the feedstock

VSS(in) = the input volatile suspended solids for the feedstock in g/L,

VSS(out) = the exit volatile suspended solids for the feedstock in g/L.

The VSS values for the input and exit streams were determine using the normal solids removal procedures.

3. Results and Discussion

3.1 Solids Analysis

The analysis of the three sludge samples was undertaken as described above. It was observed that the secondary sludge has the lowest TSS (5.79 g/L, VSS 4.66 g/L and VSS/TSS = 81%). It is interesting to see that Sieve 1 (TSS = 16.45 g/L, VSS = 11.91 g/L and VSS/TSS = 72%) and Sieve2 (TSS = 23.64 g/L ,VSS = 17.27 g/L and VSS /TSS = 73%) sludge samples had similar percentage VSS/TSS ratio despite different TSS and VSS compositions. This is because this was the same sample that was screened using sieves of different sizes. Using different sieve sizes was to effect the settleability of the samples.

3.2 Biomethane Yield, and Composition

The values for the yield of biomethane production from the original and inoculated sludge samples are plotted as cumulative yield curves as shown in Figures 15.2 a and b, respectively.

Sieve 2 (VSS/TSS = 73%) primary sludge has a higher average methane yield than the Sieve 1 (VSS/TSS = 72%) sample. This was reported by Brudeckia et.al.that 1% VSS increment increases the methane yield (Brudeckia, et al. 2015). The effect of VSS composition on methane production potential is also evident on the plots, whereby, the secondary sludge at VSS/TSS = 81% has the highest methane yield. It is evident from the figures that the addition of inoculum improved the results in terms of gas yield. It is observed that the sieve2 and secondary sludge samples exhibited no lag phase. Sieve 1 sludge showed a lag phase for the inoculated sample. According to Dutta (2008), the lag phase is the first stage of cultivation when there is little to no change in the number of cells. The reason for the lag is typically that before development can commence, the cells need to acclimate to

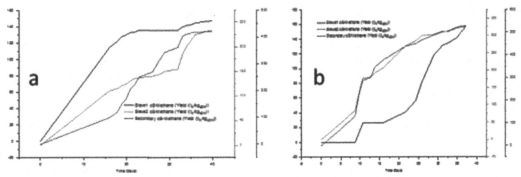

Fig. 15.2 Cumulative methane yield for three test sludges (a – no inoculum and b – inoculated)

Source: Authors compilation

the new medium (Dutta 2008). This improvement in terms of methane yield for inoculated sludge is due to the existence of active cells in the inoculum. The active cells in the inoculum facilitate immediate digestion of organic material in the inoculated sludge and inoculum produces additional gas. It is also observed from the plots that there are periods where lag occurs which could be due to an inhibitor. A modulator that lowers the activity of an enzyme is called an inhibitor. Competitively, noncompetitively, or partially competitively, it can lower the rate of reaction (Levenspiel 1999). The staged curve may be due to a multiple-phase decomposition and retarded decomposition (Enwuff 2006) . The original sieve 2 and secondary sludge samples exhibit the multiple-phase, whereas, it's inoculated counterpart shows the retarded degradation. A straight line that is proportionate to

cell concentration and constant at its maximum value should ideally represent the phase in which the number of cells increases exponentially as the cells begin to divide.

In Fig. 15.2a, the stationary phase is a bit close to the expected phenomenon between day 35 and day 40 as reported elsewhere (Dutta 2008). Fig. 15.6b shows, that the stationary phase was not reached i.e. the decomposition of the organic matter was not complete. This could be due to increased amount of VSS contributed by the inoculum addition.

The biomethane yield was on average 146.96 $L_N CH_4/kg_{ODM}$ for original sieve1 sludge and 157.55 for the inoculated sample. The average results are as summarized in Table 15.1. There is an overall improvement on average yield for all sludge samples, with sieve 2 from 234.71 to 326.04 and

Table 15.1 Summary of biogas and methane yield for tested sludge samples

Substrate	No Inoculum			Inoculated			No Inoculum	Inoculated
	oDM-Biogas	oDM-Methane	Methane	oDM-Biogas	oDM-Methane	oDM-Methane	Methane	Methane
	yield	yield	concentration	yield	yield	concentration	Vol	Vol
	I_N/kg_{FM}	IN CH_4/kg_{oDM}	Vol%	I_N/kg_{FM}	IN CH_4/kg_{oDM}	Vol%	mL	mL
Sieve1 Sludge	212,28	161, 16	72.02	309,02	137,08	69,90	425	664
Sieve1 Sludge	183,90	132,77	69,37	371,02	178,02	67,70	368	797
Average	**198,09**	**146,96**	**70.69**	**340,02**	**157,55**	**68,80**	**396**	**730**
Sieve2 Sludge	364,20	233,87	61,37	699,39	361,03	55,03	728	1468
Sieve2 Sludge	368,03	235,55	61.02	583,77	291,06	53,52	736	1226
Average	**366,12**	**234,71**	**61.19**	**641,58**	**326,04**	**54,27**	**732**	**1347**
Secondary Sludge	636,49	415,63	66.63	763,84	537,98	75, 10	1310	1572
Secondary Sludge	656,96	425,23	66, 14	713,86	519,59	75,20	1352	1469
Average	**646,73**	**420,43**	**66.38**	**738,85**	**528,79**	**75,15**	**1331**	**1520**

Source: Authors compilation

420.43 to 528.85 L_NCH_4/kg_{ODM} for the secondary sludge for original and inoculated samples, respectively. The sieve 1 increase by 7 %, sieve 2 at 28 % and secondary sludge shifted 20 % with the addition of an inoculum. The volume of produced methane gas increased from a total average of 396 to 730 mL for non-inoculated sieve 1 to inoculated sample, respectively. A similar trend with sieve 2 original (732 mL) to 1347 mL inoculated sieve 2 while the secondary shifted from 1331 (original) to 1520 mL (inoculated) as shown in Table 15.1.

According to Chlipała et al. (2019), Elsayed et al. (2019), Rodriguez-Chiang and Dahl (2015), Kedia et al. (2011), and others, biogas is generally composed of 50– 80% CH_4 and 30–50% CO_2, with traces of H_2S, O_2, H_2, NH_3, and N_2.

The analysis was carried-out when enough biogas was observed on the Erlemeyer flasks as readout, using the Geotech G5000 equipment. This equipment detects CH_4, CO_2, O_2 and H_2S and N_2. The presence of H_2S was not detected with small amount of O_2. The percentage yield of methane for the Sieve 1 remained almost the same at 70.69 and 68.80 % for the original and inoculated sludge samples, respectively. Sieve 2 sludge samples showed a decrease in methane composition of biogas as shown in Table 15.1. The secondary sludge exhibit an increase in methane productivity with the addition of the inoculum from 66.38 to 75.15% (Table 15.1). Numerous intricate networks of chemical and biological interactions as well as transport events, involving several phases and multicomponent systems, combine to produce cell kinetics (Dutta 2008). The deviations between two similar samples in Table 1 is not easy to deduce because the sludge was not homogenous. The diverse blend of young and old cells constantly changes and adapts to the media environment during growth, which is also constantly changing in terms of physical and chemical circumstances (Dutta 2008). In light of this complexity, no attempt was made to explain the high average yield of methane for the secondary sludge, contrasted with the low conversion of VSS.

The difference in terms of the %VSS/TSS before and after digestion workout to be 28 % for the two primary samples. This shows that the experimental results could be considered reliable for use in the next exercise for the optimization of the in-house design of reactor. The secondary sludge difference is 30 % which is close to that of the other samples. The comparison table (Table 15.5) and bar graph (Fig. 15.7) showing the sludge samples the before and after the digestion are provided low.

The changes are very similar for the three sludge samples before and after digestion. It is clear that a selection of sludge between these samples for further research purposes cannot be based on this criterion.

4. Conclusion

The samples were collected from the municipal wastewater works and the primary sludge was screened to remove debris. The sample was divided according to particle size, viz. sieves 1 (0.5 mm) and 2 (1 mm). The secondary sludge was used as received in the batch digestion experiment for the production of methane. The secondary sludge was superior to the other two with an accumulated average methane yield of 420.43 to 528.85 L_NCH_4/kg_{ODM} for original and inoculated samples, respectively. The non-inoculated biomethane production potential for Sieve 1 and 2 samples were determined to be 146.96 and 234.71 L_NCH_4/kg_{ODM}l, whereas, for inoculated Sieve1 and 2, values of 157.55 and 326.04 L_NCH_4/kg_{ODM} were measured. The fact that this sludge does not require any further work before use also make it attractive. The methane composition of the generated biogas was 75 % for the secondary sludge, compared to 67 % for sieve 1 and 54 % for sieve 2. The volume of produced methane gas increased from a total average of 396 to 730 mL for non-inoculated sieve 1 to inoculated sample, respectively. A similar trend with sieve 2 original (732 mL) to 1347 mL inoculated sieve 2 while the secondary shifted from 1331 (original) to 1520 mL (inoculated). The secondary sludge is to be used in future research in optimizing the designed bioreactor due to its superior performance.

Acknowledgement

This work is based in part on research funded by the Swedish International Development Cooperation Agency (Sida) through the LIRA 2030 Africa Programme, which is implemented in collaboration with the International Science Council (ISC) and the Network of African Science Academies (NASAC). The University of Johannesburg's Department of Applied Chemistry, Chemical Engineering Sciences, and Mechanical Engineering Science departments provided support for which the authors are grateful. The money and authorization to present the findings are also appreciated by the authors from the Department of Science and Innovation (DSI)/Mintek Nanotechnology Innovation Centre.

The assistance of Dr Edwin M. Mmutlane from the Department of Chemical Sciences in terms of the required infrastructure and advice is highly appreciated.

REFERENCES

1. Deutsches Institut Fur Normung , E V. 2001. "Ordinance on Environmentally Compatible Storage of Waste from Human Settlements and on Biological Waste-Treatment Facilities." Germany: Techstreet Store.

2. Anderson, G K, and G Yang. 1992. "pH Control in Anaerobic Treatment of Industrial Wastewater." *Journal of Environmental Engineering* 118 (4): 73–87.

3. Angelidaki, I, M Alves, D Bolzonella , L Borzacconi, J L Campos, A J Guwy , S Kalyuzhny, P Jenicek, and J B van Lier. 2009. "Defining the biomethane potential (BMP) of solid organic wastes and energy crops: a proposed protocol for batch assays." *Water Science & Technology* 59 (5): 927–934.

4. Brudeckia, G, R Farzanah, I Cybulska, J E Schmidt, and M H Thomsen. 2015. "Evaluation of composition and biogas production potential from seagrass (Halodule uninervis) native to Abu Dhabi." *Energy Procedia 7* 75: 760–766.

5. Chlipała, M, P Błaszczak, S F Wang, P Jasiński, and B Bochentyn. 2019. "In situ study of a composition of outlet gases from biogas fuelled Solid Oxide Fuel Cell performed by the Fourier Transform Infrared Spectroscopy." *International Journal ofHydrogen Energy* 44 (26): 13864–13874.

6. Dutta, R. 2008. *Fundamentals of Biochemical Engineering.* New Delhi: Springer.

7. Edwards, W., M. S. Sheldon, P. J. Zeelie, D. de Jager, L. G. Dekker, and C. C. Bezuidenhout. 2013.

8. *Water Reuse Using a Dual-Stage Membrane Bioreactor for Industrial Efluent Treatment.*

9. Pretoria: Water Reaserch Commission (WRC). Report No. TT556/13.

10. Elsayed, M, Y Andres, W Blel, R Hassan, and A Ahmed. 2019. "Effect of inoculum VS, organic loads and I/S on the biochemical methane potential of sludge, buckwheat husk and straw." *Desalination and Water Treatment* 157: 69–78.

11. Enwuff, VDI 4630. 2006. *Fermentation of organic materials Characterisation of the substrate, sampling, collection of material data, fermentation test.* Berlin: Verein Deutscher Ingenieure.

12. Gartiser, S, E Urich, R Alexy, and K Kumerer. 2007. "Anaerobic inhibition and biodegradation of antibiotics in ISO test schemes." *Chemosphere* 66: 1839–1848.

13. Hansena, T L, J E Schmidt, I Angelidaki, E Marca, J C Jansen, H Mosbæk, and T H Christensen. 2004. "Method for determination of methane potentials of solid organic waste." *Waste Management* 24: 393–400.

14. Kedia, G K, V P Desai, K P Hankel, and D Gadhia. 2011. "Low pressure Biogas Purification System." *Progress in Biogas Stuttgart-Hohenheim.* Valsad.

15. Levenspiel, O. 1999. *Chemical Reaction Engineering.* New York: John Wiley & Sons.

16. Meyer, F, A Noo , G Sinnaeve, P Dardenne, L Hoffmann, J Flammang, G Fourcart, P Gerins, and P Delfosse. 2011. "Evaluation of the prediction of biogas production from maize silages with Near InfraRed Spectroscopy (NIRS)." *Progress in Biogas Stuttgart-Hohenheim.* Stuttgart.

17. Muller, W R, I Frommert , and R Jorg. 2004. "Standardized methods for anaerobic biodegradability testing." *Reviews in Environmental Science and Bio/Technology* 3: 141–158.

18. Owen, W F, D C Stuckey, J B Heal, L Y Young , and P L McCarty. 1979. "Bioassay for Monitoring Biochemical Methane Potential and Anaerobic Toxicity." *Water Research* 13: 485–492.

19. Ramaraj, R, N Dussadee, N Whangchai, and Y Unpaprom. 2015. "Microalgae biomass as an alternative substrate in biogas production." *International Journal of Sustainable and Green Energy* 4 (1): 13–19.

20. Rodriguez-Chiang, L M, and O P Dahl. 2015. "Effect of Inoculum to Substrate Ratio on the Methane Potential of Microcrystalline Cellulose." *BioResources* 10 (1): 898 - 911.

21. Staff. 2010. "Laboratory Training Manual for Wastewater Treatment Plant Operators." Michigan : State of Michigan Department of Environmental Quality.

22. van der Lubbe, J, and A va Haandel. 2019. "Anaerobic biodegradability, specific methanogenic activity and sludge stability." In *Anaerobic Sewage Treatment : Optimization of process and physical design of anaerobic and complementary processes*, by J van der Lubbe and A va Haandel, 405–414. London: IWA Publishing,.

23. Vindis, P, B Mursec, C Rozman, M Janzek, and F Cus. 2008. "Biogas production with the use of mini digester." *Journal of Achievements in Materials and Manufacturing Engineering* 99–102.

24. Wulf, S, H Dohler, and U Roth. 2011. "Assessment of methane potentials - significance of batch tests." *Progress in Biogas Stuttgart-Hohenheim .* Darmstadt.

Sustainable Materials Processing and Manufacturing – Lin Zhu et al. (eds)
© 2024 Taylor & Francis Group, London, ISBN 978-1-032-88599-5

Methane Solubility in Effluent Wastewater from Anaerobic UASB Reactor Treatment—A Theoretical Perspective

Mmontshi L. Sikosana

PhD Candidate, Department of Mechanical Engineering Science,
University of Johannesburg Johannesburg, South Africa

Keneiloe Sikhwivhilu

Chief Scientist, Advanced Materials Division, DSI/Mintek Nanotechnology Innovation Centre,
Johannesburg, South Africa

Richard Moutloali

Associate Professor, Engineering and Technology, Institute for Nanotechnology and Water Sustainability,
University of South Africa, Johannesburg, South Africa

Daniel M. Madyira

Associate Professor, Department of Mechanical Engineering Science,
University of Johannesburg, Johannesburg, South Africa

ABSTRACT: The main difficulty in treating wastewater while producing methane has been getting the dissolved gas out of the effluent. This review paper's objective was to investigate previous studies that have been done in this field.. Literature search was conducted and summarized in this document. It is observed that not much research has taken place at a commercial scale and it is suggested that further work need to take place. The research based on use of a membrane seem to have attracted a lot work in recovering dissolved methane from the effluent. It is envisaged that the understanding of the solubility characteristics of methane in the effluent could shed some light in recovery strategies of this gas from the effluent.

KEYWORDS: Municipal wastewater treatment, Upflow anaerobic sludge blanket, Methane hydrate, Solubility

1. Introduction

According to Souza, Chernicharo, and Aquino (2011), biogas produced in reactors known as UASBs (Upflow Anaerobic Sludge Blanket) that treat home wastewater typically has significant methane concentrations (70–80%). Methane may be discharged with the final effluent (36–45%) due to the considerable volumes of methane that have been seen to remain dissolved in the liquid phase (Souza, Chernicharo, and Aquino 2011; Liu et al. 2014). The amount of methane that dissolves causes a 45–65% reduction in the off-gas conversion that can be utilized to produce electricity. (Chen and others, 2017a) (Chen and others, 2017d) (Gouveia and others, 2015)

(Lin and others, 2011) (Shankum and Umaiyakunjaram, 2016). The key question would be on whether it is possible to recover the methane that is dissolve in the effluent water.

The focus of this paper is to find an answer to the above-mentioned question from a theoretical perspective. It is envisaged that an understanding of how methane interacts with water could lead to the optimum recovery of this gas from the effluent during the treatment process.

2. Theoretical Interaction of Methane and Water

The majority of methane gas in aqueous media is trapped as hydrates (Kirov, Fanourgakis, and Xantheas 2008). The

[1]mmontshis@gmail.com, [2]keneiloes@mintek.co.za, [3]moutlrm@unisa.ac.za, [4]dmadyira@uj.ac.za

DOI: 10.1201/9781003538646-16

clathrate hydrate framework functions as a "host" lattice, allowing "guest" molecules to be imprisoned within its cages through weak van der Waals interactions. With a capacity of up to 180 cubic meters of gas per cubic meter of hydrates, empty water cages serve as effective gas storage devices (Songa, et al. 2019). According to Deible, Tuguldur, and Jordan (2014) as shown in Fig. 16.1, the most prevalent type of methane hydrate has a type I hydrate structure with a methane molecule at the center of each unit cell's two 5^{12} and six $5^{12}6^2$ water cages. Every water molecule in these cage-like molecular clusters lies on the cluster's surface and has a connectivity of three, meaning that it is hydrogen bound to just three neighbours. The 24-molecule $5^{12}6^2$ cage contains two opposing hexagonal faces and twelve pentagonal faces, whereas the 5^{12} cage has a dodecahedral structure. Temperature and pressure determine methane equilibrium occupancy in each cage and intrinsic characteristics of clathrate hydrate, such as guest molecule occupancy, determine the clathrate hydrate's dissociation (Komatsu, et al. 2019).

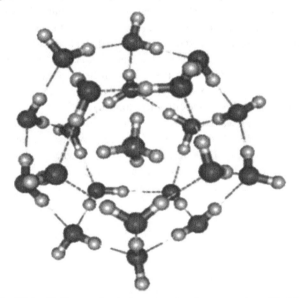

Fig. 16.1 Methane hydrate structural geometry (Deible, Tuguldur, and Jordan 2014) (Red atoms - oxygen, light gray - hydrogen and dark gray - carbon)

It has been found that dodecahedral water cage contains 30,026 symmetry unique isomers with various protonic configurations (McDonald, Ojama and Singer 1998). The isomer with lowest energy found by Kirov et al. (Kirov, Fanourgakis and Xantheas 2008) was used by Deible et al. (Deible, Tuguldur and Jordan 2014) in their investigation of theoretical binding energy of a methane molecule in a (H2O)20 Dodecahedral Cage. Second order Møller-Plesset perturbation theory (MP2), couple supermolecular second-order Møller-Plesset perturbation theory (MP2C), different dispersion corrected density functional theory (DFT) and

diffusion Monte Carlo (DMC) methods were used in the study to calculate interaction energy of a methane molecule enclosed in a dodecahedral water cage. Binding energies obtained using the MP2, MP2C, and DMC techniques were −5.04, −4.60, and −5.3 kcal/mol, in that order. The cages are in a stable bonded condition, meaning that the methane hydrate structure is resistant to disintegrating into its component protons and neutrons, indicated by negative values. Furthermore, the DFT, MP2 and coupled cluster singles - doubles with perturbative triples (CCSD(T)) methods used assess the two- and three-body contributions. It was shown that three- body contribution to the interaction energy was significantly overestimated by all of the DFT approaches that were taken into consideration. Symmetry-adapted perturbation theory (SAPT) permits decomposition into electrostatics, exchange, induction and dispersion components was used to further analyze the two- and three-body energies. The three-body contributions of induction, dispersion and exchange to the methane-cage binding energy are all significant according to SAPT calculations, with the net three-body contribution to binding energy being approximately 1 kcal/mol. This positive number, as opposed to a single-body numerical analysis, indicates an unstable structure to breaking for the two- and three-body energies.

Given that these cages are expected to be formed during the production of methane via the anaerobic treatment of wastewater, it becomes imperative that these structures get decomposed in order to recover the dissolved gas. The next sections investigate the different methods that could be employed in order to recover the methane that is trapped in the cages.

3. Dissolution of Methane from the Type I Methane Hydrate Structure

There are several methods used to recover methane from the type I Methane Hydrate Structures. The methods that are most suitable for recovery of dissolved methane during the anaerobic wastewater treatment include hydrate structural decomposition and carbon dioxide replacement or the combination thereof. These methods could form part of the anaerobic treatment system, which could reduce the methane recovery costs.

3.1 The Type I Methane Hydrate Structure's Methane Replacement

The process of replacing CH4 with CO2 from natural gas hydrate is the source of this technique for recovering dissolved methane (CH_4) from effluent during wastewater treatment (Ohgaki, et al. 1996). Computer simulations were employed by Bai et al. (Bai et al. 2012) to answer the problems regarding the formation and breakdown of CO_2 and CH_4 hydrates during the replacement process. As the CH_4 hydrate broke down, it was noticed that the CO_2 hydrate nucleated at the interface between liquid phase and CH_4 hydrate. This led to in-situ substitution of CO_2 for CH_4 molecules in the hydrate form.

Figure 16.2(a) shows that tiny 5_{12} cages are maintained in substantially longer duration (~0.4 ms) than large $5_{12}6_2$ cages, which account for the majority of broken cages. The reason for this is that some of the H_2O molecules in big cages have adverse angles for the planar hexagonal rings (Bai et al. 2012). Number of rings relative to time is displayed in Fig. 16.2(b). Even though the majority of the hydrate cages are broken, in the figure it is shown that a significant number of rings are still present in recently produced water (Fig. 16.2a). The so-called "memory effect," which is frequently observed, may have a plausible explanation in the remaining water structures following the breakdown of CH_4 hydrate.

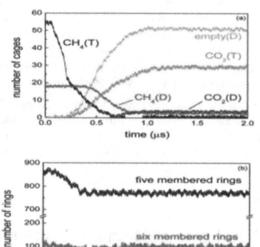

Fig. 16.2 (a) A graph showing the quantity of cages in area C over time. In the picture, the symbols "T" and "D" stand for $5_{12}6_2$ cages and 5_{12} cages, respectively. (b) Quantity of rings in area C with respect to time (Bai, et al. 2012)

3.2 Methane Hydrate Structure Type I: Molecular Simulation of Decomposition

Wei et al. (2018) conducted a molecular simulation investigation that included dynamics simulations for the breakdown of structure I methane hydrate. Table 16.1 provides a summary of the molecular dynamics simulation conditions.

The breakdown number of the hydrate cages was expressed by the cage ruptures in this simulation. This was a representation

Table 16.1 Hydrate cage decomposition numbers (n) under various simulation scenarios (Wei et al. 2018)

Group	Temperature K	Pressure MPa	n
(1)	273	0.1	102
(2)	283		180
(3)	293		329
(4)	273	5	56
(5)	283		123
(6)	293		302
(7)	273	10	52
(8)	283		64
(9)	293		260

of the methane hydrate's degree of breakdown. Table 16.1 makes it clear that, contrary to what may be expected, the breakdown number of hydrate cages rises with temperature at constant pressure. Hydrate cage breakdown numbers vary slightly throughout groups (4), (7), and (8). Methane hydrate cannot break down in these groups' settings, according to its equilibrium requirements (Dzyuba and Zektser 2013). On the simulated condition with the maximum temperature at 293 K and the lowest pressure at 0.1 MPa, there is the greatest number of hydrate cages that decompose (3). Elsewhere (Liu, et al. 2014), it was experimentally determined that the amount of dissolved methane during the anaerobic wastewater treatment using UASB reactor decreased with increasing temperature at constant pressure as shown in Fig. 16.3.

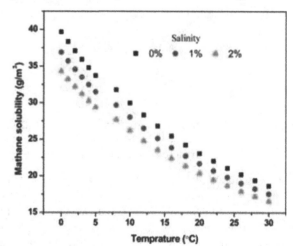

Fig. 16.3 Methane solubility in water at various salinities and temperatures (Liu et al. 2014)

For instance, at 30°C, methane is soluble at a rate of roughly 18.6 g/m^3. According to Liu et al. (2014), this indicate that in anaerobic systems running at 30°C, approximately 45% of the methane generated would presumably be present in its dissolved form. This percentage will increase at lower temperatures. Both the simulated and experimental observations indicate the need to operate at higher temperatures during the production of methane via the anaerobic wastewater treatment if the methane hydrate is to be effectively decomposed.

4. Conclusion

Dissolved methane provides a challenge in energy generation from wastewater anaerobic treatment. Models that are discussed in this document hold do show that methane could be recovered with the understanding of why up 50% of remains in the effluent. The research on use of membranes is more attractive due to its practicality. Regarding operating at higher temperature for methane recovery, the disadvantage could be the added energy, which could end up being uneconomical. It is recommended that further research needs to take place around the determination of methane type 1 hydrate in an anaerobic reactor system. This could lead to the development of efficient recovery of dissolved methane during wastewater

Acknowledgement

A portion of the study for this paper was financed by the Swedish International Development Cooperation Agency (Sida) as part of the LIRA 2030 Africa Programme. This program is run in association with the Network of African Science Academies (NASAC) and the International Science Council (ISC). The authors acknowledge the support they received from the Department of Applied Chemistry, Chemical Engineering Sciences, and Mechanical Engineering Science departments at the University of Johannesburg. The Department of Science and Innovation (DSI)/Mintek Nanotechnology Innovation Center authors also appreciate the funding and permission to present the results.

REFERENCES

1. Bai, D., X. Zhang, G. Chen, and W. Wang. (2012). "Replacement mechanism of methane hydrate with carbon dioxide from microsecond molecular dynamics simulations." Energy and Environmental Science (5): 7033 - 7041.
2. Chen, C., W. Guo, H. H. Ngo, S. W. Chang, D. D. Nguyen, P. D. Nguyen, X. T. Bui, and Y. Wu. (2017a). "Impact of reactor configurations on the performance of a granular." International Biodeterioration & Biodegradation (121): 131 - 138.
3. Chen, R, Y. Nie, H. Kato, J. Wu, T. Utashiro, J. Lu, S. Yue, H. Jiang, L. Zhang, and Y. Y. Li. (2017d). "Methanogenic degradation of toilet-paper cellulose upon sewage treatment in an anaerobic membrane bioreactor at room temperature." Bioresource Technology (228): 69–76.
4. Deible, M. J., O. Tuguldur, and K. D. Jordan. (2014). "Theoretical Study of the Binding Energy of a Methane Molecule in a (H2O)20 Dodecahedral Cage." Journal of Physical Chemistry : 1 - 7.
5. Dzyuba, A. V., and I. S. Zektser. (2013). "Variations in Submarine Groundwater Runoff as a Possible Cause of Decomposition of Marine MethaneHydrates in the Artcic." Water Resources 40 (1): 74 - 83.
6. Gambelli, A. M., B. Castellani, A. Nicolini, and F. Rossi. (2019). "Experimental study on natural gas hydrate exploitation: Optimization of methane recovery, carbon dioxide storage and deposit structure preservation." Journal of Petroleum Science and Engineering (177): 594 - 601.
7. Gouveia, J., G. Plaza, G. Garralon, F. Fdz-Polanco, and M. Pena. (2015). "Long-term operation of a pilot scale anaerobic membrane bioreactor." Bioresource Technology (185): 225–233.
8. Hopfstock, H. (1997). "Paint removal composition and system." Paint Ink International 10 (3): 1-23.
9. Kirov, M. V., G. S. Fanourgakis, and S. S. Xantheas. (2008). "Identifying the most stable networks in polyhedral water clusters." Chemical Physics Letters (461): 180– 188.
10. Komatsu, H., T. Sasagawa, S. Yamamoto, Y. Hiraga, M. Ota, T. Tsukada, and R. L. Smith Jr. (2019). "Methane clathrate hydrate dissociation analyzed with Raman spectroscopy and a thermodynamic mass transfer model considering cage occupancy." Fluid Phase Equilibria (489): 41 - 47.
11. Lin, h., J. Chen, F. Wang, L. Ding, and H. Hong. (2011). "Feasibility evaluation of submerged anaerobic membrane bioreactor for municipal secondary wastewater treatment." Desalination (280): 120– 126.
12. Liu, Z., H. Yin, Z. Dang, and L. Yu . (2014). "Dissolved Methane: A Hurdle for Anaerobic Treatment of Municipal Wastewater." Environmental Science & Technology (48): 889–890.
13. McDonald, S., L. Ojama, and S. J. Singer. (1998). "Graph Theoretical Generation and Analysis of Hydrogen-Bonded Structures with Applications to the Neutral and Protonated Water Cube and Dodecahedral Clusters." Journal of Physical Chemistry 102 (17): 2824-2832.
14. Ohgaki, K., K. Takano, H. Sangawa, T. Matsubara, and S. Nakano. (1996). "Methane Exploitation by Carbon Dioxide from gas Hydrates - Phase Equilibria for CO2-CH4 Mixed Hydrate System." Journal of Chemical Engineering of Japan 29 (3): 478 - 483.
15. Songa, S., B. Shi, W. Yu, L. Ding, Y. Chen, Y. Yu, C. Ruan, Y. Liu, W. Wang, and J. Gong. (2019). "A new methane hydrate decomposition model considering intrinsic kinetics and mass transfer." Chemical Engineering Journal (361): 1264 - 1284.
16. Souza, C. L., C. A> Chernicharo, and S. F. Aquino. (2011). "Quantification of dissolved methane in UASB reactors treating domestic wastewater under different operating conditions." Water Science & Technology 64 (11): 2259 - 2264.
17. Umaiyakunjaram, R., and P. Shanmugam. (2016). "Study on submerged anaerobic membrane bioreactor (SAMBR) treating high suspended solids raw tannery wastewater for biogas production." Bioresource Technology (216): 785–792.
18. Wei, N., W. T. Sun, Y. F. Meng, A. Q. Liu, S. W. Zhou, P. Guo, Q. Fu, and X. Lv. (2018). "Analysis of Decomposition for Structure I Methane Hydrate by Molecular Dynamics Simulation." Russian Journal of Physical Chemistry A 92 (5): 840–846.

Sustainable Materials Processing and Manufacturing – Lin Zhu et al. (eds)
© 2024 Taylor & Francis Group, London, ISBN 978-1-032-88599-5

Agriculture Monitoring System Improvement Utilizing Wireless Sensors Networks

Amo Samuel Blay[1]
Lecuturer, Accra Technical University, Accra
Mathias Bennet Michael[2]
Senior Lecuturer, Accra Technical University, Accra

ABSTRACT: Agriculture is something that can be traced back to practically every country in the world. Agriculture, which entails the growing of food and other items by means of farming, is responsible for the production of the great majority of the world's food supply. Agriculture was a crucial step in the evolution of the human practice of settling down and remaining in one location for an extended period of time. Agriculture was a labour-intensive endeavor in the early phases of human civilization. It is essential to have a goal of improving agriculture technologically in order to keep up with the rapid pace at which the globe is entering a new technological and implementation-based period. Internet of Things (IOT) is a crucial component of "smart agriculture." Sensors connected to the internet of things are able to provide information about agricultural lands.

The purpose of this paper is to demonstrate a wireless and intelligent farm system that makes use of automation. This is made possible by the implementation of a superior wireless sensor-centered farm detection and alert system. This system gathers data from a broad range of sensors that have been put at a wide variety of nodes and then transmits that data using a wireless protocol. Arduino serves as the brains of this smart agricultural system that using a sensor network. The system consists of networked sensors that detect environmental parameters including temperature and humidity. In addition to that, it has a motor and a WiFi system. These environmental factors are all analyzed as soon as it is activated. It notifies through SMS if a certain level is reached. If the water level drops below a certain threshold, a sensor will trigger the water pump to begin pumping. Any higher variations in the temperature set point, the cooling system turns on and it's shown on a display. The kind of plants being cultivated, the environment conditions may be varied. The water pump may be quickly turned off by pressing a button on the Internet of Things.

KEYWORDS: IoT, Agricultural monitoring, Wireless sensor networks

1. Introduction

Agriculture is something that can be traced back to practically every country in the world. Agriculture, which entails the growing of food and other items by means of farming, is responsible for the production of the great majority of the world's food supply. Agriculture was a crucial step in the evolution of the human practice of settling down and remaining in one location for an extended period of time.

Terrain, climate, soil, and soil water affect agricultural crop yield. These four criteria make it possible to cultivate particular crops in certain places. Lack of environmental monitoring affects agricultural produce.

Agriculture therefore needs much effort in this modern era of human civilization. To keep up with the speed at which the world is entering a new age of technologies and implementations, it is essential to have a goal of technologically modernizing

[1]sbamo@atu.edu.gh, [2]mbmichael@atu.edu.gh

DOI: 10.1201/9781003538646-17

agriculture. This will assist in improving the monitoring these environmental factors that impact on agriculture production. The capacity to improve remote monitoring of agricultural infrastructure and environmental factors may liberate farmers' time, labor, and resources, allowing them to concentrate on other activities. [1].

"Smart agriculture" requires the Internet of Things (IOT). One may get agricultural land data through internet-connected sensors. [2].

The purpose of this research is to demonstrate an agricultural monitoring system that is not only intelligent but also fully automated and wireless. A wireless sensor-based IoT-based agricultural monitoring system does this. Sensors surrounding the farms feed this system. Review of Related works

2. Literature Review

Prof. K. A. Patil et al. proposed a sustainable agriculture in [3]. [11] Agriculture and information technology have always been very important.

Farmers may have grown the same crop for decades, but environmental factors, soil conditions, and disease outbreaks have increased. Nevertheless, neither the consequences for the overall impact nor those for the hardware were investigated.

Sahitya Roy et al. [4] propose an AgroTick based on architecture with the goals of increasing agricultural output, establishing a platform for farmers to share information, establishing a cohesive farming network, and developing novel agricultural opportunities. These opportunities include: simple access to agro loans; low costs of goods; enhanced return on investment; inexpensive agricultural consultation; and agro networking. The procedures seem burdensome, and rural farmers will need more time to adapt.

The Internet of Things (IoT) and automated crop management for smart farming are two examples of cutting-edge technology that Prathibha SR et al presented ans indicated in [5]. The monitoring of environmental conditions was recognized as one of the most important factors in boosting agricultural productivity. Their study centered mostly on the use of CC3200 single-chip sensors for the purpose of monitoring temperature and humidity in agricultural regions. In order to transmit pictures to the farmers' smartphones through MMS and Wi-Fi, a camera was interfaced with CC3200. Despite the benefits of the system, combining IoT with automation will make the system difficult to use and costly to implement. Similar challenges will be encountered by local farmers who try to implement it.

An IoT-based smart farming technique was developed by Md Ashuddin Mondal et al. in [6]. Intelligent agriculture is viable

because it allows for precise crop management, important data collection, and automated farming techniques. In their research, they demonstrated an intelligent agricultural field management system that controls soil temperature and humidity. This method needs an IT expert to be of any use to farmers, which might lead to higher costs for the farmers.

In [7], Nurzaman Ahmed et al. proposed the Internet of Things (IoT), which gives "smart farming" and conventional farming a whole new dimension. Connecting agricultural and farming nodes in far areas is now conceivable because to fog computing and WiFi-based long-distance networks in the Internet of Things. A scalable network design was suggested, one that would allow for the management and monitoring of farms and agricultural activities in far-flung locations while also reducing network latency. In this, they offered a strategy for detecting and acting upon physical environments that is based on channel access and routing that operates across many layers.

The network's coverage, speed, and latency were also examined. Whilst the systems are effective at helping farmers in remote areas, they need substantial financial investment in infrastructure to enable fog computing and WiFi technologies application.

In [8], Siddhant Kumar et al. proposed a clever method dubbed gCrop that employs IoT, image processing, and machine learning to monitor the growth of greens and report on their status in real time. The gCrop system comprises of a set of high- tech cameras that can "see" individual leaves as discrete entities, measure those leaves' exact dimensions, and then statistically analyze those dimensions in relation to the species' age and maturity to anticipate what those "perfect circumstances" would be. The gCrop system, which is built on the IoLT infrastructure, uses a computer vision algorithm to track leaf development in real time. Although effective, the adoption of this technology may have a disadvantage in terms of data gathering, since machine learning needs enormous data sets for training purposes. The system may also have a high propensity for mistake. The installation of the system may also need time and money. Again, care must be taken to ensure that images are appropriately processed, tagged, and generic for ML image processing.

To help farmers increase their harvests, G.S. Nagaraja et al. [9,] presented a Smart Agricultural Management System (SAMS). Precision agriculture, which is used by the system, also aids in cutting down on waste. Several sensors provide data to the system, which is used to track prime agricultural conditions. The information collected by these sensors is represented graphically via the use of graphs.

3. Proposed Method

To improve crop yields, an automated agricultural monitoring system that makes use of wireless sensor networks is implement. Fig. 17.1 shows the systems block diagram. It will gather information from the various hardware parts and relay it to a mobile application device, along with an LCD, so that the farmers may monitor the farm's status in real time.

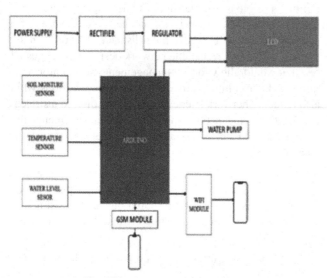

Fig. 17.1   System block diagram

Agriculture monitoring system improvement wireless sensors networks is electronic system project design to assist farmers to monitor environmental factors which will improve their farming and to also work remotely. This project is intended to operate on an ESP8266 microcontroller, and it will also include sensors for examining the temperature and humidity of the surrounding environment, in addition to a soil moisture sensor that can measure how wet the ground really is. A DHT sensor, which measures both temperature and humidity, is utilized in a manner similar to that of a soil moisture sensor. This sensor has three terminals that correspond to the Voltage in, Ground, and Signal Out pins. The ESP8266 microcontroller has a built-in WiFi chip that transmits data over the internet. It also uses digital and analog inputs, and a motor driver is included, so it may run a mechanical pump that delivers water when it is required.

The DHT VC-in pin is linked to the Esp8266 3vpin, the DHT ground pin is attached to the Esp8266 ground pin, and the DHT signal out pin is connected to pin 7 of the Esp8266. The H-brigde motor driver had terminal space for connecting as well as pulsing pins, the terminal base for DC motor is linked to the submissive DC pump, and the pins from the H-brigde motor driver are attached to pins 8 and 9 on the Esp8266 microcontroller. Figure 17.2 shows the designed diagram.

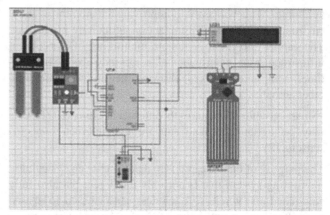

Fig. 17.2   System circuit diagram

The operation of the projects starts with the Esp8266 being programmed to connect to a particular Hotspot. Once it has successfully connected to the Hotspot, the next step is to connect to the Thingspeak internet website. Once it has successfully connected to the website, the Esp8266 will now wait for signals from the network sensors. If the soil moisture sensor detects a certain level that has been included in the code as it exceeded point, then the Esp8266 needs to pulse the H-brigde Motor drive to switch on the Submissive DC pump to send water on the soil. If the soil content gets enough water to a level that is acceptable in the code, then the Esp8266 needs to pulse the H-brigde motor driver to stop the submissive DC pump from watering the soil.

4. Results

The above figures show the designed system during testing. Figure 17.3(c) shows temperature and humidity reading during testing.

The figure below also shows an IoT web-based system Think Speak, from which the moisture and temperature reading on the farm is monitored. The indication will be off as seen in Fig. 17.4 below when the soil moisture content is less than the typical range (10–45%). This will cause the pump to water the soil in order to bring the moisture content within the average range.

Figures 17.4 and 17.5 show the amount of soil moisture at the beginning of the test as well as at the level when water had been pumped into the field to the threshold. This has been displayed both on the Thingspeak website via the green button. Figure 17.6 displays the soil's temperature and humidity as measured by a DHT sensor and uploaded to the Thingspeak website using an Internet of Things connection that was established between the

ESP8266 microcontroller with built-in WiFi chip and the Thingspeak website. This connection was made possible

(a)

(b)

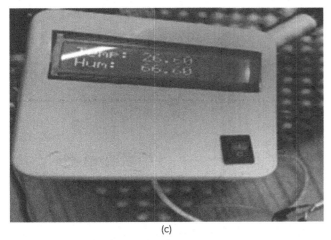

(c)

Fig. 17.3 (a) Sample soil, (b) System installed in a soil, (c) System showing readings on LCD

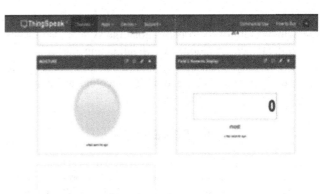

Fig. 17.4 Soil moisture content reading zero

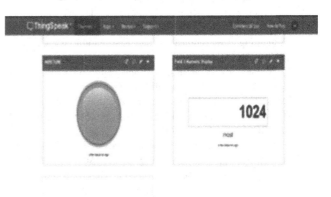

Fig. 17.5 Soil moisture content reading

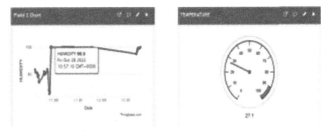

Fig. 17.6 Humidity and Temperature reading on Thinkspeak

5. Conclusion

In our project, we had implemented an Agriculture monitoring system improvement utilizing wireless sensors Networks. The simple operation of this has made it one of the most useful tools in the field of agriculture. Because of this, environmental conditions can be monitored more effectively, and farms can receive more water and nutrients automatically. As a result, crop yields can be increased, and all of this information can be viewed on an LCD display or on the Thingspeak website. All of this can be accomplished on a budget that is relatively modest. We are able to obtain information about the current temperature, humidity, and soil moisture by utilizing this Thingspeak website and the LCD display interface. This information is available to us

by an Internet of Things connection. Using wireless sensor networks, the numerous environmental conditions required for an improved agriculture system have been monitored. This will aid in the automated delivery of water and other nutrients to the crops, hence increasing agricultural yields.

whenever we want to obtain it. In addition to assisting in the achievement of the primary goal, the system also makes a significant contribution toward mitigating the effects of global warming. This, in turn, contributes to a reduction in the amount of crop devastation. The ecological balance is therefore preserved in this way.

REFERENCES

1. A. D. Boursianis et al., "Smart Irrigation System for Precision Agriculture—The ARElhOU5A IoT Platform," in IEEE Sensors Journal, vol. 21, no. 16, pp. 17539–17547, Aug, 2021, doi: 10. 1109/JSEN.2020.3033526.
2. V. Tyagi and A. Kumar, "Internet of Things and social networks: A survey," 2017 IEEE International Conference on Computing, Communication and Automation (ICCCA), pp. 1268–1270, 2017.
3. K. A. Patil and N. R. Kale, "A model for smart agriculture using IoT," 2016 International Conference on Global Trends in Signal Processing, Information Computing and Communication (ICGTSPICC), 2016, pp. 543–545, doi: 10. 1109/ICGTSPICC.2016.7955360.
4. S. Roy et al., "IoT, big data science & analytics, cloud computing and mobile app-based hybrid system for smart agriculture," 2017 8th Annual Industrial Automation and Electromechanical Engineering Conference(IEMECON),2017, pp. 303–304, doi: 10. 1109/IEMECON.2017.8079610.
5. S. R. Prathibha, A. Hongal and M. P. Jyothi, "IOT Based Monitoring System in Smart Agriculture," 2017 International Conference on Recent Advances in Electronics and Communication Technology (ICRAECT), 2017, pp. 81–84, doi: 10. 1109/ICRAECT.2017.52.
6. M. AshifuddinMondal and Z. Rehena, "IoT Based Intelligent Agriculture Field Monitoring System," 2018 8th International Conference on Cloud Computing, Data Science & Engineering (Confluence), 2018, pp. 625–629, doi: 10. 1109/CONFLUENCE.2018.8442535.
7. N. Ahmed, D. De and I. Hussain, "Internet of Things (IoT) for Smart Precision Agriculture and Farming in Rural Areas," in IEEE Internet of Things Journal, vol. 5, no. 6, pp. 4890–4899, Dec. 2018, doi: 10. 1109/JIOT.2018.2879579.
8. S. Kumar, G. Chowdhary, V. Udutalapally, D. Das and S. P. Mohanty, "gCrop: Internet-of-Leaf- Things (IoLT) for Monitoring of the Growth of Crops in Smart Agriculture," 2019 IEEE International Symposium on Smart Electronic Systems (iSES) (Formerly iNiS), 2019, pp. 53–56, doi: 10. 1109/iSES47678.2019.00024.
9. G. S. Nagaraja, Avinash B Soppimath, T. Soumya and Abhinith A, "IoT Based Smart Agriculture Management System" 2019 4th International Conference on Computational Systems and Information Technology for Sustainable Solution (CSITSS), vol. 4, pp. 1–5. Mar 2020.

Note: All the figures in this chapter were compiled by the author.

Sustainable Materials Processing and Manufacturing – Lin Zhu et al. (eds)
© 2024 Taylor & Francis Group, London, ISBN 978-1-032-88599-5

Failure Analysis and Improvement of the Sliding Door Opening and Closing of the Multiple Unit

Yueming Yao[1], Maohua Xiao[2], Yuehong Zhu, Jiapei Zhang, Yun Yang, Ye Jiao

Engineer, Changzhou Railway Higher Vocational And Technical School

ABSTRACT: Based on the overall architecture of the door system and the data processing architecture, a fault diagnosis model and sub health status of the door system are proposed to analyze the failure of the door system by using the fault tree analysis of the door PHM subsystem.Based on the method of feature extraction from sub health data and calibration data, several features that contribute significantly to the clustering process were calculated. At the same time, the status of illegal leaving and locking in place and the pressure wheel status were analyzed, and their practical significance was explained. The reliability prediction curve of the door system has been obtained, providing a basis for monitoring the door system of the multiple unit and analyzing the sub health status.

KEYWORDS: Multiple Units train unit, Door system, Typical faults, Improvement

1. Structural Characteristics and Principle Analysis of Sliding Doors for Multiple Units

The electronic control electric device of the car door adopts a microprocessor controlled motor drive device, which has self diagnosis function and fault recording function, communication function with the train bus network, and can control the car door through the train bus network or hard wire. The transmission device adopts a screw method, and the transmission device, guide device, driving device, and locking device are concentrated into a compact functional unit for easy installation and maintenance. The doors are equipped with reliable mechanical locking mechanisms, fault isolation devices, emergency unlocking, reopening and other safety facilities to ensure the safety of the door system., all components are easy to access and easy to maintain and adjust. The door system mainly consists of the following three parts: the load- bearing driving mechanism, the door leaf, and the basic components. When the door is closed, corresponding protective devices are installed to ensure that the lower part of the door leaf cannot swing out after being subjected to force.

Each door is equipped with a manually operated isolation device. The isolation device is mechanical and can be operated inside and outside the vehicle. The isolation device can only operate after the door is closed. When the train door malfunctions, the crew can operate the isolation device with a key. After the isolation device is triggered, the door is left in a permanently closed state, and the emergency unlocking device function fails, all control functions of the door are closed and disconnected from the control system. The exit service indicator light (red light) remains continuously bright and displays on the driver's display in the driver's cab that the door is in an isolated state. A door in an isolated state can't be automatically or manually opened without resetting the isolation device, even if the emergency unlocking device is operated, the door can't be opened. After the door is isolated and locked, the door can be restored using the key.

The door driving device is located above the door, and an electronic door controller is integrated and installed on the driving device to control the door movement. It adopts a

Corresponding author: [1]yaoyueming11@163.com, [2]xiaomaohua@njau.edu.cn

DOI: 10.1201/9781003538646-18

long and short guide pillar structure. The sliding action of the sliding door switch can be driven by a motor and the transmission mechanism connected to the door leaf. The door leaf with the guide wheel installed moves along the guide rail above the door leaf, driving the movement of the door carrier to achieve the opening and closing action of the sliding door.

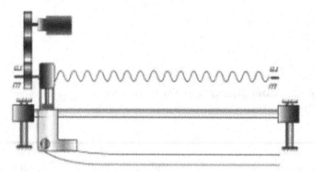

Fig. 18.1 Schematic diagram of bearing and driving mechanism

The passenger compartment doors are equipped with internal/ external emergency unlocking devices, and each set of passenger compartment doors is equipped with one internal emergency unlocking device. The emergency unlocking process inside the passenger compartment side doors is divided into two levels (unlocking request and unlocking), with different status indicators set at each level. One door emergency unlocking device is set on each side of each vehicle outside for emergency door opening operation on the outside of the vehicle. The door emergency unlocking switch on the outside of the vehicle can be manually operated by the operator[1] . The operating force of the emergency unlocking device should be moderate and easy to operate. After the emergency unlocking device is operated by passengers, when the train is in a zero speed state and the manual door opening force is not more than 150N, passengers can open the door; If the vehicle is in a non zero speed state, the door motor will generate door closing force in a short period of time, and passengers can manually operate it from inside the vehicle[2]. The status of the emergency unlocking device is monitored by the train monitoring system. When the emergency unlocking device is triggered, the train monitoring system display screen in the driver's cab will alarm and display the position of the triggered emergency unlocking device's door. At the same time, the control system of the door locking device will be immediately cut off, and the train will become inert. The emergency unlocking device has a self- protection function, and after use, the handle must be pushed back to its original working position using the key.

There is a zero speed signal connected to the door control circuit, ensuring that the train can only connect to the door opening circuit at zero speed. When the ATP system is in a non working state, the zero speed signal required by the

door system is provided by the vehicle system; When the ATP system is in operation, the zero speed signal required by the door system can be provided by the signal system. A safety relay is installed in the door closing interlocking circuit, which acts when all train doors are closed, providing a departure signal.

An eccentric wheel is set at the connection between the door frame and the sliding cylinder component, which can be rotated to adjust the door leaf so that the outer side of the door panel is parallel to the sealing surface. The distance between the outer surface of the door leaf and the vehicle body plane is measured at the farthest end of the side away from the center of the door leaf on the upper edge of the door leaf, X1. The distance between the outer surface of the door leaf and the angle seal is measured at the side near the center of the door leaf on the upper edge of the door leaf, X2, and the measured distance from the vehicle body to the angle seal (reference value mm)=b, After adjustment, the door leaf should not scratch the plane of the vehicle body when closing the door.

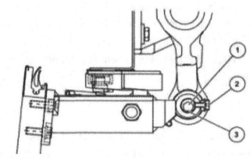

Fig. 18.2 Schematic diagram of door leaf adjustment

The side locking device integrates main components such as the main lock, auxiliary lock, and isolation lock to form a multi-point locking structure. The logical judgment of traction interlocking is completed through key control switches such as the door closing in place detection switch, lock in place detection switch, and auxiliary lock detection switch[3].

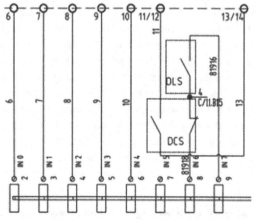

Fig. 18.3 Schematic diagram of detection switch

The door remote monitoring and fault prediction system mainly consists of intelligent door controllers, in car transmission systems, in car transmission systems, server transmission systems, etc., achieving interactive transmission between the vehicle PHM system and the door PHM subsystem within the server. The PHM system is mainly divided into three layers: data collection layer, data transmission layer, and data application layer, achieving a wider range of interconnection functions, and being able to transmit perceived information without obstacles, high reliability, and high security. After the door data collected by door diagnosis enters the server, the data is first parsed, and then used to determine whether the door function is normal. For data with normal function, sub health screening is required and normal door data features are extracted. Every morning, sub health diagnosis is conducted on the sub health data filtered out from the previous day, and the number of sub health diagnosis data needs to meet certain requirements, For data with abnormal functions, corresponding features need to be extracted. Both normal and abnormal features will enter the door fault diagnosis module for diagnosis to obtain the type of door fault.

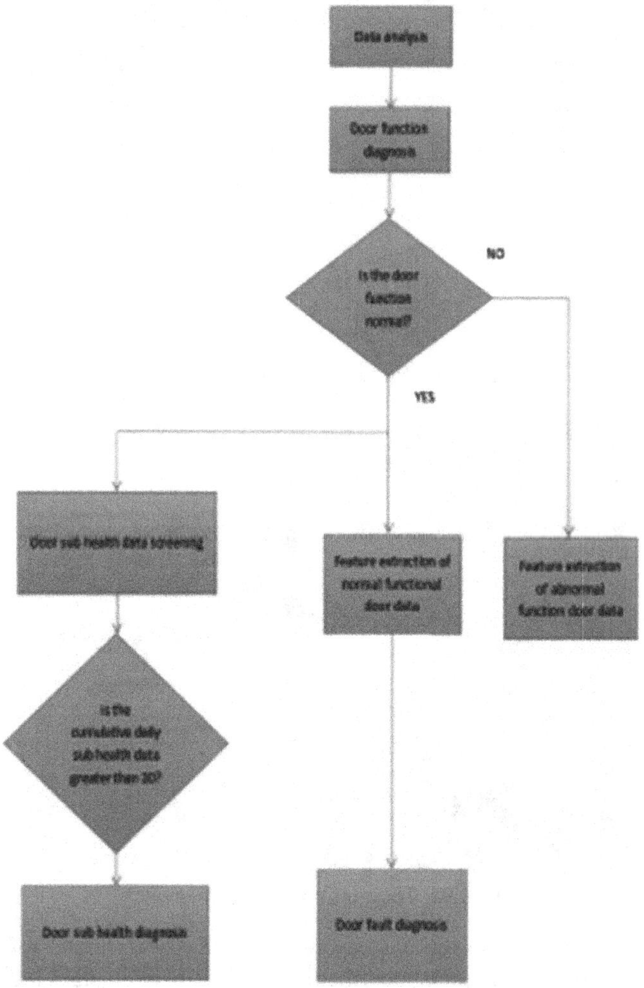

2. Diagnosis and Analysis of Common Faults in the Door System of Multiple Unit Trains

Through the analysis of previous door fault data, the common types of faults in high-speed trains are mainly caused by mechanical reasons (such as interference, size deviation, and valve switch) and electrical reasons (such as safety interlock circuit, motor drive module, and door software). The parts that are prone to malfunctions in the high-speed train unit mainly include door opening and closing failure, door opening and closing speed too fast or too slow, door controller failure, travel switch failure, and other situations[4-5]. If the door controller malfunctions, it will usually be manually locked in place and the door will be isolated through an isolation lock.

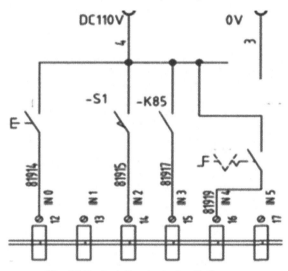
Fig. 18.4 Door diagnosis flow chart

Fig. 18.5 Isolation lock circuit diagram

The door opening and closing speed is too fast or too slow, usually due to improper motor selection or incorrect wiring method. To solve the problem of the vehicle door opening and closing speed being too fast due to excessive voltage, the 81301 and 32100 lines in the vehicle electrical comprehensive control cabinet are externally connected to the power switch and connected to the power relay.

The cluster analysis algorithm is used to identify the abnormal centering size of the door. The main curve changes are as follows: the opening decreases, the rotation speed of the section close to the door decreases, the current rises in advance, and the rotation speed increases from the opening start section to the speed rise section, and the current drops. The blue color in the figure is healthy, and the red color is abnormal centering size.

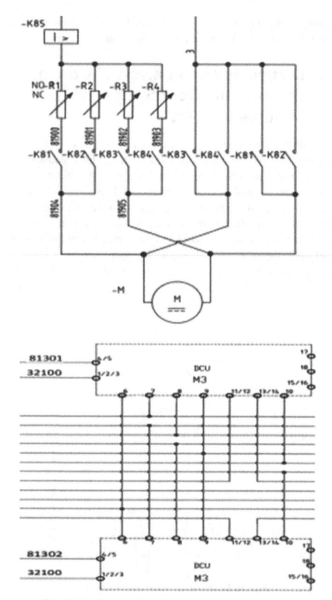

Fig. 18.6 Schematic of door opening and closing

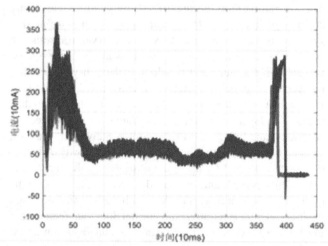

Fig. 18.7 Data chart of abnormal alignment size

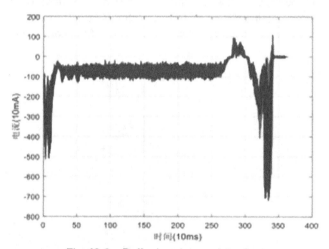

Fig. 18.8 Buffer head wear data chart

Through the cluster analysis algorithm, the main curve changes of buffer head wear are as follows: the recognition opening increases, and the operation time of opening and closing the door increases. In the figure, blue is the healthy state, and red is the buffer head wear state.

The fully closed travel switch is in the critical position for triggering, causing unstable triggering. After the rear door controller detects the signal of the door closing in place, the controller will control the motor to perform a reverse self check to confirm that the door closing position has been reached. At this time, if the travel switch leaves the triggered position, it will ensure that the reverse locking mechanism is faulty. It can be manually locked in place and the door can be isolated through an isolation lock.

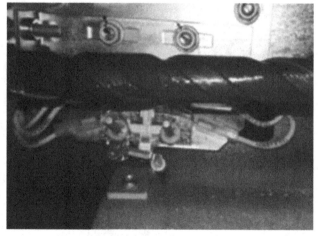

Fig. 18.9 Trigger status of travel switch

Through the cluster analysis algorithm, the overpressure of the pressing wheel is identified. The main curve changes are as follows: the current at the contact position between the opening start section and the pressing wheel increases, the current at the section close to the closing position increases significantly, and the speed decreases.

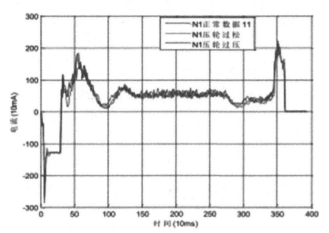

Fig. 18.10   Data of the pressure wheel

The fault phenomenon of illegally leaving the lock in place is generally when the door system is in the lock in place state and no door opening command is received, the screw rod reverses, and the lock in place switch state jumps.

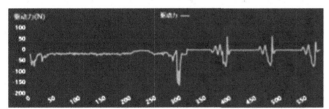

Fig. 18.11   Data chart of illegal leaving and locking in place

The most common fault in high-speed trains is the door opening and closing fault. During long-term operation of high-speed trains, it is common for drivers to operate the door opening and closing actions, but the door cannot be opened or closed. Below, we will discuss and study the door opening and closing fault of the door system from the above two types of reasons.

2.1 Electrical Faults in the Door System

The diode VD7 (model: 1N4007) in the comprehensive control cabinet of the high-speed train unit is broken down and burnt. Further review of the drawings confirms that the diode VD7 is an anti reflection diode for the main line of the centralized control power supply, with the upper port of the diode connected to+109 wire and the lower port connected to+109A wire.

Power is supplied to the main line (+109) and negative line (-109) of the train control power supply through diodes VD7 and VD8. After receiving the centralized power supply (forming a loop), the control car converts the DC110V voltage on the

main line of the centralized power supply (+109) into high-frequency signals for plug door centralized control (closing, opening right door, enabling right door, opening left door, enabling left door). The high-frequency signal of the sliding door centralized control is connected to the entire train through the sliding door centralized control line, forming a circuit with each door centralized control controller and the negative line of the centralized power supply (- 109). The high- frequency signal of the sliding door centralized control is transmitted to each door centralized control unit through control buttons in the driver's cab, and the entire train doors open and close according to instructions.

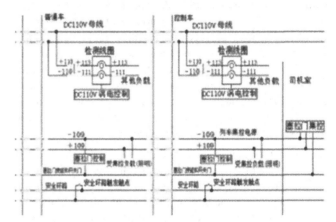

Fig. 18.12   Schematic of door centralized control topology

The rated current of the diode used in the current vehicle is relatively small, and during vehicle operation, diode VD7 undergoes overcurrent breakdown and burning, resulting in the failure of the sliding door switch.

In order to solve the problem of door switch failure caused by overcurrent breakdown and burning of diode VD7, the model of diode VD7 in the vehicle electrical comprehensive control cabinet has been replaced.

2.2 Mechanical Faults in the Door System

Download car door fault data, use car door maintenance software to analyze the fault information, and the fault data shows that 'auxiliary lock fault ' has occurred.

When the door moves to the position where the close in position switch (98% switch) is triggered and the lock in position switch is also triggered, the control command energizes the auxiliary lock locking valve, causing the auxiliary lock to enter the locking state; When the auxiliary lock in position switch is at a high level, that is, when the door enters the locked in position state, the green indicator light of the door is constantly on; Diagnostic criteria for "door not locked in place fault" : After activating the solenoid valve in the direction of auxiliary lock locking, the lock in place switch has not been triggered within the specified time.

Table 18.1 Door fault data

	Signal meaning	Meaning of '0' status	Meaning of '1' status	Current state of signal
I05	Auxiliary lock in position switch	Auxiliary lock in place	Auxiliary lock not locked in place	1
I06	Lock in position switch	Not locked in place	Locked in place	0
I08	98% in place switch	Door not closed in place	Door closed in place	1
O1	Door closing valve	Power cut	Power on	1
O2	Auxiliary lock locking valve	Power cut Power on		0

Check the data of the door controller and observe the I0 signal status at the time of the 'door not locked in place fault'. According to the analysis of the door fault data table, at the time of the 'door not locked in place fault ' fault, the auxiliary lock in place switch (I05) indicates that the auxiliary lock is not locked in place, the lock in place switch (I06) ndicates that the main lock is not locked in place, the 98% in place switch (I08) indicates that the imain lock is closed in place, and the door closing valve (01) is powered on, The auxiliary lock locking valve (02) is de-energized.

Based on the electrical schematic diagram, check the HMI screen to confirm that there are no abnormalities in the air supply circuit. Due to the indication of the door not being locked in place by the lock in place switch, after maintaining this state for 10 seconds, the door software reports a 'door not locked in place fault '. Check the size of the door: the V-shaped door panel meets the requirement that the difference between the distance between the upper and lower parts of the door panel and the door frame is ≤ 1mm; Check that the appearance of the 98% position switch is in good condition, without deformation, cracks, damage, etc. The installation bolts are complete and fastened, the anti loosening marks are clear, and there is no misalignment. The switch cantilever angle position is correct; Upon inspection, it was found that there were scratches on the door latch and frame, which did not meet the requirements; Manually close the door to easily reach the secondary lock; There is no foreign object stuck on the glide slope; The lubricating grease evenly covers the curved area of the upper guide rail and the contact surface of the lower swing arm roller. Through fault data analysis and physical inspection, it was found that the main cause of the fault was the wear resistance of the door stop and frame on the corresponding door leaf in the middle inclined wedge area during the door closing process; At the same time, the gap between the locking tabs is too large, which is in opposition to the door latch when closing the door. The main lock in place switch does not release, the auxiliary lock solenoid valve is not triggered, and the locking tab is not pressed tightly, causing the door to not close in place.

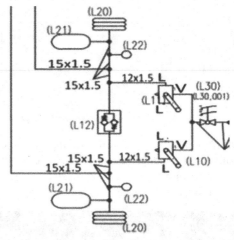

Fig. 18.13 Electrical schematic diagram

In order to ensure the safety of vehicle operation, the door stop on the corresponding door leaf in the middle inclined wedge area of the current vehicle isadjusted to eliminate the wear resistance of the door stop frame; Adjust the dimensions of the lock tongue and lock pin. After manually locking the door to the second level, the gap between the lock tongue and the lock buckle roller should be within the range of 0.5mm to 1.5mm.

3. Conclusion

Starting from the typical problem of door system opening and closing failure, this paper comprehensively analyzes the control circuit and auxiliary lock control principle of the door centralized control system, starting from the door auxiliary lock, opening and closing logic, and the internal control principle of the door controller. At the same time, other door faults are analyzed; In addition, through algorithmic analysis, possible future faults are provided, and maintenance suggestions that may cause problems are provided to ensure the reliable operation of the vehicle, which has reference significance for subsequent maintenance personnel to handle door faults.

REFERENCES

1. TB/T3108-2011,Railway Passenger Car Sliding Doors [S].
2. Liang Guiqi. Typical faults and maintenance measures for the door system of Guangzhou Metro Line 21 [J]. Modern Urban Rail Transit, 2019 (5): 64–67.
3. Zhang Liangliang, Chen Dongdong. Fault Analysis and Improvement Plan for Door Travel Switch of Urban Rail Transit Vehicles [J]. Urban Rail Transit Research, 2017 (2): 72–75.
4. Zhang Xiaoming, SHI Haiming, Li Dong. Typical troubles in plug doors for CRH5A multiple units and countermeasures[J]. Rolling Stock, 2014,52 (12): 38–39.
5. Liu Hailong. Common faults and related handling measures of subway train door systems [J]. Architectural Engineering Technology and Design, 2018 (17): 1831.

Note: All the figures and table in this chapter were compiled by the author.

Printed in the United States
by Baker & Taylor Publisher Services